# THROUGH JAGUAR EYES

# THROUGH JAGUAR EYES

## Crossing the Amazon Basin

## BENEDICT ALLEN

HarperCollins*Publishers*

HarperCollins*Publishers*
77–85 Fulham Palace Road,
Hammersmith, London W6 8JB

Published by HarperCollins*Publishers* 1994
1 3 5 7 9 8 6 4 2

A catalogue record for this book is
available from the British Library

ISBN 0 00 255193 4

Set in Linotron Galliard by
Rowland Phototypesetting Limited,
Bury St Edmunds, Suffolk

Printed in Great Britain by
HarperCollinsManufacturing Glasgow

# TO JITA,
## BRIGHTLY SHINING STAR

# CONTENTS

MAPS

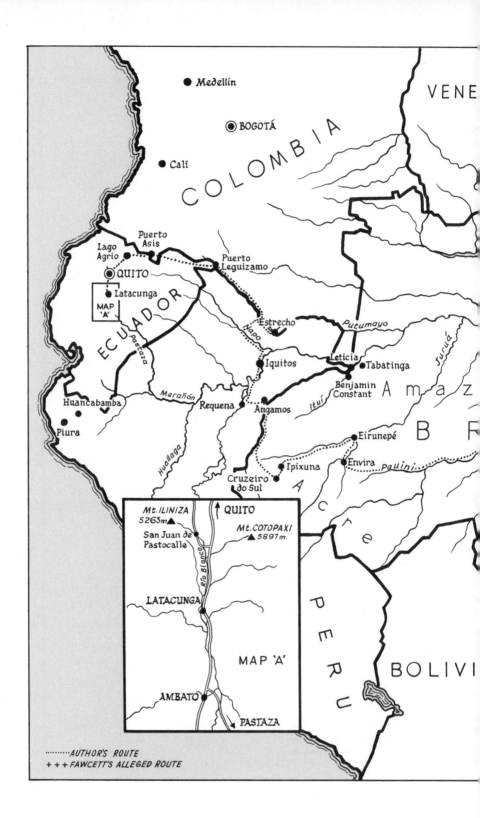

Medellín

VENE

BOGOTÁ

Cali

COLOMBIA

Puerto
Asis

Lago
Agrio

Puerto
Leguizamo

QUITO

Latacunga

MAP
'A'

ECUADOR

Estrecho

Napo

Putumayo

Jurúa

Iquitos

Leticia

Tabatinga

Benjamin
Constant

Amaz

Marañón

Pastaza

Huancabamba

Requena

Itui

B

R

Angamos

Piura

Eirunepé

Huallaga

Ipixuna

Envira

Pauini

Acre

Cruzeiro
do Sul

Mt. ILINIZA
5263m

QUITO

Mt. COTOPAXI
5897m.

San Juan de
Pastocalle

Río Blanco

LATACUNGA

MAP 'A'

AMBATO

PASTAZA

PERU

BOLIVI

········ AUTHOR'S ROUTE
+ + + FAWCETT'S ALLEGED ROUTE

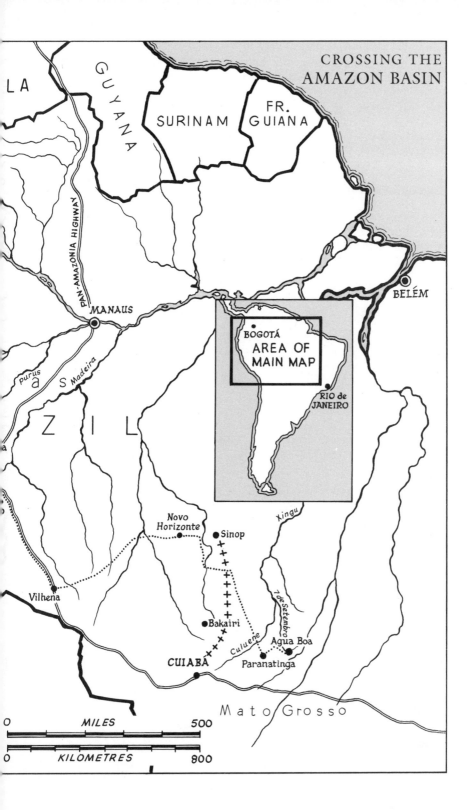

CROSSING THE
AMAZON BASIN

LA

GUYANA

SURINAM

FR.
GUIANA

BELÉM

PAN-AMAZONIA HIGHWAY

MANAUS

purus

a    S Madeira

Z  I  L

BOGOTÁ

AREA OF
MAIN MAP

RIO de
JANEIRO

Xingu

Novo
Horizonte

Sinop

7 de Setembro

Vilhena

Bakairi

Culuene

Agua Boa

CUIABÁ

Paranatinga

M a t o  Grosso

0          MILES          500

0          KILOMETRES          800

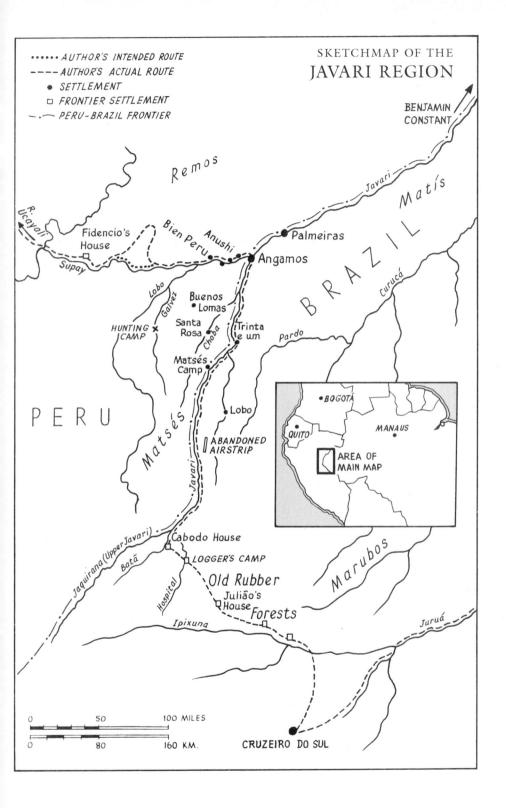

SKETCHMAP OF THE
**JAVARI REGION**

•••••• AUTHOR'S INTENDED ROUTE
- - - - AUTHOR'S ACTUAL ROUTE
● SETTLEMENT
▫ FRONTIER SETTLEMENT
—·— PERU-BRAZIL FRONTIER

BENJAMIN
CONSTANT

*Remos*

*Javari*

*Matís*

B R A Z I L

R. *Ucayali*

Fidencio's
House

*Supay*

Bien Peru  Anushi

Palmeiras

Angamos

*Lobo*

*Galvez*

Buenos
● Lomas

Santa
Rosa

*Choba*

Trinta
e um

*Curucá*

*Pardo*

HUNTING ×
CAMP

Matsés
Camp

*Matsés*

● Lobo

P E R U

*Javari*

ABANDONED
AIRSTRIP

● BOGOTÁ

QUITO

MANAUS

AREA OF
MAIN MAP

*Jaquirana (Upper Javari)*

*Batã*

Cabodo House

LOGGER'S CAMP

*Marubos*

*Hospital*

Old Rubber

Julião's
House  Forests

*Juruá*

*Ipixuna*

0        50        100 MILES

0        80        160 KM.

CRUZEIRO DO SUL

# AUTHOR'S NOTE

HERE LIE THE REMAINS of my expedition to cross the Amazon Basin. What *really* drove me to do the journey? Looking back now, having completed the book, I would still maintain that it was curiosity – that, and the challenge. This was going to be a wonderful adventure: nothing complicated, just something I could afterwards tell myself proudly that I had 'pulled off', something I could one day tell my grandchildren about.

This book differs markedly from my first Amazon one, *Mad White Giant*, which, as was obvious from its light-hearted sketches and pacey text, was not a travelogue or guide, as such, but simply an exploration of the Amazonian themes that shaped a young man's journey. *Through Jaguar Eyes*, by contrast, takes a conventional travel book's interest in trying to record accurately human and geographical features to be witnessed along the journey's route – something which wasn't a priority for the earlier book and wasn't anyway possible – I travelled at Olympic speed, often out of control, lost my notes and was very ill.

In *Through Jaguar Eyes* I've changed the surnames of Fidencio and Louis, but otherwise all descriptions and names remain unaltered. While there may well be memory lapses, and I have certainly deliberately simplified some events, everyday detail comes from my diaries.

I owe a great deal to Alyn Shipton at Basil Blackwell for allowing me to break off from his book project to go and do this journey, and also to Anna Rawlinson and Jay Scrivener-Hall for their tireless research on that volume. I would like to thank those who helped to launch me off to the Amazon: Thérèse Saba for assistance with my Spanish; my understanding dentist Stephen Charlton; Fiona Watson of Survival International; and the kind and considerate staff of British Airways, who were extraordinarily helpful throughout.

During my time in South America, the following were particularly generous to me: Jilly Forster and The Bodyshop; David Evans, from his outpost at Benjamin Constant; Susan Locke from hers above the Rio; Ron McCullagh and the staff of *Insight News*; and also the Summer Institute of Linguistics, who were very honest and hospitable to me.

After my return, Susan Kennett gave me invaluable help with the manuscript, as did Betty Palmer and, of course, my editor Richard Johnson. I would also like to thank my sister Kate Allen, Joanna Kozubska, David Livesley, Thurston Watson and Rusli for keeping me going while I wrote this book. In addition, everyone at the Royal Geographical Society library; Cathy Stastny for help correcting my appalling bush Spanish; and Scott Adams and other agents in South America from the Drugs Enforcement Administration.

Finally, for my return visit to make a BBC *Video Diary*, I would like to extend special thanks to Wolverine for patiently kitting me out with what are to me the most reliable boots around, and to IBM who, with Kodak, supported my return to 'the jaguar people' with some of the best of all equipment for some of the worst of all possible conditions.

# THROUGH JAGUAR EYES

# Return of
# 'The Man who Ate his Dog'

'GOT TO GET AWAY,' I said to myself, running out through the doors of the august Royal Geographical Society and off into Hyde Park.

Flattering to be asked, but the fact had to be faced: after two years shut away in libraries attempting to write a definitive survey of exploration books for a distinguished Oxford publisher I was going mad – the job had already driven one of my once perfectly fit and sane researchers to ill-health and a bothy in the Scottish Highlands. A stray Jehovah's Witness was coming my way down the path, a man in a shiny black leather coat. 'Jesus Saves Sinners' read the sandwich board flapping from his neck. He said to me, softly, 'The time is near, friend . . .'

Too true. Time to get away. And I'd long since had something in mind: a journey right across the Amazon Basin. People often talked about the Amazon as a frightening place, but it couldn't be as bad as months spent in a library reading about everyone else's travels. Besides, my mother would get me into a 'proper job' if I hung around much longer. I was thirty-one and feeling old. There'd be grey hairs soon.

The Amazon, though . . . I'd dreamt of those great dark forests as a child – the deft snakes, the artful mosquitoes, the coarse shriek of alarmed toucan, the teeming trees, the lost civilization of gold, El Dorado, tales of which had so bewitched the Spanish *conquistadores*. Then, after university, I had packed my rucksack and set out for South America to see it for myself, an expedition between the Orinoco and the Amazon which had been notable mainly for the disasters that occurred en route – the encounter with murderous gold-miners, the capsize of my canoe while escaping from them, the eating of my unlucky dog-companion . . . But this journey would be different, I told myself. I would cross right through the heart of the basin, the huge collection bowl that fed the main river, gathering water from the Andes in the west, the Mato Grosso in the south, the lands up to the Orinoco and Guiana highlands in the north – 1,100 rivers draining a region in which lived ten per cent of the planet's stock of living organisms. My journey would take me on a diagonal route, north-west to south-east, from the snowy slopes of the volcano Cotopaxi in the Ecuadorean Andes, down through the rain forest swathes of Colombia to Peru and the main Amazon river, then onward through Brazil to the region called the Mato Grosso, the 'Dense Forest'.

Even now, an everyday environmental news item, the word held promise, a certain magic. 'Amazon . . .' Soft, sharp, clean, more potent even than 'The Congo' or 'Borneo'.

It wasn't as if it had yet been explored – you could stop anyone and ask. To most people, the Amazon was much the same mix of horror and splendour that it had been in 1542 when the *conquistador* Orellana named the river he discovered after legendary warrior women. It was still piranhas, it was still mysterious natives. And the modern explorers, far from exploring, were still reinforcing the mystery. One need look no further than the book titles. The Amazon they told us about was sometimes a nightmare – the *Imposs-ible Adventure*, the *Green Hell* – sometimes a glorious dream, a *Lost World*. The Indians? They were *Fierce People*, *Innocent Assassins*, who were living in a backward, harsher time, a *Savage Interlude*. Alternatively they were helpless children who were easy victims of *The Missionaries*.

And if that didn't suit, the Indians were sophisticated ecologists who had perfected human existence and appeared in advertisements for high street banks, 'greens' in a *Brazilian Eden*.*

All of which was very odd, because from what I'd seen there

---

* At the time, Indians were to be seen on French television in various degrees of semi-nakedness, giving rapt endorsement to a pillar of the Western economy that was destroying their lives. See *Survival International* newsletter No.23, 1993.

were hardly any indigenous people left. The Amazon that I remembered was a mosaic of peasant farmers, loggers, gold miners, missionaries – and yes, sometimes Indians, who were in various states of cultural decadence.*

Perhaps the sheer scale of the place was what fed everyone's imagination – a hothouse in spectacular form, a gigantic pool of species left for 100 million years to evolve ever more specialized roles. The Amazon accommodated nearly half the world's 8,600 species of birds. Seventeen of its tributaries were over a thousand miles long. It disgorged two-thirds of the world's fresh water. A shipping lane for 2,300 miles. The Amazon even impressed you with the amount of it we could destroy – 80,000 square kilometres of virgin forest annually.**

It all seemed so simple, striding through Hyde Park. I would take the Amazon just as it came, using whatever local means were available, and quietly I would cross the basin, and we would see what we would see. As I walked along I imagined myself adapting to whatever people might present themselves – hopping aboard the canoe of a grim gold miner, walking in the footsteps of a humble rubber tapper, or, up quieter tributaries when I did find native people, stalking with an agile Indian – me, the clumping oaf transformed into feline hunter, making the first recorded crossing of the Amazon Basin at its widest point.

Before I had emerged from the park the Amazon had worked its magic on me as well; I had a string of my own dreams and a new spring in my stride.

'No one's done it before? *Of course* no one's done it before,' my mother said when I broke the news that I had cancelled my book contract and was off to the Amazon. 'It's pointless.'

Though it was past eleven in the morning by the time my

---

* The process by which explorers fail to explore but instead see their own ideas is one of 'projection', according to one academic. 'A mental image is transferred to an object [e.g. a physical setting] outside the self.' See Knox-Shaw, *The Explorer, and Views of Creation*.
** An estimate for 1987, from Chris C. Park, *Tropical Rain Forests*.

girlfriend Jita and I had arrived down from London, she as usual set about cooking a fried breakfast. 'You need feeding up,' she said.

I told her my journey wasn't pointless. I was going to see what the Amazon was really like because no one seemed to agree, though a lot of people thought of it as Hell, and a fair number as Eden – starting with Columbus, who didn't turn back from the Orinoco river delta just because of a nasty current. 'For I believe that the earthly paradise is there and to it, save by the will of God, no man can come.'

As I had my midday breakfast and my mother got on with her ironing, there was a heavy silence. I tried asking her to imagine my arrival in the Andes, slowing to the pace of the mountains, shedding some of this western world as I glided down a tributary into the very forests of the River Amazon. Orchids draped from emerald boughs, busy ants forging across crumbling logs . . . '"The tree",' I enthused, '"which moves some to tears of joy is in the eyes of others only a green thing that stands in the way." William Blake, 1799.' But it was no good.

'I thought you said the last expedition was your last.'

'It was the last before my Big One.'

My father arrived from walking the dogs and my mother told him I was going away. 'To the Amazon again,' she added darkly.

There was a silence, the sort you used to get in B-movies after an execution. 'The Amazon again . . .' he said slowly. I knew he was recalling what the press had had to say after my last misadventure there. 'The Man Who Ate His Dog To Survive', ran the *Daily Mail* headline. The Home Counties had been in an uproar about it: angry letters had poured in asking if my neighbours' dogs were safe and even the RSPCA had been called in to interview me.

My mother still needed reassurance and so I sat her down and told her I'd be doing exactly what had always served me well in the years since that first, rather unfortunate expedition – leaving western equipment at home and learning from the people who actually lived on the spot. River traders, gold miners, I would slip in among them and make my way by whatever means they used. There was one rather blank bit on the map beyond Iquitos – it couldn't be more than . . . well, it was at least a thousand kilometres actually, but I'd been doing some reading and the good news was that somewhere on the Javari river lived the Matsés, a semi-nomadic tribe who perhaps might be willing to teach me enough forest skills to complete the journey. The remotest subgroup of the Mayorunas – a name that some anthropologists used synonymously with Matsés – they were secretive, stealthy people who emulated the jaguar, which, I explained, being the top predator in the forest was the very best sort of animal to emulate.

'Are they *friendly*, though?' interjected Jita.

'Oh yes,' I said, hoping that all I'd heard so far was just exaggeration. 'They devote considerable energy to warfare, and take prisoners', I'd read in the authoritative – but hopefully out-of-date – *Handbook of South American Indians*. I'd uncovered a photo of a Matsés. It showed a short, pale-looking Indian with a stripe tattooed across his cheeks and jaguar whiskers fashioned from palm stems protruding from his lips. Until recently, I'd read, the Matsés had conducted a perpetual sequence of running battles and wife-stealing raids even with their own relatives, other Indians of the Panoan language group – the barely contacted Matís, the much-scorned Marúbos, the much-feared (but now perhaps extinct) Remos. All of these people also wore cat whiskers and all were hunted by tribes of vigilant missionaries.

'Of a ferocious and unsociable temper, profoundly disdainful toward civilization,' noted the traveller Paul Marcoy in 1875 concerning the Matsés, as he visited the Ucayali river missions they so sourly neglected. 'They live buried alive in their barbarism.'

It had been that way for centuries – the Indians roaming the forests imitating the jaguar, the missionaries and other frontiersmen themselves like predatory cats as they stalked about, seeking whom or what they might devour. The story only changed one day in 1963, when Sophia, a captive of the Matsés, escaped through the forests with her son. It was a chance that the latest batch of missionaries, Protestants from the evangelical Summer Institute of Linguistics, did not let slip by. The woman, a peasant who had been snatched by the Matsés group ten years before, was able to teach Harriet Fields, an American from the mission, enough of the language to enable her to attempt to open communications with the elusive tribe. In the following years, Harriet Fields and her partner Harriet Kneeland spent much time dropping presents from the air and calling out to the Indians along the river banks, but their efforts went unrewarded until 30 August 1969. Harriet Fields, in a camp in the forest, was slowly approached by a clutch of wary Indians.

Soon the missionaries had made converts of them and were now happily running a mission called Buenas Lomas in the middle of Matsés territory.

'They're not cannibals, though . . . ?' My mother was still waiting for reassurance.

'Well . . .' I faltered. A German had written a whole book on the Panoans' cannibalistic activities. 'All right, traditionally, yes they do eat human flesh. But only their own dead, and that's only because they are nomads, and want their forefathers to be near them.'

'God!'

I tried to comfort her by explaining that by all accounts, or one of them anyway, the cannibalism was done almost lovingly. I spared her the details – the Matsés carefully left the skull until the brain was rotten with maggots and then roasted it with spices – and also the story that I had uncovered only the day before about the Mayorunas' Panoan relatives and enemies the Cashibos. The British travellers Smyth and Lowe in 1836 related an anecdote from a Padre Plaza on the Ucayali river, 'of a Cashibo boy whom he had in the convento, who one day expressed a great desire to eat one of his companions, and was actually proceeding to cut his throat with a knife, which he was prevented from doing; when remonstrated with upon the atrocity of the act, he seemed by no means conscious of its impropriety, and said, "why not? He is very good to eat."'

In the end I set my mother's mind at rest by promising to talk to an American adventurer who had already met the Matsés. However, when I did track this man down he started reeling off not words of comfort but atrocities committed by drug smugglers. Once started, he couldn't stop. My diary reads: 'Talk of Indians' eyes being poked out by sticks . . . Indians laid waste by malaria; a village abandoned because [he] arrived there inauspiciously; black cayman; anacondas; drug runners with guns . . . Of fresh human heads having been sold at market. Etc, etc.'

'*Can't* be this bad,' I thought, as he went on and on. And I found myself reflecting again on how explorers down the years had created more myths than they'd ever cleared up. It wasn't all their fault, really. A lot was expected of them – they were purveyors of society's dreams. The pressure was to fulfil them, bring back a land of wonder – the hell, the paradise. Travellers were sent off abroad to bring back their traveller's tales, and the marvelling public got what they wanted. Would I do any different?

Meanwhile, the American was still talking, working himself up into a lather – and all on my phone bill. Perhaps, I thought, it would be just as well to do a reconnoitre. It needn't take long, just a quick flight into Leticia, a Colombian town near the Putumayo river and on the edge of all this 'drug country'. In Leticia, I'd be able to put these silly stories to rest.

It was around this time, mid-May 1992, that friends persuaded me that I should take along one of those new video recorders. Surely, they argued, such a little thing wouldn't impose on the Amazonians. The man from the BBC listened warily to my plans.

I told him about my journey – the expected panoramic views from Mount Cotopaxi, how it would be to look out over the steaming forest miles; of the Matsés people who knew the jaguar, copied its very gait, and slunk unnoticed through the undergrowth alert to the myriad smells and sounds, how these feline people would teach me their forest ways . . .

'Fine. But getting down to practicalities, what sort of backing have you got?'

'Do you mean back-up, or backing in cash?'

'Either.'

'Neither,' I said.

I explained my philosophy of travelling light and learning from the locals and he did finally agree to help: no money, just a list of equipment I'd need and a letter which seemed to give the BBC exclusive rights to all my material.

I looked at the list. For someone who wasn't even intending to take in a map of the route – just two local charts to help me pinpoint the Amazon Basin's furthest points, the lip of the basin near Mount Cotopaxi in the north-west and the head of the 7 de Setembro, a Xingu tributary on the far side of the Mato Grosso in the south-east

– it seemed like rather a lot of baggage. Among the heavier items were: professional video recorder, one; protective case, one; spare battery packs, five; battery belts, two (these each seemed to weigh about the same as the lead belts scuba divers wear to keep them from surfacing); generator, one; tripod and leveller, one; hours of video tape, one hundred.

As I was leaving he queried me about some hitherto ignored horrors – a cholera outbreak in Peru, and the country's Shining Path terrorists who had killed 26,000 people so far. Five per cent of the Peruvian population had been forced out of their homes by the Maoist Sendero Luminoso, who, like the Khmer Rouge, believed that it was necessary to rebuild society from almost nothing.*

I assured him that where the Amazon was concerned people were always exaggerating – why, just the other day I'd had an American on the phone talking about drug mobsters. But the next thing was two TV channels, three radio stations and five newspapers wanting to know how I was feeling with only weeks to go before the expedition. 'What a brave chap,' commented one distinguished journalist, rounding off his interview. For the first time, just for a moment, I wondered whether trying to cross the Amazon Basin was such a good idea after all.

The *Evening Standard* asked me what luxury I was planning to take. It emerged that this journalist, like many before him, was after a follow-up story to do with the dog. He read out a clipping from *The Times*: 'Canine bleu', it was entitled. 'I read somewhere you always take your Auntie Joan's tomato and apple chutney,' he suggested, trying to warm me to the theme.

I said that Auntie Joan's chutney weighed a ton, and with the video equipment I had more than enough tons already. 'Mustard powder,' I said in the end, 'that can't weigh much.'

'Mustard . . .' the reporter repeated, glumly. 'Just Colman's mustard . . . What about champagne? What about caviare?'

I pictured the stack of video gadgets back at my flat, the dents they made on the floor. 'Mustard,' I repeated, firmly.

* For further information on the group that brought a third of Peru under martial law, see Simon Strong, *The Shining Path*.

'Armed only with a tin of Colman's Mustard,' the paper read the next day, 'Benedict Allen, 31, is about to . . .' And soon after that, a letter arrived out of the blue from Colman's. They wrote that they were nominating me for a Mustard Club award, 'for services to the condiment'. They enclosed an invitation to the presentation.

The *Daily Telegraph* photographed me at the Royal Geographical Society poised over the giant globe traditionally used by the press on these occasions. The writer compared me to the explorer Colonel Percy Fawcett, who set off for the Amazon in 1925 in search of a lost city and then vanished. My mother left a phone message for me: 'What happened to Colonel Fawcett?'

The answer was, we don't know.

While other explorers are remembered for what they discovered, or what they endured in attempting to make that discovery, Colonel P. H. Fawcett DSO, Founder's Medallist of the Royal Geographical Society, is remembered for being a mystery. He is one of this century's most famous Amazon explorers only because he disappeared without trace.

He set off in search of his fabled Lost City in April 1925.

'You need have no fear of any failure . . .' he wrote in his last letter to his wife Nina, before continuing deeper into the forests. He was never heard of again. The puzzle had fascinated me as a boy. 'The forest,' I read excitedly from *Exploration Fawcett*, the account based on his journals, 'in allowing him a peep at its soul, claimed his life in payment.' To me as a boy, the mystery of Fawcett was the mystery of the Amazon.

It wasn't that I particularly admired the man's vision – his true motives, some secretive quest for a lost city, were no clearer to me than to anyone else. Nor was he my personal idea of a great explorer – instead of attempting to leave preconceptions at home, quietly absorbing only the forest, he imposed on it with baggage trains, rifles and alien ideas. No, what fascinated me was the grip the Amazon had on Fawcett's imagination. We all have our dreams, but here was a man who tenaciously pursued his dream until it destroyed him.

An officer in the artillery, Fawcett was engaged in 1906 as a surveyor for the Bolivian government. Already something of a mystic, his expeditions over the next seven years led him to believe in the existence of a hidden civilization. He wrote in his journal, 'The connection of Atlantis with parts of what is now Brazil is not to be dismissed contemptuously.'

After serving in the First World War, he returned to South America to undertake a detailed investigation, and in Rio's National Library unearthed an ancient manuscript describing purported finds deep in the Xingu forests of the northern Mato Grosso. He read that in 1753 an expedition had stumbled across a ruined city constructed of massive stone blocks; there were columns, statues, gold coins, a soaring main archway incised with mysterious characters.

Fawcett set out into the region in 1920 and although he failed to find the ruins, he did succeed in uncovering fresh stories of an ancient city. More determined than ever, he launched out again in 1925, this time with the backing of a US newspaper syndicate. Accompanied by one of his sons, Jack, and Raleigh Rimell, Jack's friend, he made his way from Cuiabá, north into the Xingu. At what Fawcett claimed was 11° 43' South and 54° 35' West they arrived at 'Dead Horse Camp', the site where Fawcett's horse had died in 1920. On around 29 May, he sent back their porters and mules, determined to continue through the dense vegetation on foot, winning over local Indians for any needed assistance. That is the last we know.

For a while Fawcett wasn't missed. He had said he might be away a year or two and was hardly in a position to send back news. He was also extremely secretive and disguised his route to frustrate attempts to follow him.

Interest was heightened in 1927 when a Frenchman called Roger Courteville described having seen an exhausted, confused man by the roadside north-east of Cuiabá. He was '50 to 60 years old with luxuriant greyish hair and a "pepper and salt" beard'. He responded when addressed in English, and said his name was Fawcett. The description fitted exactly, and although doubts were later cast on the story, Fawcett's son Brian still clung desperately to this chance. He wrote to his mother, 'Suppose Daddy is off his head with fever and the others the same, who's going to identify them? I must go.' Brian's attempts to find his father failed and meanwhile Fawcett's sponsors had dispatched an investigative expedition led by a Commander Dyott. Fawcett had most likely been killed by Indians in the neighbourhood of the Culuene river, Dyott reported, but he brought little evidence to support his findings and the mystery continued.

A missionary, the Revd Emílio Halverson, produced a boy alleged to have been fathered by Jack; twenty-five years later a distinguished Brazilian anthropologist, Orlando Villas-Boas, was entertained by Kalapalo Indians with an account of how the explorers had been clubbed to death. They even produced the bones, though under analysis these were proved not to be European. More recently, a relative of the same mystical bent as Fawcett has conjectured that he survived and went on to find a spiritual 'Temple of Ibes', there to be made welcome by a priest-king wrapped in a 'gazelle skin whiter than snow'. Stories came and went. Still no Fawcett, still no lost city. Fawcett's demise remains subject to speculation – he died of fever, he drowned, he was killed.

My journey across the Amazon would end in the Mato Grosso near where he disappeared and the question would no doubt rear its head again in due course. Indeed, with the amount of luggage I was taking, I could already see myself trudging through seemingly endless forest just like him, and fading into oblivion.


At the Mustard Club Awards Ceremony the guest of honour, Sir Clement Freud, was finishing his welcoming speech. Mustard connoisseurs, many with honorary membership and some wearing a token of yellow – a tie, a cufflink – eagerly chose from the arrays of ham and mustard sandwiches. It was a convivial gathering, everyone assembled together with a common belief in the importance of mustard – no prejudice here, whether your taste be for French, German, or English. Everyone was united by the yellow condiment.

From time to time, mingling in the contented throng, I caught tantalizing glimpses of the goings-on up on the stage, as the time drew near when Sir Clement would announce the winner of the award for outstanding services to mustard. The audience shuffled in anticipation.

'The first nomination is . . .' Sir Clement named an author of various idiosyncratic books on mustard of whom no one had ever heard. 'The second . . .' He named Benedict Allen, author of various idiosyncratic books on jungles of whom no one had ever heard. 'The third . . .' He named a dog – not known to me then or now but apparently a household name to absolutely everyone else, cherished for her TV appearances advertising mustard. The creature, a young, wilful mutt that was perhaps a boxer, was invited on stage. Spontaneous and loving applause broke out and at this it lowered its little ears and disappeared off stage with its owner flying behind.

The mustard author was announced winner and went forward to receive his stainless steel mustard pot, but this ceremony went more or less unnoticed. The dog was now running under the tables on a rewarding foray for discreetly dumped ham sandwiches. We watched the chase. A man in the crowd turned round to me and said, 'I say, aren't you the man who *ate* one of those once?'

It was 1 August 1992, only a week to go. I assembled my usual equipment (virtually none), and all the video equipment (amounting to three or four separate porterages) and lugged it from London to my parents' house in Hampshire, where there was more space. That became a journey of epic proportions in itself and left in its wake a trail of resentful British Rail employees.

The last night, 7 August, and the Allens were assembled in Hampshire for a farewell supper. My sister Katie jollied my mother along and bravely drank my health; we ate spaghetti, passed round a letter I'd secured from 10 Downing Street, expressing the Prime Minister's best wishes, then my brother and I recommenced packing and unpacking the video components in the sitting-room. My mother came to watch. 'Everything under control,' I said, battling to strap down a tripod using her spare washing line.

I got out an atlas and showed my mother the proposed route so that she could imagine my progress. Afterwards I had to help her forget it again by keeping her busily sewing up little bags of silica gel, the drying agent for photographic film – not, as it turned out, a very inspired idea, because the neatly sealed-up packages were to make every customs official from here to Rio think I was a cocaine merchant.

At dawn I woke Jita and we went out to the cornfields to be

alone together. We stopped at a stile and hugged. Across the field a roe deer lifted its head, and flicked away through the mists. Jita and I squeezed each other and promised ourselves that we'd remember the moment, the corn heads with dewdrops and the dawn light fixing them in the stillness.

Very soon after, it was all over – the people I most loved in the world were gone. The last luggage was in the car boot, I had hugged my mother, my father, my sister, my brother. At the check-in counter Jita and I were kissing our own goodbyes – not able like most parting couples to say that we would ring or write. She would get a letter from me twice, maybe three times, and I, out there in the forest, might not hear from her at all.

II

# Mount Cotopaxi

THE WAY THINGS ARE with modern travel, the very next day I found myself in the Amazon – and that wasn't hurrying to change planes. One moment the cornfields at misty dawn, the next, it seemed, I was coming in to land at a steamy tropical town for my brief recce, the Amazon running slickly by just beyond the trees and me standing beside it with jet lag.

And with nothing but a handful of memories to show for the passage of 10,000 kilometres: the Heathrow departure lounge, when I was stopped by a large Customs man. 'What are you intending to do in Colombia?' he asked. 'You seem to have a passport full of visas from drug-trafficking countries.' I said I was an explorer. He said if I thought I could take the micky out of him then I had another think coming: he had a good mind to lock me up right now.

And then there'd been an overnight stay in Bogotá. The city had no electricity that day and as my taxi driver waited his turn to charge at the policeman who was trying to control the road crossing, he pointed out the local thieves propped up against lampposts. As for the taximan himself, he was the only one of the *bogatános* around who was happy to wait in the traffic with his doors unlocked – he had long since been relieved of his wristwatch and you could see why thieves weren't keen on the car itself. It had no dashboard, no door panels, and two little wires had to be selected from all the other loose ones and joined to start the ignition. He arrived at my hotel in La Candelaria, the picturesque-sounding colonial district where I had already carefully confirmed a room by telex, and discovered the establishment had been closed for ten years – bombed, by the look of it. He took me to an alternative through streets in which waste paper tumbled in the wind and drunks swayed or leaned one hand against a wall and urinated with help from the other. One man inspected the contents of a litter bin, then he lifted it to his shoulders and walked off with it. '*Su casa*,' the taxi man murmured. His house.

The hotel was a splendid but creepy place of ancient, crumbling adobe walls, loose tiles and grand staircases. 'Silent, grim, mesmerized couple running it,' I wrote in my diary. 'Odd – inbred or something. To open my door you have to twist key vigorously, like a dagger, plunging it into the meaty innards.' Sometimes the phone rang out, a sound that gave me a feeling of hope, but the calls were rarely for the hoteliers. They knocked slowly on the wall to summon their neighbours.

I cheered myself by reflecting that I was only in transit. I just had to hold my breath a while longer, then the journey proper would be under way and I'd be surveying the Andean peaks through high, clean air.

However, I lay awake in the night, listening to Bogotá's guard-dogs barking in chorus and wondering what tomorrow's reconnoitre in this country's druglands would be like. I counted what I thought was one shotgun blast, three rifle shots and one bomb or gas explosion. The only comfort was the chickens singing out regardless from the old tiled houses scattered tightly on the hill slopes.

As the hours went by, I thought forward to the journey. In 'Phase One', as I rather grandly called it, I'd make my way down from the volcano Cotopaxi in the Ecuadorean Andes, through Colombia by way of the River Putumayo towards Leticia, site of my recce on the main Amazon river, but half-way down the Putumayo I would turn south to Iquitos. There I'd gain sufficient information to launch out east through the Peruvian forests to the River Javari and the Matsés, the 'Jaguar People'. In Phase Three I would use my newly-acquired Matsés jungle skills to continue east through Brazil towards the Mato Grosso. I fell asleep still contentedly dreaming of the Amazon. After all, whatever dangers really were out there, they just had to be less than those offered by Bogotá tonight.

The next morning I found myself flying onward to Leticia, the Amazon forests down below, at first just a layer of flat green floor material, and then, as we began our descent, thickening into a textured carpet, and thickening and thickening again until it had a 100-foot pile and was all around us on the runway. Then the doors were open and the forest's hot breath was wet on our faces.

With all my video luggage to be checked at customs, I was the last through. By then it was dark. A customs officer helped me with my bags – and left them half-way to the taxi, muttering to a colleague that he'd ruined his back. He went off for a little lie down.

The taximan was made of sterner stuff. He managed to fit all my luggage into his VW Beetle and even an Austrian missionary as well. Together we squinted out through the windows, bracing ourselves for the first sighting of Leticia, drug country. If the stories were true, it would be a fetid shanty town, a jungle squat where home-grown cocaine exchanged hands for the first time in a long chain that ended in the most fashionable parties of Manhattan, or the squalid bedsit of a ruined junkie anywhere in the western world.

However, so far no jaundiced addicts marauding the streets: all I could see were children running along, satchels flapping. I unloaded myself at a hotel, and ventured out for a closer look. The road to the port was lined with friendly bars with people beckoning me to join them for drinks. On the right was a TV showroom. On the left, chic girls cycled by on bikes painted in the fashionable fluorescent colours. They were serenaded by boys hissing waggishly at them from porches. Mopeds, trail bikes – all spanking new. It was as if I had got off at the wrong stop. Just as I'd suspected, this wasn't the place the American adventurer had described – all primeval forest and stubbly-chinned cocaine dealers; there were no skulls for sale in the gift shops. I'd come all this way from Hampshire and now I was in middle-class Amazonia. The main hazard seemed to be dodgy tour operators, who came at you out of the dark with their brochures and asked if you needed a one, three or five day Amazon trip.

Over the next few days, I systematically gathered all the information I could. It did seem as if the Putumayo was safe. And the other options were not: I'd have to descend to the main Amazon via one of the parallel tributaries further to the south – either enter

Peru illegally by way of the Rio Napo, which flowed through land disputed between Peru and Ecuador, or down one of the Peruvian tributaries further south still, these haunted by the Shining Path terrorists. So I would come down the Putumayo as planned. But not with all this video equipment, thank you. I couldn't stand the thought any longer. I had 6,000-odd kilometres by foot or river boat ahead of me and already, like the customs man, I felt like a little lie down. No, I would take my normal backpack, containing my mosquito net, jungle boots, water bottle, survival kit and my ordinary camera equipment, and, reluctantly, squeeze in the video camera, a tripod, a dozen or so tapes and a few batteries.

Having stored away the rest of the video equipment – the generator, ninety hours of tape, miscellaneous cables and three strange black boxes of unknown use – I went into the night to have one last look at the Amazon before the start of my journey. There was no view, but a few lighted boats gave depth to the darkness. I stood looking out, wondering what lay ahead of me. Certainly the warnings about the drug traffickers had been exaggerated. What did I have to lose by coming through Colombia down the Putumayo?

The answer was, in fact, my life. But for the moment, blissfully ignorant of the mishaps in store – the broken bones, the chase, the rest – it all seemed very satisfactory. My Spanish was settling in well, and I had dumped most of that alien technology. All set, I thought, for a first-rate expedition.

I couldn't have known that I had already seen one sign of the other, hidden, face of Leticia. By itself it had meant nothing, just a bit of local colour for my diary. I had been at a clothing store near the river, down by the neat line of booths where you exchanged your dollars. In the store sat a woman, and beneath her manicured nails was a glass counter, and beneath this she displayed a photograph of the previous occupant, her husband. One day he'd answered the door of their family home and been shot dead. No one enquired further. For all was not as nice as it seemed in Leticia.

I flew back to Bogotá – no electricity today either – and took another flight onward to Quito, Ecuador. At last, alone with my few things, I was in a bus heading to Latacunga, a town at the foot of Cotopaxi, over 3,000 kilometres from the Mato Grosso of Brazil and the approximate point at which the Amazon Basin was at its widest. Soon I'd be at the start of my journey.

I sped on through what would have been the old Inca empire, an area reaching through modern Ecuador, Peru, and portions of Bolivia, Chile and Argentina – all this, and its emperor Atahualpa too, overrun by the illiterate Francisco Pizarro with fewer than 200 soldiers. After Atahualpa's death, his general Ruminahui – 'face of stone' – fought on, Quito, the seat of the northern half of the empire, being destroyed in the struggle. Within nine years Pizarro had removed almost all trace of Inca culture – it was over by 1540, less than two decades since Cortés had done the same to the Aztecs.

But now my mind was on the volcano Cotopaxi, and I strained to see outside between the other passengers. Mostly they were children, girls on their way to school opening and closing exercise books, mouthing words for a test. As we sped along the tarmac road, the girls' grey school socks slackening down their fat legs, I peered to see the cone of Cotopaxi through the last morning mist that was enfolding the land which rose on both sides. Potato plots lay embedded up the steep lower slopes; clothes were spread-eagled on cactus spikes to dry; a soil which was occasionally laden with grey lava dust blew in the mountain winds. Then, unmistakably, Cotopaxi – a majestic hat of snow rising sharply on our left. I watched the mountain, the snow that was yellow in the early sun. It was said that when the mountain erupted in 1877, the lava sped into Latacunga at 80 kilometres an hour, carrying with it huge blocks of ice from the summit. Some of these giant ice cubes were left stranded 50 kilometres away, and took months to melt.

'The start of the expedition,' I thought, proudly looking up at the snow cap. 'Phase One: from the widest point of the basin – in effect, the most north-westerly Amazon source – down through the Colombian drug lands towards Leticia and to my first destination, Iquitos.' My starting-point must be a little brook out of the way up there somewhere.

Soon I had seen quite a few little brooks out of the way up there somewhere, none of them on the map. And I couldn't help noticing that the people who lived up in the windswept grasslands were very different from the friendly schoolgirls on the bus. They seemed a quiet, buttoned-up people. They looked out of sorts, the poor of a variety you'd expect only in huge cities. A girl with her hair wound into a knot was walking into the hills balancing a bit of cow leg on her shoulder. A man was doubled up below a battered door, walking in the same direction – into the apparently empty hills.

The bus drew up in the central market of Latacunga. I looked around. A woman stopped to adjust the handwoven webbing around her waist and dropped her potatoes. Shoeshine boys, with black palms and smudged black faces, ran after them.

My journey was going to depend on ingratiating myself with these people – not over months, as I had always done when settled with a remote tribe, but over days, as I passed on through. And how many of these people agreed with the graffiti I'd seen in Quito: *500 años de hambre y miseria*, 'Five hundred years of hunger and misery'. And *500 años de ruas – y qué más?* 'Five hundred years of roads – and what more?' The *conquistadores* had arrived in 1532 to subdue the Incas, and they were still subdued. Being poor meant being an *indígeno*, being indigenous. Yet the *indígenos* I'd seen in Quito's old quarter had been struggling along quite cheerfully, I'd thought, even those beggars sitting against the church of La Compañía where seven tons of their gold decorated the altar.

I booked into a cheap hotel, and a man with mange gave me a room with a view of a backstreet and of the people I was going to try to get to help me – people perhaps heading for their 501st year of hunger and misery. A boy cripple was being carried on his brother's shoulder like baggage. Other cripples inched by in home-made chariots. One girl had a skirt made of a plastic bag. A madman walked by on his knees, five keys hung from his neck on a metal collar. He was reading the day's newspaper, then eating it.

For a moment, as I stood looking out of the window, I felt like Mathieu in Sartre's *The Age of Reason,* a dispirited man of about my age who appears to have 'just realized he was living on ideas that don't pay'.

I must pull myself together, I thought. These people were hardly likely to be representative and the Indians at the market stalls with their red ponchos and white felt hats were smiling as they talked among themselves. I spread the map on the damp bed sheets and stared at its lines and symbols, western man's strange, rationalized interpretation of natural and human endeavours. Outside my hotel room a pony-sized guard dog stomped up and down, the floor boards creaking under its weight. The dog's frayed-rope tail was thumping outside, as if the beast was intent on breaking into someone's room.

Eventually I got out my pencil and circled a valley beyond San Juan de Pastocalle. This was a village below a peak called Iliniza, which sat back in a range running to the west of Cotopaxi, and whose slopes must hold the most north-westerly source of Amazon water.

The next morning I woke early and went in search of a bus to San Juan de Pastocalle. A policeman stopped what he was doing – cleaning his teeth with string from a flour sack – and directed me across the bridge to a bus. I climbed aboard and found myself beside a woman who smelt of smoked wood and cheese. She had some half-a-dozen cardigans on and could block the view just by breathing. A drunk stumbled on to the bus, and offered his watch for the price of his fare home. Mothers barged aboard, the babies on their backs chewing their pigtails and using their little fists to help their mothers push and shove.

The bus wound up into the hills, its exhaust pipe blowing out sooty clouds. More villagers piled in. Each time the door closed it made a violent scream, as if someone's fingers had been caught in it.

The grimy, rosy-cheeked passengers were studying me thoroughly. They were easy-going among themselves, but when I tried to help a girl by picking up a dropped shawl it reduced the bus to silence. The girl herself had a scar across her wind-polished cheek and beautiful, bright, inquisitive eyes. Sometimes she looked at me, but when our eyes met she hardened her gaze.

My nose began to bleed from the altitude. Four thousand, four and a half thousand metres – we wound into the bare hills. A girl tottered along the road, strapped by rope to a milk churn. Sometimes we passed eucalyptus, planted by energetic Belgian conservationists, now known to drain the soil of water and deposit leaves which inhibit all other plant growth.

Then up to the high altitude grasses, the only habitation the occasional grass-roofed hamlet. Far away we were eye to eye with the snowy peaks – Cotopaxi, 5,897 metres, and Mount Iliniza itself, 5,263 metres. My neighbour blocked the view as she reached to dip into her polythene bag of coca leaves, munching them like sweets, but I already knew that Iliniza was receding, not getting nearer. I was on the wrong bus.

Though the view was spectacular I couldn't see enough of it to work out where I was going. None of the people pressed against me spoke Spanish. I was wedged aboard a bus bound for . . . where? – the west, it looked like – and I was helpless.

Finally, I struggled to the door, and stopped the bus. Outside, I was suddenly alone, winds sweeping over the mountain pass, wanting to take me with them. When clouds covered the sun the weather immediately became bitterly cold. I flailed around in the wind for a few hours, orientating myself with Cotopaxi to the east, and the Amazon source to the north. I waited for a bus back to Latacunga, watching, as the day proceeded, the clouds budding around the summit of Cotopaxi, like rose blooms.

A girl came by, leading a donkey, its quick trotting steps organized by her wielding a heavy rope. She was in a hurry to get out of the wind. I asked her if there was a bus coming. She made no effort to understand but stood staring, not afraid but with a poker face set in silent resentment. All those graffiti in Quito, *500 años de miseria y hambre*, were locked away behind those child's eyes – not expressed openly for me to see, but there none the less, shiny black mirrors in which I could see my feelings of guilt.

Another two children came by, these with a llama flock. The girl talked cheerily in Quechua to the boy, who was chopping a huge knife at a little piece of root. When I was near enough to see the wind parting the hair on the llamas, I called to her. She stared as they passed me, veering off the road and away into the wind.

It was an unpromising start to the expedition. I sat waiting in the wind for the bus, and thinking of the first girl's speechless black eyes. Whether or not she was just a bad-tempered girl, the fact was, her people had been robbed by my kind for just too many centuries. I felt terribly uncomfortable. Even the word 'Indian' wasn't one of their own choosing – just a lost Columbus thinking he'd found

India in 1492. My expedition had hardly begun and already I felt I needed a holiday.

Back in town I heard there was to be a cockfight. I decided to go along and get to know a few Latacungans. My progress here could only improve. The owner of the cockpit, a hearty man called Martínez, beckoned me in out of the dark and showed me around. This was a family business, and two little girls served up rum and also bread and local cheese with portions of – it seemed in poor taste – chicken soup. I was taken down a passage lined with the padlocked cages of the feathered contestants. Referees, farmers in fraying suits, were busy fixing on tortoiseshell and bone spurs. These were handed to them from natty cases held open by the owners, people who bustled about with an air of importance – it was an old saying that cocks took after their owners, and the owners had to keep looking plucky if only for the sake of their birds.

Before the first fight, I met an English-speaking man who was originally from Puerto Rico. I told him about my journey and he nodded, understandingly. 'Dat's okay. You godda have ya dreams. Ya dreams, they important when ya young.' He sounded as if he'd learnt his English from an illiterate Italian living in Chicago.

'Me. I'm happy here with my family. I ain't goin' nowhere for no one,' he said. 'Except for dollars,' he added, on reflection. He asked how far I had got on my journey, and I told him about my bad day on the bus up in the hills.

'You ain't even started den!'

After thinking about it for a bit, he said, 'Say, you got enough dough for anudder bottle of rum?' And after a little while longer he said, 'I gat what ya need!'

'You have?' What did a drunk Puerto Rican have that would help me cross the Amazon Basin?

'A llama! I got a spare one.'

Dominic felt that a llama could take my bags and allow me to walk the hills with enough food for a week, say. I'd be totally independent, I could see that, and I said the idea was worth a go.

The cockfighting began. There was a special cash prize if one of the cocks was killed in less than twenty seconds and a giant clock above the pit ticked away like a TV quiz show timepiece. During the first four fights, none of the cocks gave up in that time, though some looked as if they wanted to.

The big fight was coming up now. It was between a veteran of six battles – each of them to the death – and a much more sprightly bird. The veteran looked like an ailing buzzard. He had only one eye, and not enough meat on him for even two servings of the soup. Today, defeated by a bus ride and with the whole of the Amazon yet to cross, I felt a little like that cockerel – a knackered old bird that was past his prime.

The match started. The clock ticked away, and within seconds, all too predictably, the old bird was a gory mess. His adversary pecked away at his head; blood spurted over the red cockpit. As the assault went on, the old cock bent his head lower and lower. Surely it wouldn't be long before his one remaining eye was out. Then something peculiar happened – so odd, it played on my mind for days afterwards, seeming to gain a significance of almost religious dimensions. The veteran, one-eyed cock took control of the fight. It was as if he had changed his mind about dying right now. Fate would just have to lump it.

The old cockerel raised his head and threw off the young bird – Spartacus throwing off his destiny. For a full second the young opponent seemed to stop and goggle astounded at the old bird. Then, quicker than I could see, the cockerel stirred himself. He appeared just to flick his feet up, but it was a movement that killed the other outright. The young cock lay upside down with his legs quivering feebly in the air, and still with that astounded look in his eye. So it was the young, tender bird that ended up as soup that time.

I went out into the night stirred by this unlikely triumph, and the following morning Dominic drove me along the bus route, and on beyond San Juan de Pastocalle towards the slopes where the source lay. 'Funny that your spare llama is kept so close to where I want to go,' I said.

'I make it easy for you,' Dominic said. 'Who knows? If you happy, maybe you pass dollars my way.' Where long grasses blew in the wind and potato crops grew on almost vertical slopes, we got out of the car. Off to the left, the west, was Iliniza, and that boggy source, the most north-westerly point of the Amazon Basin.

He led me over the grassland to a single hut which had a grass-thatched roof and earth walls. A sheep pen was pressed up against the building, but there was no one to be seen. Dominic called out.

'Your friends aren't in,' I said.

'They is here all right,' he said, and marched up to the low, hidden entrance. A young man came out. One of his eyes was dry, the eyelid unblinking and useless. Dominic talked to him in Spanish while I looked around. The air was dry and clear. Five hundred feet up, a rancher was rounding up two head of cattle. A thousand feet up a woman rode on a mule, a bandana over her face against the wind, her little round hat held down with a red shawl. Somewhere up there was my bog.

'He says you gotta pay seventy bucks,' Dominic said, eventually.

'I thought this was your llama.'

'You gotta the money or not?'

'Fifty?'

'Sixty, he says. No way he takes less, he says.' But the Indian hadn't said anything, and I wondered if he even understood Spanish. He looked as though he'd never seen Dominic before in his life.

I handed Dominic my cash, and he pocketed virtually all of it, passing on just a couple of notes to the Indian. I interceded on the Indian's behalf, and for a while I was haggling with the Puerto Rican as if on an unsavoury downtown street corner. 'Who you try'n ta kid?' he said, reluctantly handing over more money to the Indian. 'Shit – I don' believe I'm doin' dis.'

The Indian was surprised at more money coming his way, but not grateful. He seemed to have come to expect the town people to come up here to rob him and without complaint went away to get the animal from beyond the horizon.

It must have been grazing a long way off, because it was over half an hour before he returned. It was a large animal, and it was followed by a smaller one, its baby.

'You're lucky, man. You got two.'

I asked how I fed a llama. 'Plenty grass for him, don't you worry.' He spread a fat arm out to encompass some of the 360-degree view of wind-blown grass.

I asked Dominic to explain to the owner I'd return the llama in a few days. 'Don't bodder. He don't speak Spanish too good, and I don't speak none of his language neither.'

And the Indian disappeared, content, it seemed, to have got away with this robbery so lightly.

Ten minutes later, Dominic had disappeared as well, having charged me for petrol, and I was standing alone with my luggage on the bleak hillside, the uncertain owner of a llama with one dependant.


Wandering the windswept Andean slopes with a llama is less easy than you might imagine. There was nothing to tie their lead reins to except grass, and as I stopped to investigate the first of three rivers trickling down the slope the two llamas drifted away from me, as if carried by the wind.

It didn't help that I felt like an intruder here. I *was* an intruder here. And while the llamas soon became bored with me I was of considerable interest to the local shepherds, who watched me suspiciously, along with their flocks, as I guiltily stalked about their land examining which peaty brook arose where. A short-eared owl abandoned its quarry, veering away as I walked through the reed tufts, over bristly grass mounds and sumps of black mud, head bent low against the wind, and for no other reason than to satisfy myself that I was doing this journey properly. That night I left the llamas tethered by their former owner's hut, and retreated down the road to a house where a farmer put me up for the night.

I set out the next morning with a packed lunch of boiled eggs and bread and for that day and the next jumped in and out of black mires, tramped over the moorland grasses, openly followed now by children. They kept their distance and stood gazing silently, waiting for the next time I fell into a bog. They wore hats which they kept low over their eyes, like gangsters, and had thick hair on their arms. I asked them gently where the highest point of water was, but no one would say a word. But they loved to laugh at me stumbling about, daubed in bog moss, the llamas pulling me back down the slope, and on the fourth day a little girl from the family who had owned the llamas escorted me to the highest running water on the slope, a spring nestling in a hollow and decked with reeds. I sat down on the sheltered spot, an imaginary 'X' on the llama-chewed turf. To the girl it was the highest water source for her flock, to the people who made maps back in the western world it was the Rio Blanco, a northern source of the Pastaza, which led to the Marañón, which flowed into the great Amazonas.

With excitement gathering in me, I ran downhill with the llamas happily trotting behind, only too pleased I was disappearing from their lives.

There was no one in the hut. 'Keep!' I said to the small girl when she arrived off the hillside. 'Have!' I put the leading rein into her grubby little hand. I noticed she wasn't very much a child at all, but aged by the wind into an adult. She stood there, curious but distrustful, while I wrote a note in Spanish for her. '*Gracias por la llama*', I wrote. Thanks for the llama.

The girl was still waiting: town people didn't just appear, buy llamas from them, and give them back. She was still waiting as I walked off out of the winds, waving goodbye.


Phase One was under way. I journeyed back to Latacunga and then went on to climb up Cotopaxi, hoping to glimpse something of the great forests that I'd soon be among. I hastened up through tangerine-coloured lava fields to the snowline, and at last reached a beleaguered hummock of moss, where I sat down and looked out from the racing clouds, down through the deep layers of mist to the Amazon Basin.

No clear view, only a lone condor swinging around through the winds, but as my trousers began to soak up water from the cold moss I thought back to the past few days spent scrabbling with the llamas and knew I had to slow down. The local people had helped me in the end, but I had come here in precisely the way I'd always been trying to avoid. So much for not imposing with my alien map and ideas. Here I was, yet another galloping westerner, clumping about on the Inca mountains just like a *conquistador*. I wasn't going to get very far across the Amazon like that – not alone, not without 'back-up'. I could still remember that child's black, stark eyes.

And there was something else. Passing through Latacunga I had got into conversation with a local policeman, the one who picked his teeth with string from a plastic flour sack. This stout man virtually reeled in a dead faint when I said I was heading down into the lowlands. It was those drug trafficker stories again. The worrying part was that the policeman, a country bumpkin who looked as though he'd yet to see the capital, actually knew what he was talking about – his wife came from the Colombian frontier.

'So, it's a very genuine problem, you're saying,' I said.

'It is for me,' he said grimly. He spat out his plastic string. 'My brother's wife was shot three years ago.' I expressed my deepest sympathy. 'Five bullets,' he said. It happened in a place called Lago Agrio. 'But that's where I'm going,' I said. The policeman expressed his deepest sympathy.

My crossing would start off easily enough. Phase One was a road journey from here in the Andes down into the lowlands, providing me with an excellent chance to meet my first modern citizen of the Amazon, the bus conductor. The bus would get me all the way to Lago Agrio, in the steamy lowlands near the border, and the plan had been to enter Colombia and travel by trading boat, floating peacefully down the Putumayo river along the Peru–Colombia border towards Leticia, with the idea of finding a short cut south through Peru to Iquitos. Although the policeman clammed up about the details of his sister-in-law's sorry demise, his warnings had been generously supplemented by a German traveller, a girl who seemed permanently adhered to her huge backpack, from which her bandy legs hung, weighted by heavy walking boots. She didn't talk much of Lago Agrio, but she did about the Putumayo, likening the traffickers to merciless rocks along both sides of a white-water river. She had been strictly forbidden by her consul to cross the frontier, and though she didn't have much evidence that the river was really dangerous, like me she was hearing stories that seemed to made it a likely possibility.

Having pondered about these things on the slopes of Cotopaxi, I got out my diary and wrote, solemnly, 'I fear I'm moving rapidly on a collision course with reality.'

A need to slow down, then. To begin to blend a little better with my surroundings. Time enough to see the Amazon lowlands, the forests that the missionary Kenneth Grubb in 1930 called those 'dark and endless leagues', a forest which held 'more than the human eye can see . . . more than any explorer can reveal'.

So first I would head a little south along the Andes to the *lagunas*, a collection of sacred healing lakes known as the Huaringas just over the frontier in Peru. Not in themselves without human interest, a visit would give me a chance of spending a quiet time with indigenous people, slowing to local ways. I would gather myself together before facing the steamy drug world and the rest of the arduous journey – or so I thought.

# III

# A Cure to End All Cures

THE *LAGUNAS* WERE NEAR HUANCABAMBA, perched in the Andes of northern Peru, and this was best approached from Piura, a town in the dry flatlands to the west of the mountain chain. A village bus took me through scrub country with dry watercourses and oases of savannah-like thorny trees. Large, blue-bodied king-fishers sat with their heads in their shoulders, watching for move-ment in the water. Small ochre birds spun through the white heat. Dispirited mules stood outside clay sheds, and in corrals of brittle, bent branches there were black pigs with upturned noses. A cactus budded like a fat thumb from a rock. There was so little rain here, roofs were simply parallel sticks that provided a bit of shade.

Many of my fellow passengers had come to be purified in the sacred waters of the *lagunas*, but they admitted this only quietly at first. They were city folk, typified by my immediate neighbours, a husband and wife whose luggage consisted almost entirely of jum-pers for the mountains. The husband was called Jesus and his teeth were intermixed with fake plastic-looking ones. Among the fifteen pilgrims was a splendid 70-year-old *señor* with a dapper waistcoat, tie and impeccable English, a young technician who worked for the Japanese electronics company Canon, and a scary silent woman with dyed red hair who was a compulsive orange eater and had paid for, and took up, two seats. With her were two spoilt, bickering teenage girls who looked in need of more than your average bit of spiritual cleansing.

Why were they coming for a purification? Perhaps like me they were preparing for an undertaking that, on second thoughts, seemed a little too ambitious. Or perhaps disaster dogged their lives and they wanted a clean start. I'd yet to prise the truth from anyone, though I certainly hadn't given up.

For the present, bouncing along in the bus, everyone was more than occupied. The ladies' frocks were getting spoiled, and dust was coating their hair-dos. 'Uugh!' they cried as we swerved to miss another goat and their oranges tumbled. 'UUUUGH!!' For most of the people here, you got the feeling, the pilgrimage to the pagan lakes was a last resort.

As hours went by and our sweating faces were overlayered by the dust, we began to confer. '*Primera vez?* First time?' I found myself entering a little into the spirit of things – we were beginning to discover the nature of the purifications ahead of us. For although the *curandero*, the breed of shamanic healer who would conduct the rituals at the lakes, was well known, he was not as well known as the notorious hallucinogenic cactus he used, San Pedro. 'It's a purge,' the second-timers said, beginning to mope at the prospect ahead.

'A purge? But I've come for a rest,' I said. 'Some tranquillity before I summon all my energy.'

The second-timers shook their heads. 'We will vomit,' they lamented. 'Oh, how we will vomit.'

Among the first-timers, only the large woman was unmoved at this appalling news. She continued peeling and consuming her oranges with a frightening rapaciousness, never saying a word, just spreading her huge bottom on an ever-increasing surface area.

'A first purification,' my neighbour, Jesus, intoned with a tragic air. He nodded at her sack of sour oranges. 'Before the ordeal ahead.'

Most of the travellers kept themselves to themselves, and listened to the locals, who wore sandals made from car tyres and pale, stiff, wide-brimmed hats of enormous dimensions which made them look like munchkins; as the air grew cooler some men donned woollen caps with flaps over the ears, like those worn by imps and pixies.

The road wound into the hills. We continued up it, scattering turkeys and chickens. Higher into the sierra, and now moss grew from the rocks instead of cacti; higher still, and the tiles of the houses were made from cactus sheaths. Telegraph wires fostered lichens, which looked like sheep wool caught in a farmer's fence.

The bus wound along the slopes and dropped into Huancabamba, easing through the narrow streets and circling the plaza, which had bushes around it, a topiary of monkeys. Some local wit had given one monkey bush a sheep's jawbone. As we came to a halt, first-timers like me craned to see the famous cleansing lakes – only to learn they were still miles away.

A farmer would take us a further leg, for a fee, starting at four in the morning. Then it would be a trek on horseback through the sierra. Hearing the news, for the first time the fat, orange-munching lady showed signs of emotion. She was about to speak. We waited as she removed her teeth, clenched them in both hands, and said, 'But I've come here *because* I have a fear of horses.'

The townsfolk were well used to the routine. Urchins, primed with a reward by hotels, relieved us of our bags and took them off to the more expensive establishments; the police registered our names in case we were terrorists, then told other urchins to take us to the farmhouse where the *curandero* lived. Juan Manuel García was a tall man with beautiful but bleary eyes and black, straight hair which seemed permanently wet. He didn't have much to say to us except that we should pay him whatever seemed right. For my benefit – I fear he sensed cynicism – he said he had been practising for twenty-five years; he pointed to a certificate on the wall which showed he was a maestro. The art was passed on down through his family – usually the males. He was now training his thirteen-year-old son, he said. I noticed the son also had bleary eyes.

Before daybreak a truck hooted outside the hotel, and, half asleep, we threw ourselves into the back and set off. As we woke up and the dawn rose I was surprised to find I was sitting next to an Englishwoman. While the truck wound up into the hills I learnt how, back in London, Sandi organized seminars on shamanic practices; now she was studying the various healers in Huancabamba.

Some, she said, used dice to help them divine the future, some used the cactus San Pedro, and some didn't use anything very much but took her off into the hills then asked for money. She had had to call in the policeman to deal with them, but the policeman had fallen in love with her. He would call at her hotel room, politely removing the bullets from his revolver before sitting on her bed. She welcomed a day out at the healing lake.

Dawn came up over the hills and the damp that had settled on us began to rise. Women in the dirt road stood aside to let us pass, spinning wool with spindles that rose and fell, rose and fell in front of their skirts. Here the houses were of mud-brick and clay tiled; they had chimneys consisting of a raised lid of tiling perched on four crossed sticks.

We passed a stand of the hallucinogenic cactus San Pedro. Grimly, we watched in silence as it went by, its tall, fluted tubes projecting into the clear skies. Jesus began moaning to himself.

Everyone was now chewing limes that they had brought along. Sandi, an old hand at this sort of thing, said it was a preparation, an initial cleansing. It was reassuring, listening to the unflustered tones of a professional. She said San Pedro wasn't that bad, really. It was much like peyote, the cactus hallucinogen used in Central America. 'It sounds like this man is thorough, which is good.'

'Is it?'

She surveyed our companions, who, like me, were clutching at themselves as they froze, waiting for the sun to show above the ridges. 'Worth sticking around if only to see how this lot cope.'

On the roadside were Indian girls swathed in inelegant jerseys and with two or three layers of socks pulled up over their plump calves. With all their clothing it was difficult to tell which were adults. No one grew very tall, and both women and children wore their hair in braids, the two ends often tied together.

Now, nearing our destination, Jesus seemed to be cracking up. He said he wanted to tell me what had gone wrong with his life. Everyone listened in with morbid curiosity.

Jesus said he had been a laboratory supervisor for a petroleum company, and began to be bullied by colleagues at work. During this time, his wife, running a store, also found that she had no customers. However much she lowered her prices, they still wouldn't come in and shop. Then their four children began to have accidents. Each one of them broke an arm or a leg.

'Then my husband went mad,' Jesus's wife cut in. 'Lost his sanity. You know what he did? He got involved with another woman.'

'It's all true!' Jesus wailed.

'She bewitched him,' the wife said, simply. 'Even wanted a baby by him. Had to get rid of her.'

We listened, engrossed, wondering what means she had chosen.

'Got help from another shaman,' she said. 'But even he got our bad luck in the end.'

Jesus moaned, 'Was arrested by the police for witchcraft.'

We all settled back, thinking that was the end of the sorry tale, but Jesus went on, 'It was then that strange things began to happen.'

The couple told us how they started suffering sharp pains, as if a hot poker was being jabbed at them. Their arms, legs, groins. They had to sell the shop because customers would come nowhere near. Then, one day, salt was found in a circle around their house.

'The work of the devil,' Jesus said.

'The work of their worried neighbours, more like,' said Sandi. 'Salt, the oldest cleansing agent known to man.'

As a last try before resorting to this present treatment, Jesus had called on a distinguished witch to help them. However, the witch had been scared of entering their salt circle as well.

We pulled up at a desolate farmhouse, Manuel's second home. Geese ran at us, dogs lunged at us, and, as we waited for the *curandero* in the shelter of the farm sheds, we were pursued by fleas.

All day we waited for *el maestro*, as everyone now reverently called the *curandero*, and also for our ride to the lake on the horses – we had already seen them grazing in the fields and they looked wild brutes.

As we waited, guinea pigs scuttled in and out of the farmhouse kitchen. I took a peek inside: it was like a proper wizard's cave, light in shafts from broken tiles, cobwebs hanging with stalactites of grease and dust, and more guinea pigs squeaking in the dark of their own little cave, which was set into the mud-brick.

We waited all day, and were joined by two infirm peasants who had been riding since dawn. They swung in hammocks, carving flutes, and told us the lakes were dangerous. A foreigner had been sucked down into one of them called La Negra.

I wasn't too surprised that these lakes were attributed mysterious powers. The legend of El Dorado itself – that Indian tale which so fired the imagination of the *conquistadores* and which, fatally, was to draw them deeper into the continent and reveal to them the Amazon – was based on stories of a sacred lake, perhaps the Chibcha of the northern Andes. A tribal king, El Dorado or 'the Golden One', was taken to the lake waters at sunrise and, in a ceremony dedicated to the sun god, sprinkled with gold dust. Here in Huanca-bamba it was said that when the Spanish began to search and plunder, the *lagunas* were used as hiding places for their own gold.

When *el maestro* did turn up he murmured something about today not being auspicious and retired to one of his ancient rooms. Sandi said he was drunk.

Night came and local farmers fed us soup and distributed ponchos. I huddled as best I could on a straw mattress, while Sandi – already a victim to fleas from the farmhouses of other *curanderos* – opted for a convenient table she found in the dark round the back. She woke the next morning to find a stuffed dog dangling over her head from the rafters, also a monkey, squirrels, other hairy animals half-devoured by moths, and a python – like a bit of old lead piping. All were here to accommodate the animal spirits that guided the shaman in his trances. For, as Sandi evacuated (at last the fleas had tracked her down), she found she'd been sleeping on the *mesa*, the shaman's sacred altar.

The horses were arriving and were being saddled up. Sandi's mount began panting in an unpleasant, rather sexual, manner. The other beasts were a whimsical, cynical lot. The large lady had a horse with a rabid froth on its muzzle and she began wailing, saying she was going to walk. She needn't have worried: the horse whose lot it was to convey her was virtually immobilized under her weight, and it staggered along with the guidance of a peasant – grateful, it seemed, for any help it could get in delivering the load. I was given a large mount, an animal that had the same beautiful but bleary eyes as its owner, *el maestro*. We trotted off in a long trail through the hills.

For a while all was well as we meandered along the slopes looking out on the dry hill valleys below, peasants running alongside us trying to restrain the horses. Downslope, three horses harnessed together threshed corn that was laid in a circle under their hoofs. And now a vista opened before us, a steep slope of garden plots like an embroidered quilt hung up to dry.

I got out my video camera, which I had carefully placed in a leather saddlebag for just such a moment. I loosened the reins as I grappled with the camera, just the type of western technology that I had spent an entire career in exploration avoiding.

The horse – afflicted perhaps by the insanity I later came to believe was inherent in its owner – sensed its moment. It broke into a canter. We were on a narrow track which quickly developed into a tricky cliff path. The horse sped onward as I tried to recover the reins. Ahead was a sudden left bend, and a drop of fifty or a hundred feet. The horse was content to charge into oblivion. I leapt before the end came, and landed heavily on the track, striking my chest on the camera. While I fingered my ribs – three of them felt as if they weren't there – the horse executed a calm emergency stop. As I lay moaning in the dust, the creature turned round and began ambling home.

I was given a replacement horse, but could only mount it at all because I was still in a state of shock. For the rest of the way I was in screaming agony, too wretched even to be able to get off again. It seemed only a matter of time before the bewitched couple, Jesus and his wife, met their next disaster. Sure enough, Jesus was soon moaning on the ground where his horse had flung him and the girth strap on his wife's horse snapped, sending her rolling down the hillside.

We arrived at Chimbe, the main healing lake, towards the valley head. Here the land was bare and boggy, a little like the Lake District, and Chimbe a large upland pool which nestled in a watermeadow.

Having been lifted off my horse, I trailed behind the others, padding through a peat bog to the lakeside and wanting to go home. Now everyone was suddenly producing talismans that they'd had, all this time, secreted about their persons. Out of their jackets came a range of antiques – huge crucifixes, conquistador swords, wooden macumba figurines with huge African bottoms. They were all placed at the water's edge with money and photographs and other precious things to be sanctified, then sprinkled with perfume.

I sat in a sorry heap, watching all this, long since having stopped trying to be brave. Sandi gamely placed some small change on the pile for me. 'What next?' I said, unenthusiastically. A chilly wind was blowing up.

'Clothes off!' said *el maestro*.

To my surprise, not to say horror, everyone obeyed this command without hesitation. Long fingernails clicked against pearl buttons, designer cardigans were abandoned in the grass. The middle class of Peru lolloped into the icy water in their underpants, rubbing themselves with a purifying leaf, *wauwau*. They seemed to have come here wanting to punish themselves. I tiptoed through the shallows, occasionally splashing water on my ribs to numb the pain.

By the time I was ashore, everyone was shivering in a queue and the first in line, the upright old man from Lima, was having a purifying dose of Johnson's baby powder blown in his face. Then one of the *curandero*'s apostles brutally rolled a sword over the old man's back, symbolically cutting away all evil. He instructed him to leap to the north, south, east and west, exhaling deeply, ridding himself of all his fears and doubts. 'PAH!!' wheezed the ancient pensioner. And again, 'Pah!!' He was having to take his time, now. 'Pah!' he gasped. And finally, limply: 'Parrr . . .'

'That old man won't survive all this,' said Sandi.

'*I* won't survive all this,' I said.

When my turn at last came I could hardly stand up straight any more, let alone lift off the ground. Luckily the apostle took one look at my chest, scored with markings from a New Guinea initiation ceremony, and backed right away.

'*Vamos!*' *el maestro* called crossly in my direction. 'We're waiting to begin.'

'We haven't even begun?'

We were formed into a line facing the lake, and each given a shell to use as a cup. Into these, the *curandero* squeezed juice from lengths of tobacco – they dripped in the breeze like straps of fetid seaweed.

'Sniff it up your left nose,' the apostle said.

'Did he just say sniff it up your left nostril?' I asked Sandi. She was standing further up the line, staring sadly at her bivalve.

Sniffing acrid tobacco juice up your nose was just like you'd imagine it to be. As we were recovering, we had to do it again for the right nostril. The women stamped their feet in discomfort, like restless horses.

The *curandero* began waving a rattle, walking up and down in his heavy black lace-up boots. He was beginning a mantra, '*Por su trabajo, su familia, su novia* . . . For your work, your family, your girlfriend . . .'

He charged himself periodically with his own tobacco purges, raising a huge goat horn to his nose. Sword in his hand, he tipped it back, his head to the sky. His eyes and nose streamed as he chanted; we were blown at with talcum powder, sprayed with mouthfuls of perfume.

When the end finally did come, it seemed to be only the chilly breeze that was keeping me conscious.

'You ought to see a doctor,' said one of the healer's disciples, as we gathered ourselves to leave.


It wasn't just me. For most of us on the pilgrimage, our problems were not diminishing, they were accumulating. Some women did throw their bras and underwear into the lake, feeling renewed. Not me. I was among those now back to my worldly worries – namely, our return hike on the horses and the taking of San Pedro.

On the return trip, as I trailed at the back with the old and infirm, we were ambushed by a gang of drunk peasants who demanded money. I handed over some loose change, not caring if it wasn't enough – by this stage I wouldn't have cared if they'd been Shining Path terrorists.

Eventually we were back at the farm. 'You can't imagine how I feel,' the old man said to Sandi, as his stiff frame was eased off the horse. But I could. And *el maestro* was now sitting at his cauldron, cutting off the spines of tonight's San Pedro.

We had been forbidden to eat all day, but Sandi said I'd faint soon if I didn't and she searched in my bag for some biscuits I had remembered seeing somewhere. No luck.

Around the back of the farmhouse, the *mesa* was now stacked up with charms and photographs, all to be charged with spiritual power. Through the night we lined up and were cleansed in the way that was already all too familiar to us – purification by talcum powder, purification by sword, cheap perfume and tobacco juice. But this time the Peruvians *really* threw themselves into it. There was a special rail to be sick over. Time and time again they came back for more, happy enough to put themselves through hell.

I had been invalided out long since, and even Sandi was picking and choosing which rituals she would join in – 'all in the name of objectivity'. She sat with me at the base of a damp wall, studying it all, and warding off Peruvians who were looking for a place to vomit.

When it was time to take the San Pedro, a noxious sludge that was still warm and made most people throw up, I did my duty and went to swallow a little gulp down. Sandi took her dose and immediately ran off to be sick – or so she said, though it looked to me like she just spat it out. Then the paraffin lamps were turned down, and we all sat in the dark waiting for our hallucinogenic visions.

The *curandero* seated himself in an armchair lined with a spotted cat's skin. Suddenly he exhaled loudly, as if yawning. His breath came out like a cooing dove, and his lips made a flutter like a bird's wings. 'His power animal,' Sandi whispered. 'A dove. All shamans have a power animal, a spirit with the semblance of one animal or other, and that guides them as they enter the spirit world.'

'Ssh!' someone hissed.

*El maestro* was pacing about. Suddenly he seemed, in the moonlight, to have become much, much shorter. 'Woof!' He was making the husky bark of a suspicious dog. He walked about, feeling his way with his hands, like a child playing blind man's buff. And – was this the effect of San Pedro? – I suddenly felt very attentive, the pain of my ribs gone. And something more, the sensation of having made a monumental discovery – that unfocused moment of glee you sometimes get when something's on the tip of your tongue. But what?

Then it was gone. And we were taking turns to talk with the *curandero*. Still in his entranced state, he burbled to each of us from his chair, breathlessly revealing our past and future – and announcing for everyone to hear our alleged sexual problems, deranged lovers, and morbid fears. He told me I had a red car, though I've never owned a car at all, and that my father was a doctor, which he wasn't, and when I told him so he said I was sick and should go and sit down. And then a miracle occurred: I found the packet of biscuits in my spare trousers. As Sandi and I stood in the dark, hiding from another purging, I unwrapped them beneath my poncho. They kept us going until dawn, and a final celebratory dance led by *el maestro* on the mouth organ.

Daylight at last. Soon we would be leaving. Sandi and I climbed into the back of the truck and waited for the others. We were delirious from lack of sleep, excess of hardship, and the prospect of getting away from there. As we trundled down the mountain, and everyone else was reminding themselves that they weren't to eat anything too sweet or acidic for two days, Sandi and I disgraced ourselves by eating the remainder of the biscuits.

It was more a sign of desperation than disrespect. For, although it had to be said that many of these people were leaving in a much worse state than they came – indeed, some now needed urgent conventional medicine – everyone had come away from the *lagunas* with renewed hope. And, just for a moment, there had been something extraordinary here – that dog bark, that dove fluttering. Despite everything, Indian medicine had filtered through to the *conquistador* class, the rich European stock of the city. And the result was that every one of those here was coming away more positive about their blighted lives.

'All in all, what do you think?' I asked. 'Marks out of ten as a shaman, Sandi?'

'Eight,' she said. And that wasn't a bad impression to have made on two cynical old travellers who'd munched chocolate biscuits through the ceremony and come away from a healer with broken ribs and gaping flea bites.

# IV

# The Plunge

ON 6 SEPTEMBER, or thereabouts, the journey was under way. Having taken things easy for a couple of weeks while my ribs started to heal, I returned to Ecuador and the volcano Cotopaxi, near the true starting-point of my journey. Onward by road to Quito, and at the main bus terminal, among the thieves, vendors and litter larks, I found a bus that would take me down through the Andes to Lago Agrio, towards the Colombian frontier. And those drug men. I climbed aboard.

The bus conductor, my first representative citizen of the true, modern Amazon, stepped off the bus just as we lurched off into the twilight. He wasn't seen again. This left only two waifs walking the aisle. They'd developed a primitive form of busking and, until they were ejected by the driver, the younger child screeched a repetitive incantation and proffered a cardboard juice container as a begging bowl. The older girl checked donations to see if they were dud foreign currency.

I pressed my nose to the window, looking out at the dry mountain surroundings as the slums fell away. I was happy to be on the move at last, even if drug people were awaiting me. This was my passage into the forests of the Oriente, the headwaters of the Napo and Putumayo. I waited for the air to grow warm on my face, and remembered how the first Europeans to descend the Amazon had also left from Quito, though not in a bus.

Gonzalo Pizarro, whose older brother Francisco had already vanquished the huge Inca empire, had been enthralled by the stories of El Dorado, that elusive kingdom of gold. There was also talk of La Canela, a mysterious land of cinnamon – one of the prized spices that had been the inspiration for Columbus's original voyage.

In February 1541, Gonzalo Pizarro launched out from Quito at the head of a column of more than 200 Spaniards and 4,000 Indian porters, whom he carefully kept shackled. Down they went into the unknown, humid lowlands, forging their way into a new world, an oppressive forest of unimaginable dimensions feeding river courses that were seemingly endless. The year drew towards a close and still Pizarro had seen no sign of El Dorado. But now his stores were depleted, he was bogged down by rain and most of his Indian porter-slaves were dead from hunger and exhaustion. His subordinate Francisco de Orellana volunteered to set off down the Napo in search of food. Sixty men left with him, and they never came back. Captain Orellana's home-made brigantine was swept downriver by strong currents, and while they drifted on, the starving men driven to eat their shoes in desperation, Pizarro was left to struggle back home as best he could. Orellana's progress was no fairer. Although they were reasonably certain that they would eventually arrive at the Atlantic if they continued downriver, seven Spaniards had already died of starvation before assistance came from a group of Indians who, like all the others they were to encounter along the Amazon, were stunned at their first sight of white men – their helmets, guns, beards. Persuaded by the Spaniards that they were descendants of the Sun, the tribe offered up food.

As the expedition proceeded onwards, some tribes reacted by treating the strange figures as gods, some by attacking in canoe fleets. Increasingly, Orellana pillaged villages for food, and, as his reputation went before him downriver, increasingly a violent reception awaited him. It was eight months before he reached the sea, and was able to tell of the prosperous Omagua Indians who had handsome candelabras and pottery decorated with fine glaze, and of Indian women they had fought who were akin to the Amazon warriors of classical legend. The Spaniards recounted how, in front of their eyes, these females had clubbed to death any men who dared run from their ranks. They spoke of other Indians of whom they'd heard, tribes composed entirely of women who killed all their male babies and raised only female children. From time to time these Amazons made war with neighbouring tribes, and brought back male captives to enjoy at their leisure.

The legend of the 'River of Amazons' was to live on for some years. In the meantime, fired by Orellana's tales of strange peoples, more *conquistadores* were drawn into the Amazon Basin – they were more certain than ever that El Dorado was out there somewhere.

As I made my own descent into the Oriente I began chatting with my neighbour, Mari-elena. Smoky-haired, an Andean Indian, she had a child of three who scrambled back and forth over the passengers. Her hair flew out of the window, dry and loose like a horse's mane, as we sped downhill into the tropical air of the lowland forests where so many of her people had died with Gonzalo's *conquistadores*, breathing their last as they lay in manacles.

Times hadn't changed, just the names of the invaders. Now there were oilfields in these lowlands where Gonzalo might have wandered, and Mari-elena's husband worked for an American company as an engineer. Last week he had gone missing, believed kidnapped by Waorani Indians. A decade or so ago the Waorani were so isolated they were known just as 'Aucas', a Quechua word meaning 'savages'. Now there was an oil invasion, and the Waorani were no happier about it than they were with all the previous ones.

There had been the 'great challenge of the dread Aucas' to which Protestant missionaries more than amply responded, some of them dying in an Indian ambush. Then there'd been the even more dread Jivaro 'headshrinkers' – the task of 'bridging the gulf between abject heathen bondage and the life of liberty in Jesus Christ'. Then there had been Conoco Oil. And the latest? An invasion of Texas oilmen from the Maxus Energy Corporation, who had taken over the controlling interest of 'Block 16', south of the Napo river, amidst indigenous territory. All these invasions and more. In short, if poor Roberto had been picked off by the Waorani, perhaps it was seen by them as self-defence.

As the night came on Mari-elena's hand lay against mine, brushing my palm with the smooth curve of her wrist. As the bus began to turn downhill, she told me she didn't know what she would do if Roberto never came back, and that set me wondering what I would do if I didn't come back. I told her about my journey and she said I'd be safe from the traffickers until Colombia. As we talked, sleepily, our faces tilted closer and closer, gradually lolling together. I woke up to find her drawing my head into the warm sweet smell of her hair. Her eyes were closed, and she was mumbling into my face, 'Roberto.'

Twice in the night we were stopped at checkpoints. Soldiers climbed on board, and, seeing I was a foreigner, took me off the bus for questioning. On both occasions the soldiers took an instant dislike to my tripod. They examined the mounting, obsessed with the idea that it would fit a machine gun. While they detained me, the bus driver revved impatiently. It was a dark, wet night, and the soldiers gave up and let me get back on board. I would be dealt with at the Colombian frontier, they said.

It was still dark when we arrived at Lago Agrio. There was some street lighting, not much. Mari-elena gathered her bags and left, saying I should sleep here in the bus until daylight. 'It offers better protection.'

'Against what?' I called. But she was gone – 'Adiós!' – and everyone else was trying to get back to sleep.

Against what? I wondered. The famous traffickers? Robbers? Indians? Missionaries? I fell asleep before I had finished reeling the categories off. I woke in misty daylight, a muggy dawn in the tropics, a dirt street with Wild West wooden shops, and a forest around us. The hills steamed, and I peered through them for Cotopaxi and the line of white peaks. But this was not clear mountain air and I could see only the haze of the thick vegetation perspiring.

Within an hour I was riding along towards the Colombian frontier in another bus, this one home-made. It was small, makeshift and open-sided and it afforded good views of the farmsteads along the rutted road. Here people were actively moving against the forest, assaulting it block by block. The trees were in visible retreat – they were on fire, or being sawn or their saplings were being munched by slow but determined cows: all the forces of man seemed to have been mobilized.

There were two young people beside me in the bus. They'd been watching me for some time. 'Ask him,' the girl said to the boy. She had thick flesh, good wide lips, sugar-eroded teeth. 'Ask him,' she repeated. 'Pregunta!'

'He'll chuck me out of the window! El es un gigante! . . . He's a giant!'

'Pregunta! Ask!'

45

He asked, cautiously, in English. 'Excuse me. Er, why do you Americans –'

'English,' I said.

'– English dress badly?'

I looked at my clothes – long-sleeved shirt and thick trousers that had been waiting weeks for this jungle. The truth was, since I'd broken my ribs I'd rather let myself go. I must try harder. And at the next checkpoint I took the opportunity of going round the back of the bus and changing into a bright tropical shirt normally reserved for visits to missionaries.

The young man bent forward so as not to be overheard and hissed mischievously, 'Now you look like you are from the DEA!'

He walked off down the road with his girl.

'DEA?' I wondered. Do they mean the American Drug Enforcement Administration? Must have misheard, I thought.

There were more roadblocks, and I got through these as well. The Colombian frontier, too – just a row of wooden shacks where my tripod was disassembled three times – and then a ride in an overloaded ferry boat, and another bus. So far, so good. '*Americano*,' the soldiers agreed at the next checkpoint as they frisked me and began to strip down my tripod. Then I was on my way.

Though some soldiers were rough, searching me, I wasn't complaining. They frogmarched other passengers away into their little sheds. I came to see the presence of the military everywhere as reassuring: in my mind the army were still the 'goodies', a protection force against these hidden drug mobsters.

'DEA,' a scratchy-voiced man nodded knowingly to his friend as I climbed aboard once again.

His friend said, 'It is true? Are you from the DEA?'

'The what?'

'Anti-narcotics. The Americans.'

I chuckled. 'Good heavens no!' I settled back to enjoy what there was left of the jungle here. Squads of cobalt-winged parakeets shot low overhead.

'They think you are.' The man tilted his head at the checkpoint we were now leaving. The guards were sauntering through our dust cloud back to their sentry box. 'DEA. They come here from time to time.'

I thought about this, and after a while said, 'Excuse me. Is it good to be from the DEA?'

'Oh yes, very good.'

'That's all right, then.'

'In America. But not good *here*, of course.'

I said, because I couldn't think of a more tactful way to put it, 'So, er . . . these drugs people are still powerful here?'

He said it was best just not to talk about it. 'Besides,' he said, cheerily, 'you're all right. You said you're not from the DEA.'

But what if someone thought I was? The American field agents worked in co-operation with the Colombian government through two offices, one in Bogotá and another in Barranquilla – both a long way to run to. While I chewed this over, wondering where I could change back to filthy clothes without raising suspicions, we stopped at another checkpoint. A smartly dressed girl of about half my height murmured, 'Mister, you shut up about the DEA. It's making people worried.'

'It's making *me* worried.'

To change the subject, she promptly asked who I was and what I was doing. She was called Francesca and she was dressed as if on the way back from a May Ball, with a black lacy top which puffed out at the shoulders according to the current fashion. She was perhaps sixteen, with the dallying eyes of a flirt, a noble Inca nose, fine brow bones and small ears with earrings like miniature chandeliers. As we left the checkpoint, a soldier, bristling with grenades, ran up and gave her an ice lolly. She threw the wrapper out of the window with breathtaking elegance. At last we were through the final checkpoint, and entered the town of Puerto Asis, on the upper Putumayo.

It had a lively plaza for courting in, a thriving market, and men here felt secure enough from street thieves to wear their gold necklaces. Not a drugs gangster in sight. 'Just as I thought,' I said to myself, contentedly surveying the family scene. 'As usual, the stories are thoroughly exaggerated.' I booked into a hotel. It had clean basins and showers, but these were fully occupied by prostitutes who were beautifying themselves for their night's work. They also filled the armchairs in the hotel lobby, slouching in front of the TV while their hair dried.

I went for a walk to stretch my ribs and, down at the market, bumped into Francesca. She looked very small standing in her expensive Spanish outfit among the dirty wheelbarrows and brawny men. She said she'd take me to see her children.

Children? How many children could you have at sixteen?

She led on like a princess, imperiously flicking her fingers to clear the road of carts. But I was already guessing: rich families did not allow their daughters out to get pregnant. And so we did not have a taxi ride to a hacienda with long verandas but a short walk up a dark, rutted backstreet. Francesca's clothes were a front, her only material asset.

Her house door was made of iron, and heavily bolted. The light was weak, and issued erratically from candles in bottles. The walls were hardboard, with Bible texts for decorations. She introduced me to a toddler, one of hers, then a sulky young woman with her legs up on the table. 'My mother,' Francesca said.

The mother didn't look very much older than Francesca. Getting pregnant in childhood seemed to run in the family. Francesca was putting on a cream jacket which was flared out to spread over her all-too-childbearing hips. I was distressed to find she was about to leave me with her mother, who had reached for a tube of handy lipstick, applied it and was now standing far too close for comfort. For a while it was an uneventful evening, and worthy of comment only because I gained my first hard information on the drug traffickers. She talked openly, seeming to hope that her information would soften me. As she talked, her eyes remained sly, up to no good.

'The drugs trade is not a bad thing, Benedito. For example, do you see addicts here? No. The drug dealers lead the country's export drive. America wants to destroy our economy.'

'You know, I don't think so.'

'Well, I do think so, Benedito,' she said, playfully reprimanding me. Her fingers crept towards my hand. 'Oh, Benedito, Benedito . . .'

While she chased my hand slowly along the chair arm she talked of how Colombia was divided into two parts not labelled on any map – one owned by the Cali cartel, the other by the Medellín. The two groups accounted for a large part of the country's violence, and things hadn't got better with the disappearance of the head of the Medellín cartel, she said.

She was talking of one of the ten richest men in the world, Pablo Escobar, head of a $3 billion operation, whose car fleet included a 1933 Pontiac once owned by his idol Al Capone. Unlike the Cali cartel, who maintained a pretence of controlling their operations merely through their sharp accountancy practices, the Medellín cartel were brazen in their use of violence. Escobar controlled two-thirds of the world's cocaine, 80 per cent of America's supply. Who knew how many junkies around the world were dependent on him? Five million perhaps? Ten million?

The Americans had put a $5 million price on his head, but in June 1991, in exchange for not being extradited, Escobar arranged with the Colombian government to retire to a luxury open prison. He had walked out a few months ago.

'Don't ask me where he's hiding,' the woman said. 'I don't know, and I don't want to know.' I decided I didn't want to know either.

In due course she did reveal, however, that he was on the run not just from troops, but from his business enemies – the rival Cali cartel was beginning to supplant the Medellín as suppliers to the world. And funnily enough, the Putumayo river, where I was heading, was popular with escapees because of its proximity to Brazil and Peru.* 'You'll be safe enough, though. Just don't get involved.' Then she gave me a pout with her lipstick-fattened lips, and her hand renewed the chase. 'But Benedito, my love, stay a while. Stay . . .' The conversation went downhill from then on, and ended when a drunk began hammering at the door and calling abusively for her. Francesca came running in from the back entrance. She

---

* Pablo Escobar was killed just over a year later, on 2 December 1993, shot by troops in a chase over the rooftops. Afterwards, the marksmen reputedly fired shots in the air, and cried, 'We've won.' According to the *Guardian* (London), 4 December, 'He died alone, outgrown by the drugs trade that he had done so much to create. In the end it grew too sophisticated for a man who could rise to head a $3 billion operation, but could never rise above his origins as a petty thief.' However, the slum-dwellers of Medellín regarded Escobar as a Robin Hood figure; he inspired so much loyalty among the poor that four separate funeral masses were held. 'Such was the crush of mourners queueing to pay their respects to the bullet-ridden corpse . . . that the funeral was delayed for two hours.'

seized a huge ashtray, handed it to me – 'a gift' she said – and packed me off towards the first lit street. Then she ran back to defend the home.

'*Buenas noches, amor*,' said a prostitute, hanging about in the hotel doorway, her hand stroking her bare thigh.

'*Buenas noches*,' I said, handing her the hefty ashtray.

I went to bed, and lay on my good, right-hand side, believing nothing too terrible stood between me and my journey down the river towards Leticia.

The Putumayo was a large river, and at this time of year it lay beside a wide dry-season shore on which was pitched a line of food stalls served by women with teeth decorated with gold stars and borders. Trading boats swung in the current from anchors of scrap metal. Bananas, pigs, oil drums, were tossed from decks and were floated ashore. Maize made its way to land on the backs of stevedores, boisterous youths with no muscle but terrifying strength who yelled macho greetings from beneath their loads. '*Negra!* Blacky!' they called to the darker girls, '*Gordo!* Fatty!' to the plumper youths. '*Mono!* Monkey!' to the deckhands. '*El mister!*' Mister? That was me.

I said I was looking for a boat down the river. I was heading towards Leticia, on my way to Iquitos, Peru. They whistled and sighed. *Lejos!* Long way. However, it happened there was a trading boat leaving today for Estrecho, ten days downriver. The owner said he'd take me that far, and I'd have to ask there about possible paths into Peru.

Soon we were away. Silky rolls of water unwound from the boat as we chugged off into midriver. A blue haze lifted from the riverside roofs of the occasional homesteads that perched on the banks hemmed in by the walls of forest.

It was a cramped little vessel with three other passengers, a boatload of produce to sell and permanent living space for the young boat owner, his wife and their pesky two-year-old who was gradually plundering the stores, '*Me, me, me!*' There was also the boat pilot and the delicate male cook who wore his pretty apron like a skirt. He had paper-thin skin that stretched tightly over his cheekbones and he left talcum powder and sometimes nail clippings in the food.

The first few days passed peacefully. I spent them lying sleepily on the boat roof with the other passengers, a remarkably well-educated Indian from downriver who played chess with me, and two local fishermen with thin, stubbly beards and long scars on their arms. They were *mestizos*, that is, peasants of mixed Indian and Spanish stock, and they spent their time teasing the cook, calling out to him if pretty boys were dabbling on the river bank. Very occasionally, if the boys were very special, the shy cook dared to hiss over the water at them, knowing that the thumping engine would hide the sound.

We all watched the trees and plants that were fighting for daylight on the river bank. The humans were fighting for light, too, the forest pressing in on them and their thatched houses with sandy brown and white cows lying underneath. So far, no sign of any Indians. Yet the density of the riverside population recorded by Friar Carvajal, the chronicler of Orellana's expedition, was a continual feature of his account. It's thought that five million Indians lived in the Amazon five centuries ago. Now there were around 250,000, just 5 per cent of that total.*

For the wealth of El Dorado had proved to be not the Indian gold, but the Indians themselves. Many died directly at the hands of those moving in on the Amazon in the wake of the *conquistadores* – particularly the slavers, who enthusiastically seized Indians for the tobacco and sugar plantations of the continent's newly arrived colonialists. The greatest killer, though, was imported disease. No sooner had the indigenous population been decimated by smallpox, than malaria, unknown before the eighteenth century, swept through them.

Missionaries, too, were rounding the tribes up – Jesuits from the emerging Spanish colonies of the Andes, the rival Portuguese

---

* Survival International puts the Brazilian Indian population at 220,000 (comprising some 200 distinct groups with more than 100 different languages). Compare this to the number of 'wildcat' gold prospectors working alluvial mines throughout the Brazilian Amazon: 400,000. See Macmillan, 'Counting the cost of mercury gold mining'.

Carmelites and others ascending the river through Brazil. While some missions were a valuable sanctuary for the Indians, very often the missionaries gleefully joined in the slave trade themselves. The bodies of the Indians might wither and die, but at least their souls had been saved. Many were quite legally enslaved through the practice of 'ransoming', a euphemism for seizing Indians to save them from (generally non-existent) cannibals. In 1750 clashes between parties vying over the Indians were reduced by the Treaty of Madrid, which fixed the border between the Spanish and Portuguese colonies along the Javari river, though missionaries and their allies were to carry on slaughtering each other's flocks for some time.

Few Indians on the Putumayo, then, just the forest and occasional *mestizos*. Their houses were shaped to the terrain and hewed roughly from the trees, outsiders still bending to the force of the forest, which was strong and aloof.

Macaws flew out of it, monkeys crashed through the tree crowns, but these were glimpses from another world – the forest was inaccessible to us on the river, its scratching sounds muffled and its smells wrapped up inside those leaf walls, only occasionally attracting our attention when some animal in there issued a shrieking call of alarm.

A Colombian army checkpoint. Conscripts searched the boat, and the officers checked all our identity documents, taking them away and asking us one by one into their little shack. In due course, I was demonstrating my tripod. The officer was a friendly man who looked like a young bank teller, and we were getting along very well when he said, 'Just a bit of friendly advice. Better not to show your video camera too much. Bad people, you know.'

I wanted him to be a bit more specific about the bad people, and as he seemed like a nice sort of man I bent closer and whispered, 'You mean drug traffickers, or just thieves?'

'Just use your common sense, that's all I mean.'

'Well, while I'm here, perhaps I can ask . . . There's no problem with, you know, trafficking on the River Putumayo, is there?'

'Look, forget I mentioned it,' he said, getting up from behind his school desk and leading me to the door. 'Really there's no problem here, none at all.'

'No problem, then. Many thanks!'

Outside, a military policeman also warned me against filming. I said I was very grateful, but it was all right, the army captain had just reassured me there wasn't a problem with trafficking along the main river.

'He *did?*'

'Well, more or less,' I said. 'Why, *is* there a problem?'

'Oh no, no, no,' he said, hastily. 'No problem here. You carry on filming if he said so. No problem here.'

Strange lot, policemen.

Onward, lazing through the days, watching distant king vultures twirl high over the forest, stopping each night at riverside houses where we hitched up our mosquito nets and slept on the plank floors.

Now we had reached the point where the river was marking the frontier: on the right was Peru, the world's greatest grower of coca, from which cocaine is derived; and on our left Colombia, the world's greatest exporter of the drug.

On we went, lying on the boat roof, playing chess and jokingly pairing each other off with girls on the river banks, washerwomen at work on log pontoons, their clothes getting soaked with suds, their breasts dark against their wet blouses. The settlers waved our boat to the river bank and called down to us for Imperial cigarettes, sugar and flour; mothers, who had hurriedly put on lipstick, rummaged through our box of second-hand clothes. Rag-doll children followed cautiously behind, staring from the river bank, hair in long wisps, and whined for sweets, '*Mamá!*'

The Indians rarely waved to stop us, but when they did we saw men with tranquil, enchanted faces and women who copied the *mestizos* and applied make-up, but using the red grease from prickly pods of the achiote tree. Dabbed on like rouge it made them look like dolls.

This was my Amazon so far: shy Indians side by side with the other poor – the fishermen, the homesteaders who struggled to feed their families. There was no material for newspaper headlines, no wholesale rain forest destruction and no strings of logs being floated downriver to market. No Indians running for cover, no grizzly *garimpeiros*, the desperate gold miners who polluted rivers with the mercury they used to separate out the gold – the lonely men who were up to their waists all day in mud, who got foot rot, whose cuts went septic, who misused medicines and died of drug-resistant malaria. The 40,000 who invaded Yanomami lands at the end of the 1980s, the 50,000 who were prepared to try their luck slaving as donkeys in the open-cast mine of Serra Pelada. Here the Indians, like the forest, were disappearing in a polite, decent-seeming manner. It was a gradual, silent evaporation.

Watching the quiet banks of the Putumayo, it was hard to remember that the real impact of the white man wasn't in present times. The forest might be threatened in the Amazon nowadays, but the Indians went years ago.

In the last century the depleted Indians had faced yet another wave of immigrants – these, like the others, discovering their El Dorado was the labour to be had out of the Indian population. On the Putumayo, almost more than anywhere else on the Amazon, these newcomers were to surpass themselves. They managed to shock the world with their cruelty even in an era when enslavement of Indian children went unremarked.

The story begins with Charles de la Condamine. A French scientist who had been sent to Quito by Louis XV to work with the Spanish to measure the Equator, he descended the Amazon in 1743 and although not impressed by the Indians themselves – he found them 'enemies of work, indifferent to all motives of glory, honour or gratitude' – he was fascinated by the legend of the Amazon women warriors. Interrogating Indians on the subject he came to believe there had indeed once been a tribe of fighting women, as related to the first explorers. He was also impressed by an extraordinary product used by the Omagua Indians. This 'cahout-chou' was waterproof and elastic; the Indians shaped the substance into bouncing balls and pear-shaped syringes full of drink, which they handed round at gatherings.

The first object to be made of the material in Europe was a pencil eraser, invented by the English chemist Joseph Priestley, who called it an 'India-rubber'. In 1823, Charles Macintosh manufactured a rubber-sealed textile fabric and in 1839 the American Charles Goodyear discovered the process of vulcanizing – elasticizing and strengthening the crude material. The growing popularity of bicycles and then motorcars triggered a surge in demand; by 1850 the rubber boom had begun. In 1887 a Scottish veterinary surgeon, while trying to improve one of his son's toys, invented the first successful pneumatic tyre, made of rubber tubing bound with linen tape. The demand rocketed further and, with a monopoly on wild rubber trees, Amazonia was again proving a gold mine. The rubber was collected from the forests of Colombia, Ecuador, Peru and Bolivia – rivers such as the Javari, where the Matsés lived, and the Putumayo, where I was now. The rubber was floated down the Amazon to Manaus, no longer a slow, garrison backwater built to monitor the mischievous Spanish, but suddenly a metropolis with an opera house, Portuguese paving stones, cafés and electric trams.

In 1906, as the market continued to thrive, a Peruvian river trader called Júlio César Arana bought 31,000 square kilometres of Putumayo forest lands and set up a company with British directors. The wild rubber of the region was known to be of inferior quality, but the site had the considerable advantage of being occupied by tribes of a placid nature. As Arana soon proved, these people could easily be induced to act as a labour force. He hired 200 militiamen to go into the forest and round up the Indians; some 30,000, most of the population, were brought into his camps.

By 1907 stories of atrocities had already begun to leak out about the Peruvian Amazon Company, but were successfully hushed up before they left the area. Then an American railway engineer, Walter Hardenburg, travelled down the Putumayo and unexpectedly found himself witnessing a massacre. He began to collect evidence and in 1909 his findings were published in the English magazine *Truth*.

The Indians were robbed of their crops, their women and their children. They were flogged 'inhumanly until their bones [were] laid bare'. They were left to die, eaten by maggots, then served as food for the dogs. Their children were grasped by the feet and their heads were dashed against trees and walls until their brains flew out. Men, women and children were shot at to provide amusement. They were burned with kerosene so that the employees might 'enjoy their desperate agony'.

Was this exaggeration, another example of the curious effect the forest had on people's imaginations? It seems not.

Such was the public outrage, the British company directors were forced to send out a commission of enquiry and in 1911 the team, which included the experienced diplomat Roger Casement, published their report. The findings were damning, Hardenburg's accounts verified, but little came of it. The Peruvian government, who had supported the venture to bolster their claims to the region, failed to convict anyone. A mere 8,000 of the original population of 50,000 Indians remained. The Andoke, the tribe to which my chess opponent Joel belonged, was reduced from an estimated 10,000 to the present population, a few hundred.

As Joel went about winning another game of chess, I talked to him about the massacres. He said that as far as he was concerned, the rubber boom was only history. Older members of his family did talk about those times, but they were the olden days; nowadays, he said, there were opportunities.

Ah, Joel's opportunities. I was wondering about that.

Joel was the only person on board whose Spanish I could easily understand. Everyone else spoke slang – for example '*má*' instead of '*más*', more. Joel had an education above mission school standards, could beat me effortlessly at chess – no one else here could even manage draughts – and he even wore Reebok running shoes. I'd been saving to buy some for years.

Yet he came from a simple family who lived on the river bank. We stopped off there one day. They had a giant *maloca*, a building like a huge haystack that was in fact a cosy communal home. The boat paused for Joel to leap to the shore with sugar, salt and T-shirts. I waited to see if any Indians would creep into sight.

He came back with three chickens, which his sister helped carry. She stood away from the bank as she handed them over, watching us shyly through her fringe. She had a leaning-back stance from carrying baskets suspended by a string across her forehead, a loose dress hanging like a home-made curtain off her back. It was a far cry from Joel and his Reeboks.

One night, lying in our mosquito nets in one of the homesteads, and watching distant lightning linger in the sky, Joel told me about his 'opportunities'.

'Trafficking,' he said.

I was flattered that he trusted me with the information. 'That must be dangerous, trafficking.'

He asked dreamily, 'Dangerous? Why should it be dangerous?'

'The police . . .'

He propped himself up on his elbow. 'Benedito. It's a policeman whom I traffic *with*.'

I could see I had a lot to learn about drug trafficking. 'The drug cartels, then. It must be dangerous to get involved with them.' I could remember photographs from the Bogotá paper *La Prensa*: men in business suits slumped in their car, blood running down their ears, a bomb crater in the road.

'On the contrary,' Joel said. 'Safer to do my job than spend all day fishing in a little canoe. God, have you seen the size of the catfish here – if they get a chance to upset your canoe, they gulp you down!'

'You're saying that trafficking is safe?' I noticed that while I talked in a whisper, Joel didn't bother.

'If a policeman checking my bags doesn't accept the money I give him, then he knows he's taking a risk with the *traquetas*, the dealers.'

'What sort of risk? They're not . . . you know, killed or anything, are they?'

'People have these stories about executions, but look, you don't ask these questions. I do know it's safe if you follow the rules of the *traquetas*. Safe for the little man, safe for the police.'

'Straightforward, anyway,' I said.

Coca was grown mainly on the Peru side, as I'd suspected. And *carajo*, did it grow! It was the perfect crop. Coca percolated money into remote rural areas in just the way that Third World aid failed to do. The plant didn't even need tending. You kept the little shrubs in a garden as you might any vegetable, stripping the leaf crop as it suited you and taking the bundle across the river as you went about your fishing. Colombians took it off your hands and disappeared into their forests. In their simple laboratories it was dried, powdered, heated and distilled into pure cocaine. From there it was despatched to a secret airstrip. Only this last stage was tricky, because you were now dealing with strangers, the *traquetas*, the dealers from the towns. The rest of the story I knew about: up to 3,000 illegal flights carried cocaine into the US every year, and many more than that attempted the journey by boat.

In short, here on the Putumayo, getting your cocaine made up for you was much the same as, in the UK, dropping in on the high street chemist to get your family photos processed.

The next morning I brought out my video camera. The drug trade being such a happy cottage industry, it was obviously safe to take footage of the forest as we went on by – the high tree screens with their still leaves, the fishermen in hats idly paddling their canoes. Besides, coca was a part of indigenous tribal life – the Andean Indians chewed the leaves to fend off hunger and soothe headaches, and on hunting trips the Tukano of the Colombian lowlands were sustained for days just on the ground powder.

The boat owner at first said I should be careful and keep my camera from sight, but Joel said there was no problem and after a while he grew less concerned, and let me carry on regardless.

# V

# The Death Penalty

'EVER HEARD OF PHANTOM BEACHES?' asked the boat's pilot that day. He was a man who prided himself on 'knowing water' – the way it rolled, turned, tucked in on itself.

'Phantom beaches? Nope.'

'You've never even heard of them, but I've seen them! Whole banks of sand rise up in the night, run you aground. Once I was steering a boat in the middle of the channel. Bang! We had hit a sandbank. Hadn't been there yesterday. We thought we'd hit a log, but no, out there under the moon was a bed of sand.'

'Mist?' I suggested.

'Sand. I got out to see. I climbed on to it – felt the grains between my toes. It was cold, though. Wet. I walked over it – I couldn't see an end. And I had got some yards, when something happened that make me stop dead. It started bubbling. The whole island was sinking. I got off there quick! Swung back on the boat, looked around – nothing there. Just that cold sand still between my toes.'

'What was the cause, then. Currents?'

'*Phantom* beach,' the pilot said, frowning. 'Didn't I tell you?'

On we went down the river, the chickens each morning calling from their bamboo cage, bracing themselves for their daily sluice down; the forest sizzling, waiting there for us, freshwater dolphins rising from the water to take air and, on the bank, *mestizos* scratching about for a living and the occasional clump of Indians with clothes hanging carelessly off them.

We came into Puerto Leguizamo, the first settlement of any substance, on about the fifth day.

Though it wasn't market day today, you wondered if it ever was.

There were billiards bars, men bent over dusty green spreads, but everyone seemed to be waiting. Scavenger birds, too heavy for the wires, sat atop poles, wings stretched in the morning sun. It was more than a one-horse town – there were perhaps thirty, in all; but one of them was dying of heat exhaustion in the empty market square and it seemed symptomatic of the place.

As we got under way again a couple of pigs were brought on board, dragged by their ears and doused with water to keep them cool. We also had another passenger. He wore brand new wellington boots, dark suit trousers and carried a pile of magazines.

'*Evangelista*,' one of the fishermen said, scratching his hooked nose, and then tried to find somewhere to duck out of sight.

But there was nowhere for any of us to go. The evangelist, called Joseph, was soon dishing out copies of tracts and beginning to address us like a congregation. One and a half joints were missing from his right index finger. He was more sinew than muscle. 'I wouldn't let him near my soul,' I wrote in my diary. 'His hands shake.'

Joseph went on preaching by himself for a bit, standing by the pigs in the breeze, then suddenly gave up, and asked if he could join in the game of draughts.

Two more days passed, days spent trying to keep our distance from the preacher. Each morning Joseph rasped his hands over his skin-tight jaw and decided he needed to shave, and each morning he asked if I knew his bible school teacher. 'Mr Paul,' he said. 'He was from America too. You know him, brother?'

'I haven't yet had the pleasure.'

'Brother, Mr Paul is a good man. He saved me for the Lord.'

At night, now just after the full moon, he slept in bright white underwear, something that alarmed the farmsteaders' dogs.


One afternoon, as we were playing chess, the boat owner came up to visit us. It was a rare honour, mainly because to make such a visit he had to battle through the stores pulled down by his child. '*El Dueño!*' Joel called. 'A game of chess?'

*El Dueño* was a friendly man with a downy moustache and a growing trade business, but just now he looked under strain. '*El*

*Mister,*' he said. He'd come to see me. I realized then that something was wrong.

'What have you been filming with that camera?' He turned to Joel. 'The pilot says someone has been following us – all the way from El Encanto. Or that's where he noticed it.'

'That's two days away,' Joel said.

'A canoe and outboard. He was nowhere to be seen yesterday afternoon – the pilot only mentioned it because he thought he saw him again just now. Red cap.'

I said, 'Well I've been very sensible with the camera. And the army said there was no danger from traffickers around here, so that's all right.'

Beside me, Joel was stifling a laugh. 'You asked the *army* if there were drugs people around here! And they said no!'

'Have I said something funny?'

*El Dueño* was less amused. 'Jesus! He asked the army.'

'And the police,' I said. 'They also said there was no problem. The man I spoke to clearly told me I could film. You see, I've been very careful.'

Joel broke into a fresh shriek of laughter. The two fishermen started joining in. 'He asked the army!' 'And then he asked the police!'

'Let's forget it,' *El Dueño* said. 'If anyone had wanted to catch up with us they could have done it easily.' But he offered me a word of advice. Don't get into conversations about drugs. Just turn a blind eye to whatever I chanced across. It could only get me into deep water.

He ducked down and forged his way back through the boat. His voice trailed behind, as he stumbled through the packets of rice and sugar and second-hand clothes. 'And, *El Mister*, no more filming please.'

'Forget about it,' Joel repeated. 'I've never heard of people being followed by a *traqueta* on this river.' He pushed forward the chess board. 'Your move.'

I did forget, watching the slow, untroubled rise and fall of Amazon dolphins, marine mammals adapted to waters 3,000 kilometres from the sea, their echo systems guiding them through the shifting currents of brown clay. And, wrestling with the fishermen, the huge flat-bellied catfish with barbels like whips.

Sometimes I mused on the ways of this distant figure Pablo Escobar and the people who had died at his hands: a newspaper editor, a presidential candidate, a judge, 107 in an airliner. I knew of these particular murders, and I hadn't even made a study of the subject. And then there were all the addicts, wasting away in the west, their lives ruined or ended.

I remembered how, when I'd told Joel that some Asian countries like Malaysia had the death penalty for trafficking, he simply couldn't believe it. 'The death penalty . . .' he repeated again and again. 'The *death* penalty . . .'

Here it was part of life. It would never be possible to ban the trade. If you didn't export it, you used it yourself the Indian way, chewing the leaf for energy or, if you had a headache, drinking an infusion, like a herbal teabag.

In Colombia it was the police who got the death penalty. And that was when they didn't help smugglers.

But all this seemed a long way away from the sunny Putumayo, our little boat with Joseph the evangelist. I'm afraid Joseph was rather stupid, and kept confusing the left and right side of the bank, Colombia and Peru. I was never convinced he knew the difference between Mary the Mother of Jesus and Mary Magdalene, Jesus' friend from his later, ministering days. Altogether, Joseph the evangelist wasn't the sort of man you'd want your life to depend on – and that, as things turned out, was unfortunate.


We eased down the Putumayo, and came at last to Estrecho, Peru. It was time to part. I shook hands with Joel and we went our own ways. 'The *death* penalty . . .' he said, chuckling again.

In the short distance into town with my backpack I discovered that my ribs were still in a bad way. I hobbled along, lifting the pack with my hands to take its weight off me, and saw the local delights.

I won't dwell on Estrecho – there wasn't much to dwell on. Rotting sandbags formed a little shield around the police station, where the police sat trying to get their pet, a spider monkey, drunk. The town did have a primitive sort of plaza and a medical clinic with a doctor, but the doctor was nicknamed the Killer on account of his track record and anyone with any life-threatening complaint instead begged for mercy from the Catholic mission.

I stayed two days, long enough to discover that the track towards Iquitos was back upriver; it led south-west through Peru to the River Napo, and from there it would be only a day or two onward by boat to the town. Phase One, I mused. Almost within my grasp – and then the push from Iquitos to the Matsés.

The owner of the boat came looking for me. '*El Mister*. That man found you yet?'

'Which one?'

'The man that knows you. He was the one the pilot saw yesterday and the day before. With the canoe, and wearing a red cap. He's a friend of yours, nothing to do with drugs after all.'

A friend of mine? Here in the heart of Colombia? I said I didn't know anything about it. I was probably being muddled up with the Canadian priests at the mission: 'We all look the same.'

'Oh well. I promised the soldiers I'd tell you. The man with the red cap was asking questions about you – or about the priests or whoever.'

'It's very odd,' I said to *El Dueño*. 'Why would he ask for information about his friend? I don't like the sound of this *at all*.' Disturbing visions rocketed through my mind. What if I'd accidentally filmed Pablo Escobar, the big Number One? In my head I saw thuggish hitmen, I saw men who would stop at nothing.

'Hey, relax!' *El Dueño* said.

'I'm trying, I'm trying.'

'Mind you,' he said, laughing to himself, 'we were worried sick about the way he seemed to be following us in the canoe. No harm in telling you now: we thought he was after us. We almost had to throw you overboard!'

Very funny.

'But it's all over now, and there's another thing I came to say: the soldiers I mentioned, they are heading upriver. They say they'll give you a lift to the path.'

In the morning, I climbed aboard the army launch – and found

Joseph there. He had already finished his evangelical business and was heading back upriver to a Colombian settlement opposite Puerto Arturo. 'It's near the beginning of the track, brother. I'll show you around.'

'Oh, I'm sure I'll manage,' I said, but what with my ribs I could hardly lift my bags aboard. Joseph leapt to my aid. 'You need a helping hand, brother,' he said.

In the space of a few hours in the powerful launch, we had undone two days' river-boat journey. The soldiers were newly posted and didn't know the path. We were deposited where Joseph requested – not at Puerto Arturo, but near a couple of silent *mestizo* huts populated chiefly by midges. 'Puerto Arturo is just along the river, on the Peru side,' Joseph said, brightly. 'Or the Colombian side. And the track must be here somewhere.'

I stood sadly on the Peruvian river bank, watching the launch go. Joseph didn't have a clue.

'Come,' he said, picking up my bag. 'Meet my friends. They are brothers in Christ,' pointing up the path.

Any introduction was better than none, you would have thought. Wrong. The first house had a family-sized woman blocking the doorway. She did little more than extend a hand to Joseph. She may have been a Brother In Christ but she was not going to move and risk allowing Joseph to sneak in.

'Sister . . .' he tried. 'I'm Joseph.'

'I know,' she said.

We walked on to the next-door house, my bare feet being pecked by chickens along the way. There were no other houses. This was our last chance.

The woman here was much thinner. She had a Roman nose that was badly set on her face, slanting off to one side. We located her round the back, by the kitchen, helping to hold a four-foot fish which was being chopped up by a girl of the same length. The fish was scarred by a bloodsucker which had left a track where perhaps it had been drawn backwards by the river current.

We were invited in for coffee and sat at a bench, while children, armoured with long trousers against the midges, came in to watch us. 'I have a son who is at university,' she said proudly. 'Bogotá.' While I tried to work out how she could afford to keep a child at university, she fed a baby, fending the midges from her breast with her spare hand. I learnt that the Rio Napo was three days' walk down the path. I'd need someone to guide me and I'd have to talk to her husband before setting out. She spoke as if it was his path, his property.

While we waited for the husband I got out my diary and wrote: 'In cupboard are stacked plates with left-over meals from yesterday, future meals for today. Grimy utensils. So far, each member of the family has wiped their hands on same corner of dirty table-cloth. Stove is firewood in clay. Dogs queue up for scraps. And her son is at university – she claims.'

A belligerent old man came in. While the woman's back was turned he snatched a banana from a child, and left again.

My eyes caught a bag of white powder sitting on top of the cupboard in a polythene bag. I wouldn't have thought anything of it but then the woman saw me looking and shrugged. She said, simply, 'It's no problem here.'

Cocaine. It was a relief to come face to face with it at last. And it looked so innocent there, snowy white on an old kitchen cupboard. A powder that I might have accidentally poured into the sink as washing detergent but which would soon be bundled off in a plane that would end up in the States, landing under partial cover of dark.

I couldn't stop looking at it. As we waited there in the palm-roofed shack, that little heap of white dust on the crockery cupboard was mesmeric – worth a fortune back home, here it was common-place, not even locked up. Although maths had always been my weak subject, if this was a kilo it must be worth £60,000 on the London streets. Supposing that bag was torn on a nail, and a tablespoon sprinkled out – £1,000, a ticket for Jita to come and visit me. Even getting a tenth of the London street-price, that one little polybag could change these poor people's lives. It could change mine, even.

Joseph didn't share my sociological interest. He made his excuses and left, unexpectedly spouting gospel school English as he went. 'Praise be,' he said, bowing out through the door.

Perhaps I'd better take my leave as well.

While I waited under the shade of a lime tree, congratulating myself for following Joel's advice and not asking questions, Joseph again went to try his luck at the first house. When he was out of sight I was invited back indoors and offered some fish. It was pacu, a type of piranha, but a vegetarian and less bony. I noticed the polythene bag had gone.

A man arrived with sweat on his forehead. Flecks of dirt had splattered on his trousers, some of it wiped by wet grass. He had run to get here. He looked at me hard as he entered, then thumped his shotgun down. He was not happy with me being here. He muttered to his wife, and I heard her say I was dropped here by the army. Suddenly, I wanted to leave.

'You cannot walk through towards Iquitos,' he said, sitting down to face me better. '*No es posible. Es prohibido.*' He left no room for questions, and as I didn't have any, I decided to depart.

'No, please eat,' he said as I rose. 'Eat.' He forced a smile, looking a little unhappy for a second that he'd come across as inhospitable. But there was silence now. He had a necklace around his neck, a gold chain with a rhino beetle head on it. He spun the beetle head rapidly in his fingers. He was waiting for me to go. Then he seemed to change his mind, and poured some coffee from a thermos. He told me to join him on the side bench. '*De dónde?* From where?'

England, I said.

'*Estados Unidos?* United States?'

I said no. But he looked meaningfully at his wife and said, '*Americano . . .*'

He asked what I was doing here, and I told him I was a student. I didn't think saying I was a writer was a particularly good idea at this stage.

'Which university?'

I was on my guard now. I named the University of East Anglia.

The questions went on. '*Antropología? Arqueología? Biología?*'

I chose anthropology.

'What do you call the tribe you study?'

I answered that I was on my way to the Matsés.

'I've never heard of them.'

'They are a long way away. River Javari.'

Soon it was an interrogation – question following question, each one firm, persistent, while he twiddled the necklace. Sometimes he realized he had pushed a bit hard, and he chatted matily for a while. 'Have you heard about the Indians here – how the men do unnatural things with the female dolphins?'

This was a story I had heard more than once, one that only seemed to serve the purpose of reminding the *mestizos* there were other people more primitive than they; it was more slander than folklore.

And still he was fiddling with that beetle head. 'What's in all that luggage?'

He might well ask. I said, nothing very much. But he persisted. Sticking out from the rucksack was the tripod, that mysterious, treacherous object that had no place here.

'You have a *máquina?*' He meant camera. I saw no point in raising tension by denying it. I got out my still camera, and showed him, passing it to his wife, trying to involve her and the children and thereby lighten the tone here. He turned the camera over in his hands, but this was not the *máquina* he meant. 'Not a moving camera? You haven't got a moving camera?'

Then I was certain. This man knew of me, and he knew of my filming on the river. He felt I was a threat to his cocaine – his son's education, his pension. That necklace must be worth a bob or two, as well. I fobbed him off for a while with the tripod, hoping Joseph would come back any second. The man undid the three legs, jiggling them about – up and down, up and down.

'I'll be going now,' I said. 'I wonder where Joseph is?'

'Who?' He looked sharply at his wife.

'*Evangelista,*' she said. Then she shook her head, in answer to some unspoken question of his. '*No problema. El es un estúpido.*'

God knows, I was no fan of Joseph, but he was a kind of innocent ally in all of this, and I didn't like my only companion being dismissed as no problem because he was stupid. It left just me.

Things went from bad to worse extremely rapidly, kicking off with the next question from my host. 'Who says you haven't been recording things – things you shouldn't have been recording?'

'The army said there was no problem,' I said.

'I say there is.'

The business was made so much worse because I sensed that this man was half-decent. He didn't want to chuck me out. I was the one at fault, the one disrupting his chance to make it out of poverty. I knew he wanted to give me another chance.

Amicably, I brought out the video camera and carefully moved myself over to the kids. They were absolutely engrossed by the drama brought them by this stranger and I thought I'd show them my latest footage, clear the air. I fumbled nervously with the knobs, half-hoping this would endear me to everyone – I was an inoffensive uncle showing his home movies. 'Gather round everyone, that's it.'

I ran the monitor. It only made things worse – shaky views of river banks, men lurking suspiciously in their cowboy hats, exchanging packages. It did not look good.

'Why are you filming like this? You are something like a spy.'

I remembered a story about a traveller in Africa – the Congo, I think. He had a very enjoyable trip until he reached a border crossing when the local policeman grandly perused the passport. 'Tourist, you say? *I* think you are spying.' The tourist began snorting with amusement. 'Spy? Spy? I'm a chartered accountant, for God's sake. How would I get the time to be a spy?' The officer stripped his luggage down. The tourist wasn't laughing any more. 'What's there to spy on in this hole anyway? Just *tell* me!'

'So you want me to tell you? So you admit it. You *are* interested!'

'Imbecile!'

At this point, the officer found a coded message on one of his shirt collars. 'What is this?'

Fate continued to conspire to undo the chartered accountant. 'I swear,' the man said, leaning over to have a look. 'There's nothing there.'

But he was wrong. It was a laundry tag, with a clearly encoded laundry message. Within seconds, the Englishman was behind bars. 'It's from my launderette!'

As I remember, the tourist was released after a lot of string-pulling from the British High Commission. But here in the forest I was in the hands of a man with cocaine in his crockery cupboard, the happy proceeds spent on his necklace and his son's education. I was a threat to that – a *gringo* all alone, with uncertain army support, and my video camera once again seeking to ruin me.

The *traqueta* was still transfixed, watching as the wretched machine poured forth the evidence. 'I'm in the police,' he said. 'You must tell me what you are doing here.'

Not for a moment did I believe this man was in the police. And I was still wondering what my next move should be, when Joseph appeared in the door. I said it was time I was leaving. I plucked back my camera, and thanked the wife. I forced my hand into the husband's. He accepted it, uncertain, caught on the hop, then I quickly packed my video camera away. I thought everything was going to be all right.

Joseph had come to say he was leaving. He too had found he wasn't welcome here. Someone had even volunteered to take us away.

We climbed into the dugout canoe. I laughed nervously to Joseph. 'That man seemed to think I was from the DEA!'

Joseph hadn't heard of the DEA, but he had seen the man with the glittering necklace. 'What trouble have you got yourself in?'

'Well, let's hope it's all behind me.'

I couldn't begin to untangle this. The man with the red cap, who was that? The army, were they goodies or not? I hid my video recorder and tapes in the bottom of my bag. We stopped after an hour at a little *mestizo* house with a couple of cows in front. The canoeist walked us up to the farmstead. A large family came out as we drew nearer. They wore long trousers, socks, long shirts. It was as if they were in high fever – the stage of malaria when you can't keep warm enough, even in the midday sun. Children were similarly covered, and scratched at themselves or cried. When we stopped in front of the house, the midges dived on us.

We were given a hospitable welcome, though most of those here were puny, and generally speaking toothless. I gave the woman of the house a bag of sugar, and we were served fresh fish. Her husband was also friendly enough. He had wrinkles criss-crossing his face, like a piece of unfolded waste-paper.

At dusk a man called in from upriver. He had a scrawny, turkey throat and a beard perched on his chin like a wind-blown grass hummock. His face looked world-worn, denuded by life – that beard on the crag – but he wore a red shirt that was fresh from the factory, not faded by the tropical sun or washerwomen. The dogs took badly to him, and he had to fight them off in the doorway.

Instead of addressing the head of the household as he came in, he said, 'So you are here, *gringo*.'

I knew I was in trouble again. 'We've met before?'

He didn't answer the question. 'There's a man who is saying you've taken something of his. Pinched it.'

I told him I hadn't stolen anything.

'Doesn't matter to me if you did,' he said. I could see he meant it. It really didn't matter to him. Not a flicker of interest – not in my predicament, nor the dogs who had tried to maul him, nor the household here – as if life was passing him by and he was glad to be getting rid of it.

'Well, I didn't steal anything.'

'Yes, yes. The point is, he says you did.' He added, 'Film.'

'In that case,' the head of the household said, 'I wouldn't stay around here, if I were you.'

'Are we talking about the man with the gold necklace with the beetle on?'

Neither man could remember a necklace.

'A red cap?'

Yes, he usually wore that when out in his canoe. He was a city man, not from the Putumayo. He lived a day upriver.

'What should I do?'

The visitor said, 'As I told you, leave the area. That's what I would do. Leave.' He said he'd take me a short way himself. 'You can stay with a friend of mine. I'll present you. Also, I'll ask him to take you downriver. You'd better get back to Estrecho.'

'You'd better go right now,' said our host.

I was being shipped out again.

Joseph no longer wanted to be my travelling companion, and I left that same night just with the red-shirted man. He took me to his friend, downriver. We were welcomed, and given another boiled fish supper, but the friend said it was out of the question to take me anywhere tomorrow. He was leaving before dawn, and had too much cargo to take. I offered his petrol costs, and $20. Then $50. He wasn't interested. He smiled apologetically to the red-shirted man. He said I could wait at his house for two days until his return, but he wouldn't take me anywhere tomorrow.

I walked to the river bank with the man who'd so kindly

brought me. He refused money for petrol. 'Save it. You should use it to get out of here.' He sped away upriver without waiting for a goodbye.

As I went back indoors, I thought: perhaps the army launch will come looking for me, wondering how I got on. They must know this was a risky place at times. They wouldn't want a *gringo*'s death on their hands.

Back indoors, I was offered another coffee. 'A good friend of Jaime, yes?' the man said.

'Who?' I'd never heard of Jaime.

'The man who brought you here.'

'Oh yes. Very close. Very.'

He watched me in the paraffin light across the table. Outside there was a large moon, and he sometimes went out to have a good look at that as well. Then he said, 'You can come a short way.'

We left in the very early morning, while it was still dark, and even I had guessed by now that something fishy was going on. The sand on the riverbanks was bright, gleaming with moonlight. Fireflies zipped between palm fronds, insects tinkled like bells, the little canoe engine churned away. Before the sun rose, the mist still on our faces, I found out why he had been so reluctant to take me. I was sitting on a sizeable packet of white powder.

He steered the canoe to the bank on the Colombian side. It was a strange place to stop. This was just forest, a curtain of leaves on thorny strings and a log sticking out like the cracked rib of a dinosaur. We stayed there in the shallows, the only sound the insects and the water flow rumpled by the huge log in the river. After a while, the man said, 'No camera.'

No camera, I agreed, and waited to see what was going to happen.

Very soon, before the sun had steamed the damp from the log, we heard an engine. A boat was approaching from up the river: it was very fast. It came into sight. But it wasn't a trafficker.

The possibility that we might bump into the security forces hadn't occurred to me. I had prayed for their help, and they had answered my prayers – just at the moment when I could not afford to be seen by them. I was sitting on thousands of dollars of cocaine – not a good position to be in. If he wanted, the trafficker could deny having anything to do with the drug himself: if he wanted, I could be a very useful scapegoat. I began to sweat.

Now they were bearing down on us. There was no point in making a run for it. I sat there, sweat steaming off me, wondering how I was going to get myself out of this one. I'd say I'd been told it was *cal*, lime used for whitewash. As an excuse it was pathetic, but with the launch bearing down on me it was the best I could come up with.

There were only two men on board, neither in full uniform, just in green drill T-shirts. Whether Peruvian or Colombian, I'm not sure. The soldier in the prow stood operating a steering wheel, watching us carefully. He slowed the motor, and a tidal wave sped off ahead of the craft and almost swamped us. The second soldier, in the stern, leaned out to hold fast our canoe. Just for a second, as I reached for my passport, the boats rubbed against each other. Then it was all over. The canoeist handed him what was undoubtedly a fat roll of banknotes, and then, as quickly as they had appeared, the army boys were gone.

The canoeist turned to me, shrugged his shoulders. He said, disgustedly, 'They are not soldiers, they are money men.'

We travelled on for a couple of hours, a time I passed trying to work out what was going on. Why didn't the two soldiers baulk at having a *gringo* witnessing the transaction? Was the DEA in the take as well? All I could understand was that people here on the river were good people. They lived their simple lives and welcomed strangers and struggled to make ends meet. Some of them had a way to supplement their incomes, a nice little earner, at last. Cocaine had come to their rescue. And I had come along to ruin it for them.

I was dropped off at a *mestizo* hamlet on the Peru side. From here, the driver said, I'd soon get a lift down to Estrecho. I turned to the houses – only two of them, and chiefly inhabited as far as I could see by children and dogs. They all sat together hunched over small green parakeets that were captive in a wicker cage.

As I struggled to pick up my pack, I saw a canoe speeding down-river on the far side. The driver, in the rear, had a red cap on. Was this the man, the *traqueta*, who had been following me? He was too far away to tell. I left the luggage and shrank away from the river bank. I stood to the side of one of the houses, being eyed by a territorial pig, and all the dogs and all the children. I squinted over the glaring water. The canoe was coming back up the far bank. I watched as it slowed, then turned in to the shore, then pulled away again and shot off upriver.

There was no doubt about it. They were looking for me. They had been looking for me for six days now.

I kept watching the glare of the water, waiting for the canoe to slip across it again, and tried to understand: those people were dangerous people, with dangerous amounts of money at stake. I was meant to be scared but, now that I was no longer with anyone who was actually angry, it wasn't all that easy. I had to remind myself to be worried. There were no guns, no grisly hitmen playing dice with human knuckles. Who were the baddies? Not those people. They were no different from the army, the police, the farmers, the fishermen. They were the good, law-abiding citizens of Amazonia – because drugs were part of life here. They didn't know of the lives that were shattered and broken in the west, at the other end of their drug chain. Here the only baddies were common thieves, and people like me, *gringos* who were a threat to the rural economy.

I suppose I must be in trouble, I thought, picking up my bags. It was difficult to believe it.

Before I had moved from the river bank a fuel-carrying launch came up. A deckhand yelled out that they needed a chicken for supper. While the children ran about chasing their chickens, I talked to the captain. He was a very big man with fat, almost bulbous hands, but thin, trim little ankles. He said that with a fuel cargo, he wasn't permitted passengers. So I parted with some more dollars.

I snoozed my way through most of the day, lying with my nose squashed up to the reeking oil barrels. You could only laugh. So far this video had broken my ribs and all I'd managed to do with it was to take kindergarten standard footage of misty riverbank – and now it was prized by the local drug baron. Lying in the hot reek of the oil fumes, I racked my memory. *Had* I chanced on something? Had I filmed Escobar himself, even? Here I was in the sunshine, a calm river in a quiet rural backwater – surely I wasn't being hunted.

No thugs patrolling clandestine cocaine fields, enslaved workers crying in the night. It would have been easier if it was like that. Lying back on the riverboat, the glorious forest sweeping by, I had to talk myself into believing the situation. 'These people are powerful. If they want to get rid of me, they can do it even in Estrecho. I could be gunned down in front of witnesses, right in the middle of the lamentable plaza. There'd be a bit of a commotion – not all that much. Reuters would pick the news up, wire it across the world – Englishman shot dead after meddling with Drug Barons – and that would be that.* Wake up! This is cocaine country. If they think I've found Pablo Escobar they'll kill me. If it costs a few lives and $3 million to cover up, that will be worth it – just one-tenth of a per cent of his annual profit.'

But it was no use. 'Cocaine country', 'gunned down' – these were silly, cowboy phrases that you heard on the telly. I was a 'gringo who knew too much' – another cliché. I heard a canoe come along-side. The captain throttled down the motor. A voice said, quite clearly, 'Is the *gringo* here?'

I lay exactly where I was. This was a bit more like it. But it was still TV, a parody of a matinée Western.

'Who?' The captain said. He wasn't meant to be carrying passengers. He said, gruffly, it was none of their business. There was a pause; I guessed the canoe was manoeuvring to come alongside.

The question was repeated. 'Where is he?'

'You aren't the police, so get out of here.'

I heard the canoe peel away, back up the river.

After a minute, I got up to have a peek at the retreating canoe. It had already gone round a river bend. I went to thank the captain. He said, 'You in trouble with the narcos?'

'Trouble? Me?'

Very soon after that, I was dumped on the river bank.

---

* As it happened, it was not I that was to feature in the next dispatch from Reuters. On 17 December 1993 two government patrol boats, returning home for Christmas, came under attack from grenade launchers and automatic weapon fire directed from a Colombian gang waiting in ambush on the upper Putumayo. 'Nine Ecuadorean police officers and soldiers were killed, five others were injured and 24 are missing,' the report read with a tantalizing brevity. *Guardian* (London), 18 December 1993.

I turned towards the settlement. About thirty people were standing in front of their homes, watching me suspiciously. There were three palm-roofed dwellings with kitchens at the back, water dripping from their abandoned washing-up.

Two thin middle-aged women made up the nearest party. They had their arms folded. They said, simply, *'Problema?'*

I didn't propose to tell them I was being chased by drugs men, so I said that the driver wasn't allowed to carry passengers and decided he couldn't take me further. The women repeated the excuse loudly to the others, everyone nodded, and most of them turned to go back indoors. One of the two women told her children to carry in my pack. The other asked me in for a meal.

I said I had a relative who was sick in Iquitos, and couldn't stay. I'd pay $40 for a ride downriver to the track in the night. That only left $150 to see me through to Iquitos.

They said I should eat first, and there were no canoes here, not until this evening.

Tonight, then?

Now they were suspicious. 'What kind of trouble are you in?'

I repeated that I wasn't in any trouble.

'Then you won't mind staying to eat.'

While we waited for the fish to boil I noticed for the first time that, though these *mestizo* houses were simple and the children had the usual messy erosion between their front teeth, the young girls had bleached strands in their hair. They wore skirts with lacy folds, or the bright, tight bicycle shorts which were *la moda* in Europe. Their dogs were also in good condition. The tips of their ears were clipped off, perhaps against fly infection, or perhaps because the dogs too were *la moda*.

While eating my fish and manioc I learned I was still a day's paddle from Estrecho. On the other hand I was a few hours from a second, very minor track that connected with the Rio Napo. This route started from Flor de Agosto and was a two days' walk. Within about four days I could be in Iquitos. Now I wasn't seeing Iquitos just as an urban instalment of my Amazon journey, I was looking to it for more. I was hanging on until I could get there.

Things might have begun to look cheerier with the news about the convenient path, but I now discovered that the two women had invited me in just so as to learn more from me. Now they were looking to each other, preparing to broach an awkward subject. I could guess what the subject was.

'About your friend . . .' began one, softly.

'My friend?' So they did know.

'The *traqueta*,' said the second woman. 'He says you have film of his.' She was quite suddenly very blunt and hard in tone, but I didn't mind this. It was honest – her stance was clear in a place of deceptive values.

I asked what else he had said. She said, 'Really, it's "they", not "he". And "they" want to see you.'

'If it's the tapes they want, perhaps I can leave them here. They can pick them up.'

The first woman kept her soft tone. She said gently, 'They want to talk to you. Better you wait here for them.'

This didn't sound a very good idea. I remembered from somewhere that 60 per cent of ransom victims of Colombian narcotics gangs were killed regardless of payment.

That evening I did secure a ride for the next day, largely because I took off my shirt and showed them the bruising on my ribs. At last I had my mosquito net up; I closed my eyes and waited for a better day to dawn.

Before I left in the early morning, I put all the used tape on the kitchen table.

The canoe brought me to the house which marked the end of the path. It was still the first hours of day, the mist rising in smoky tongues from the warm river. Children were already up, dragging sticks, walking embraced in twos or threes down to the water to clean their teeth.

Again, I was offered a meal. The woman here said it was true, there was a track and she'd get her son to help guide me. But it would have to be tomorrow, he was away fishing all day.

'Not long now before I'm out of here,' I told myself. 'Just hang on.' I tried to pass the time by going for a stroll. I walked around the back of the house, and discovered that there was another house a little behind. It was occupied by a flirtatious girl in her twenties who said she was a teacher. She liked my blue eyes, she said, sitting down heavily on the steps as she sighed.

'Can I pick a lime?' I asked, stretching to a branch overhead.

'I am a lime,' she said. She giggled. 'You can pick me!'

Really I wasn't in the mood for this, but she meant no harm and we talked a while. She said she would keep an eye on my luggage and put it under her bed.

Most of the rest of the morning I slept in the main house. I woke suddenly, hearing a motorized canoe draw up. I ran to the window.

It was Joseph, of all people. I went out to greet him, bounding up. 'So good to see you!'

He felt rather differently. 'You still in trouble?' he said cautiously.

He walked towards the house, eyeing me suspiciously. I said I was leaving tomorrow on foot. If he wanted a job I could pay him a little to accompany me.

He said, 'There's two men who've been asking for you.'

I said I knew. He said, 'They are city men.'

I told him it was all over. They had wanted some tapes back. I had left them in another house.

When the worst of the sun was off the water, I borrowed a small canoe and went fishing with Joseph. We went up a side creek, fishing for piranha. It was something I hadn't done for ten years and I was determined to enjoy this, my first outing into the forest. Excitedly, I wound wire reinforcement around the line where it joined the hook, and threaded on fishmeat bait.

It was too near the heat of the day to have much luck with piranhas but I was content, sitting back here on the clear stream water, jade dragonflies trembling in the still air, a huge spider's web draped like a dust sheet over a shrub, veils of leaves around me. A pair of scarlet macaws were climbing up a branch, grasping it with their beaks and shifting their feet forward. A tyrant flycatcher spun after an insect, flipped and curtsied and was out of sight again. These were little things, but they were real things. They seemed important just now, away from the Putumayo.

Joseph was moaning about needing to relieve himself in the bushes. We steered the canoe to the bank, hacked a hole in the wall of creepers, and he jumped through them to the shore. While he was still out of sight I heard another canoe coming into the creek, two men in it talking loudly. They were nearby, but the river's course meandered back on itself and the distance between us by water was perhaps 75 yards. I called Joseph to come.

'*Espera!* Wait!' he called back. 'Not finished.' I heard a rustle in the bushes. 'What's the hurry?'

'Just hurry. And keep your voice down.'

I could now hear urine splashing on to rain forest leaf litter; there seemed to be gallons of it. Come on, come on. Suddenly I realized I was scared.

The canoe must have been just around the corner now. 'Keep going,' a voice said.

I still didn't know for certain if it was the two traffickers, but I was in a hot sweat now. Just as I raised my paddle to get myself out of there, Joseph came through the creepers yanking up his flies. The paddle was still in my hand, hovering over the water, as I listened for the men. Joseph's foot was slowly stretching for the canoe. Suddenly I couldn't wait a moment longer.

I dug the paddle in the water, and shot the canoe into reverse. The canoe surged back. I swung it round and started digging at the water. I had my ears peeled and I was tongue-tied. I felt like a bolting rabbit. I was also strangely aware of Joseph's predicament. He was grappling with creepers, his balance lost. Finally, there was an enormous splash. 'Shit!' he said. It was the second time I heard him use English.

After that I heard nothing. I was intent only on vanishing.

The men must have heard the commotion ahead, because they called out, '*Gringo?*' For a moment I re-established control. I told myself to be calm, listen to the pitch in their voices. I listened, hearing my heart, and my paddle chopping at the water, stirring it.

They must have reached Joseph by now, and were trying to work out what on earth was going on.

The stretch of water ahead of me was absolutely straight. They would see me before I could turn the corner.

I raced, but even before I was half way I heard a call – just that one word, '*Gringo!*' It came from directly behind. They were within sight.

I turned, expecting to see two red-faced middle-aged men trying to outpaddle me. Instead I got a clear view only of the man in front, squinting as he pointed, strangely hunched, at me.

He was aiming a gun: but before I had taken this in, there was a loud bang. I almost died there and then. But there was no impact. I kept on paddling, not able to respond sensibly. 'This can't be happening,' I said aloud. But it was. And another shot was going to come any moment. It was taking a long time to come. This seemed to add another strand of farce to a situation I was still finding difficult to grasp as real. The man with the gun was having to put it down so as to steer the canoe with the paddle.

I was around the corner, out of direct view. A short curve now, and a few moments' cover.

My mouth was dry, and I was beginning to cry. I suddenly found myself thinking of the most unlikely things. I remembered eating the chocolate biscuits while queuing for *el maestro*. I thought of Francesca chucking the ice lolly wrapper so beautifully from her slim fingers, of the deer that last dawn in a cornfield in Hampshire, with Jita. I remembered Colonel Fawcett – that I hadn't done any better than him. I was going to disappear too.

Now the creek straightened, and I was a target again.

'Could have been a warning shot,' I said aloud. 'Mustn't exaggerate. This isn't as bad as it looks.'

Time went by, and no shot came. Soon I was out of sight again. This time, without even looking for a suitable opening in the undergrowth, I leapt to the shore. The canoe skidded from under me, and I landed half in the water. I tore apart the leaves and was gone into the forest.


I'd come to the Amazon to see the forest, and suddenly here it was. The Amazon rain forest. It was another world. Dark and muffled, but secret and safe. I headed to the right, straight along the line of the river, getting as much distance as I could between myself and them. Soon, though, I stopped. This riverside vegetation was thick. It was easy cover. I couldn't squat because of my ribs. I waited, hunched up, trying to breath fully and slow my panting. Sometimes I held my breath to listen. There was only the racing of my blood, the cicada-hissing background, a yapping of passing macaws. Further away, a flock of little birds hopping about excitedly. I recognized the enthusiastic call of a bicoloured antbird. Somewhere very near an army of ants was on its way through; the birds were assembled to pick off the insects running out of the leaf litter to escape the ant column.

I found myself thinking of Jita waiting for me back home. What were her last words? I wasn't sure. Then I remembered. 'Just get home safely,' she'd said.

And now here I was. A finger-length caterpillar waved its rear at me, shedding its toxic brown fur. When I stepped away a large black ant latched on to my heel and made a deep incision. It was difficult not to think of Fawcett again. Very few people subscribed to the theory put forward by Fawcett's fellow mystic and family relation Timothy Paterson: 'As regards Uncle Percy Fawcett's "disappearance" in 1925, it is now known that he lived at Ibez-in-Roncador [the 'subterranean city' of 'the resplendent Golden Man', none other than El Dorado itself] until 1957, when, at the age of ninety, he finally gained release from the physical vehicle.'

I waited a little while, getting my bearings. Then I began to move around with less caution, investigating my surroundings.

The men would search a little bit longer, and then, having struggled to find a place to turn their canoe around, they'd go back to the settlement and wait for me. I realized suddenly I must get back immediately – it wouldn't be difficult to slip into the teacher's house at the back. I could grab my boots and make my way along the river bank to the next settlement. It was bound to have its own shortcut to the Rio Napo path.

I'd better get a move on. I followed the river back, slipping quickly through sparse ground cover. Ahead was low, thick vegetation – messy secondary forest of degenerated gardens. This was slower going, but I walked along a pathway made by a felled tree. Whenever I slipped, my ribs screamed out at me, but after what must have been about ten minutes, I reached the back of the houses.

I was expecting dogs, questions from the houseowners. But in the event things were made surprisingly easy for me. The teacher's house was quiet. I stepped indoors.

ABOVE: The author with reluctant horse companion – in the Andean highlands while looking for the north-west Amazon source.

LEFT: Mountain girl with Cotopaxi friends in Ecuador, at the start of the journey.

ABOVE: Mount Cotopaxi, with the town of Latacunga below.

LEFT: An Indian family on the track from Huancabamba to the Healing Lakes, over the border from Ecuador in Peru.

RIGHT: The shaman of the Healing Lakes with his staff of office.

BELOW: Apostle to the shamanic healer of the highland lakes.

LEFT: River boat of the type used by the author to descend the Putumayo in Colombia. This photograph was taken on the Javari, with typical mestizo small-holding behind.

BELOW: Iquitos riverside at dawn.

RIGHT: The riverside markets of Iquitos.

BELOW RIGHT: Fidencio, the 'conquistador of the Matsés', with his extensive brood.

ABOVE: The author assessing alternative jungle medicines, Iquitos.

RIGHT: A hunter from Fidencio's hamlet with white-lipped peccaries.

ABOVE: A 'missionised' Matsés child playing with clay model of a jaguar.

RIGHT: The largest of the three Matsés scouts carrying a tapir head - on the Lobo, en route to the Javari.

BELOW: Charo and Armando on the raft during the descent of the Matanza.

The author having capsized into the Matanza River, en route to the Matsés.

'*Mamá?*' A child lay lolling in a hammock, swinging it back and forward with a foot.

I didn't answer, but pulled my bag out from under the bed. '*Mamá?*'

'*El Mister,*' I said softly. The child peered, half asleep. I asked where the others had gone. 'They went to see. They heard a noise from a gun.' The girl added accusingly, '*She* said it was a rifle, but she doesn't know anything.'

Oh yes she does, I thought. I looked outside, and the houses were still unusually quiet. I was suddenly lightheaded. I think I knew then that I was going to get away.

I'd take my pack as well as my boots, I decided. There was time.

My pack weighed only some forty pounds, but the weight pressed into my ribs with every stride. I trotted as best I could, supporting the weight with my hands. Down the river-bank path, through rough gardens and secondary forest bisected by paths. I stopped to lace up my boots and noticed a tree whose bark had been partly pulled away in strips. I saw what people had been doing: cutting into the tree-trunk and tearing off lengths of bark in order to make head straps for carrying home baskets of crops.

I did the same, pulling the bark away easily, even without a machete. With the weight on my head, not my back, I was on the move again, still following the hunting paths that criss-crossed along the line of the Putumayo. Soon I stopped, and left my pack against a tree. I'd come back if I could.

I came to the first house, knowing I was chancing it to make my presence known, but did I have any other choice? No time to think: over an hour had gone by since my encounter with the drug men and they would be arriving downriver any minute – they would moor up just over there at the open stretch of riverbank, at that very mooring post. I walked up to the house, and called in through the door to a young woman who was hunched over a pot on her clay stove.

'*Hola?*'

She turned around sharply. I knew I was shaking, and I tried to speak slowly to hide my nerves. I heard a voice coming out of me that was horribly polite and formal, an archetypal Englishman.

'Good afternoon.'

'What?' She stared, in a state of shock. I was the shock. 'Good afternoon,' she gasped.

'I'm a bit lost. Can you tell me how to get to the path to the Rio Napo?'

'The path to the Rio Napo?'

'Yes.'

'You want to go to the Rio Napo?'

'Yes.'

'Did I just see you come out from the trees?'

The conversation looked set to continue fruitlessly like this for some time. I could see that she was blissfully ignorant of me and my troubles now, but in a few minutes this would change. I said I wanted to go there immediately.

It was too late to go anywhere now. Perhaps tomorrow her son could take me.

I tried to say it as calmly as possible: 'Well, I really do want to go tonight, you see.'

She sent a little girl to hurry the boy back from the gardens.

It all took agonizingly long. The son came slowly, pulling a basket of maize. I walked up to him. My eyes were still on the river. It was a miracle they hadn't come yet.

He wasn't very keen on walking to the Napo. I said I could afford to pay $60 maybe.

'But it's anyway easier for you to go down the river and walk on the main track.'

'I'd prefer the short cut.'

'But it's late.'

'Just take me to the nearest house.'

'It's five hours' walk away!'

After I'd promised him half my clothing, the boy and I set off, taking some plantains to eat.

Iquitos, I thought. Not far away now. There was said to be a building designed by the French architect Eiffel. I would have a little potter around.

I trudged on, making my escape. That night we stayed at a relative of the boy's, arriving as dusk fell. An aunt made a herbal brew for us. The boy drank it like medicine. 'Coca,' she said, simply, pointing at the leaves sitting at the bottom like autumnal mulch.

Fortified by another glass of coca, the very substance that I was trying to run away from, we left at first light. At midday we met the main track, and the next evening but one I was out of harm's way, sleeping on a trading boat on the Napo, feeling as wretched as Orellano's crew members, the first explorers who had entered the Amazon down this same river and had eaten their shoes in despair.

The day after that we drew up at Santa María, a little port just downriver from Iquitos, which had a bustling market in low-quality river goods. I stepped down the gangplank and ashore. I was being watched by a totally jawless girl, with a toothbrush flapping in her empty jowls. A dead dog was lying in the road, a tyre track over it. Another dog was staring at it. But I was on a tarmac road to Iquitos and by now Iquitos sounded like paradise.

# VI

# The Predators

FOR DAYS I HAD BEEN LIMPING along through dark forest, dreaming of Iquitos, and now here it was, my dream, sitting proudly on the river bank, and I was wondering what to do with it. My three-wheeled motor-cycle taxi circled the Plaza de Armas while I stared – a flagpole, snoozing shoe-shine boys, an inept statue of a dolphin. 'Where to?' the taxi boy was asking.

But I was still staring: a girl was passing the church, adjusting her necklace and devoutly crossing herself in one go. A barefoot Indian was tracking tourists, padding by with two stuffed alligators for sale. All these things were signs of a place in order – even the palm trees were marshalled into rows – and after the topsy-turvy rules of the Putumayo this was bliss.

'Where to?' Finally, the driver made the decision for me, and I was dumped at a cheap hotel just north of Prospero, the main commercial street.

The hotelier put me in a room with a permanently dribbling shower and with that fishy smell which tells you something electrical is about to explode. I didn't mind; these urban hazards told me I was in the west, back home where I belonged. In a minute I would summon energy to undo my jungle boots and have a shower. Then I'd go to the telephone office and call Jita.

Very soon, though, I was asleep, and when I next woke up it was dawn of the next day. After my shower I went outside and was surprised to find the shops shut and the streets empty. I was still living according to forest hours.

A lone leaf-sweeper directed me across the plaza to the house designed by Eiffel. A rubber baron had bought it and had the whole cast-iron structure shipped to Iquitos. However, it wasn't at all like the Eiffel Tower, it was more like Eiffel's Hut. The building was painted silver, and was all metal-cladding and bolts. It had now been converted into a modest café whose metal walls were like a rotting ship's hull. But Eiffel's Hut, like the plaza and the river-front promenade, held a hint of past splendour. These things suggested strength, not weakness. Iquitos, this bastion against nature, had been around a while, and in my fragile state this was rather comforting.

I took a table with a view of the plaza and dived into my lemon meringue pie, at the same time having my jungle boots restored by a shoe-shine boy.

It was a happy scene – considerably more happy than that presented by the Putumayo. For a while I sat absorbing it, jotting down details in my diary, starting with the cheerful shoe-shine boy, who had an old label stuck on his wooden box that said 'Visa cards welcome'.

'Shoe-shine boy uses a biro to scrape jungle mud from my boots,' I wrote contentedly. 'He sits square on the ground, legs split open on either side of the box. He yanks my leg about to show he's working hard . . .

'Girls vaguely mouthing English words from pop songs they don't understand. Smell of clinical alcohol from the chemist.

'Metal bottle tops deeply embedded in the plaza tarmac.'

I began enjoying myself, relaxing into the sanctuary provided by this town. The odd thing was, I hadn't even observed the forest through which I'd got here. I couldn't remember a single smell, the shape of a single leaf. The path had taken me through a couple of days' worth of vegetation, but I had hardly noticed. It had been just an emergency exit, an escape chute. After the problems caused me by the Putumayo, I hadn't dared look.

'Iquitos, at last,' I sighed. Later I'd talk to the beggars and the barefoot banana carriers – the Amazonians who never got into the Amazon books. So much yet to be written about: I watched as a boy went by pushing another limbless boy along on a little cart. He looked carelessly ahead down the road, pushing him with one casual finger, as if playing with a toy.

But into my second helping of pie, my enthusiasm began to slow. I had completed only Phase One, not even a remote portion of the crossing. And how had I coped? I had broken three ribs and managed to get myself chased by cocaine dealers. There was two-thirds of the journey ahead of me, x thousand miles to go, this time through virgin forest. It could only get worse.

Suddenly, I went off my lemon meringue. I sat the shoe-shine boy down to eat it. The thought of organizing a push to the Matsés, somewhere in the headwaters of the Javari, was too much to bear. And in my present state, the more I thought about the Matsés the less I was sure they were going to be my salvation. 'Jaguar People' they might be, but they were people who got by in life through restricting themselves to swamplands rich in palm fruits – this according to Steward's definitive and surprisingly large *Handbook of South American Indians*. 'Seemingly exceedingly primitive', 'semi-horticultural', the book said, and they were lacking 'many of the hunting devices, technological accomplishments, musical instruments, rites and religious concepts characteristic of their neighbours.' And who were their neighbours? The three more powerful members of the Panoan language family, from which the Matsés hid – people like the Shipibo, who in 1657 quickly disposed of the first missionaries and soldiers to visit them; and the Setebo and Conibo, who preyed on those weaker tribes who'd naïvely thought they might gain refuge from them by becoming Christians and hiding away in missions. The Mayorunas featured in the book as 'proto-Panoan', perhaps the most primitive in a long list of the lesser tribes, many presumed extinct: Chamicura, Cashibo, Capanawa, Puyumanawa, Remos, Mananava, Managua, Amahuaca, Maspo, Amenguaca, Ruanagua, Pichobo, Soboyo, Comobo, Mochobo, Nocomán. Were these shyer subordinates really up to training a white man with broken ribs in the art of the forest?

I sloped off to try to ring Jita. At the other end of the line there was only an answering machine. I phoned again, just to hear her recorded voice. When it came to leaving a message I was suddenly unable to speak. I just said, 'It's me. It's Benedict.' And then I began to choke.

'Feel lonely and lost,' I wrote forlornly in my diary. 'This fast deteriorating vision shared by no one else.' Certainly, I wasn't going to get anywhere very far with broken ribs. I went back to Eiffel's Hut and found myself gorging on another unwanted lemon meringue pie. There it slowly became clear: I must go to see Harriet Kneeland and Harriet Fields, the two intrepid female missionaries from the Summer Institute of Linguistics who had made contact with the Matsés. They knew this forest like no other outsiders. All those efforts on their isolated jungle river bank had been rewarded. And why? Because they knew that forest. These American ladies were sure to inspire me.

Unless of course I was just too old. Perhaps that was it. I watched the shoe-shine boy go up to a nun, and gently try to coax her into having her black lace-ups polished here in the plaza. She blushed at the very thought, and flapped him away. Some things in life were indeed impossible.


Near Pucallpa, a town to the south up the Ucayali tributary river, was Lake Yarinacocha, and on its shore, the headquarters of the Summer Institute of Linguistics.

I arrived by plane in pouring rain and waited at the gate, while enquiries were made about me on the guard's little telephone. He was not going to allow me to walk straight in. For one thing, the SIL, American Protestants engaged in a crusade to translate the Bible into every known language, had blasted a bible belt right through the forest without waiting for an invitation from the Indians. This made them extremely unpopular with, among others, the tribal rights organization Survival International.*

While the missionaries worked out whether I was a spy or not, I stood in the guard's hut, peering out through the rain. I saw grass verges, houses with fresh licks of paint. In brighter weather there would have been the sounds of lawnmowers, the sounds of a ball game. The view looked like the threshold to the American Dream, not the Amazon. Suddenly I wasn't so sure I'd come to the right place.

* It was a campaign that had its roots in the very foundation of Survival International, an organization brought about largely by the publication of an article in the *Sunday Times* (London) in 1968 entitled 'Genocide in Brazil', about alleged atrocities by other US-based Protestants, the New Tribes Mission, in Paraguay. The New Tribes Mission was also actively searching for 'Brown Gold' in the Javari region. See also Hvalkof and Aaby, *Is God an American?*

The telephone rang, and I passed through into the closed world of the Summer Institute of Linguistics. Beyond the lawns were classrooms, halls, a village store and a post office. Nearby was a range of low, modern offices. I was conducted through to wait in a room full of computer consoles. They marched in: Harriet Kneeland and Harriet Fields. They were not as I'd hoped, shy and lithe, like creatures adapted to the forest in which they normally dwelt. 'The Two Harriets', as they were known affectionately, seemed to be indoor women with office-bound faces.

Harriet Kneeland in a business-like manner went to get on with other things. Harriet Fields kindly sat me down to help me where she could. She had grey hair in a clump, practical glasses, plump, pale calves.

I told her my plans and she got out a floppy disc and tapped nimbly at a laptop computer, drawing out names of people who might be of help. Her software was not encouraging. The only Matsés that she was in touch with were those at Buenas Lomas, her mission off the Javari's Choba tributary. Harriet had to think hard to remember if there was anyone who could still make a bow and arrow.

'Not very good people to teach me, then.'

'Not at my mission.' However, she had a word of comfort. As I'd once hoped when I'd first read of them back in London, the fact that the Matsés hadn't burdened themselves with musical instruments, weapons and artefacts made them better hunters, not worse ones. They relied on their dexterity, senses, and knowledge. Hearing this, I knew my expedition was alive again. I found myself daydreaming, smiling to myself and recalling the words of the nine-teenth-century naturalist Waterton about the Indians of Guyana. 'He is now laid low in the dust; he has left no record behind him, either on parchment, or on a stone, or in earthenware, to say what he has done . . . Their total want of civilization has assimilated them to the forests in which they wander.'

As we settled deeper into conversation, I said, 'I can't help wondering what has been the most important thing you've learnt yourself. Over twenty years with them in the forest, that's quite something.'

'I've made good friends,' she said, and nodded to herself, letting a smile slip around her face for the first time. She pointed to an inch-long tattoo on the underside of her right arm. The tattoo was reassuring to me: as a missionary she had well and truly left America's mark on the Matsés – her converts couldn't even make bows and arrows! – but they had also left their mark on her.

'What else have you learnt, I wonder?'

She thought again. The Matsés had a particular swaying motion when they walked, she said fondly. She adopted this sometimes and it helped her walk in the forest.

So far, we had an inch of tattoo and a swaying motion. What about something a little more profound. Philosophy, perhaps? Wisdom? I waited. But there was a silence, and I had a terrible sinking feeling. I was furrowing very stony ground.

Back to her stronger suit: practicalities. She felt my best hope was somehow to cross Peru to the missionized Matsés of the Javari, as planned, and then with their help locate the remoter Brazilian Matsés further east on my route. She knew some of them because they used to live in Peru – 'before there was a fight'. She explained that the Matsés in the two main Brazilian settlements were a wild bunch.

'Wild?' I said. 'Did you just say "wild"?'

'Both at Trinta e um and Lobo,' she said. 'Threw out a photographer who tried to get in there, and they've been known to come into Peru on raids to capture women. If missionaries ever go there, they usually end up hysterical.'

'The missionaries?'

'The Matsés. They scream for machetes and clothes. They don't like FUNAI, even though officially they have a presence there.' (This was the Fundaçao Nacional dos Indios, the Brazilian government department that, with limited funds and an almost as limited track record, dealt with indigenous affairs.) 'Yeah, if you went with FUNAI, my guess is you'd be attacked for sure.'

I wondered what the Matsés were like when Harriet first saw them, that momentous day when they had stared at each other, out there alone in the forest by her little camp.

'They were scared. We found frightened Indians. Scared of the frontiersmen – the rubber tappers and the *patrónes*, the big bosses in general.'

'Scared of becoming slave labour?'

'Much later they explained that they had decided to come out to talk to me that first day because they were tired of running away and hiding. The *patrónes* used to snatch Matsés children, take them away to make them "Spanish".'

Like the missionaries do, I thought.

'It was years before it got to the stage when I saw any Mayoruna customs – even ones they had copied from the *patrónes*, such as burying their dead. Before that of course,' she added vaguely, 'they ate them.'

'So it's not just a traveller's tale?' I wanted a few details – at last, the truth of the Amazon from this first-hand witness. And were they eaten roasted or raw? My mother was bound to ask.

Harriet just said, 'The Mayorunas say it was better they ate them than the worms.' She went back to her computer, tapping at her keyboard, extracting more data. Roasted was the answer – anyway, according to the nineteenth-century British naturalist Henry Walter Bates.

The Mayorunas, who were now facing the biggest threat yet, the rubber boom, were 'a fierce, indomitable, and hostile people,' he wrote in 1891. 'The navigation of the Jauarí is rendered impossible on account of the Majerónas lying in wait on its banks to intercept and murder all travellers, especially whites.' Bates observed that, just recently 'two young fellows had been shot with arrows, roasted and eaten by the savages.' The National Guard was called out. They reached the 'settlement of the horde', who had now taken flight. They found one girl, from whom they gathered that the two young men had 'brought their fate on themselves through improper conduct towards the Majeróna women.' The girl, duly brought downriver and baptized, acted as a maid to Bates for a while, filling his water jugs, making the fire.

I also gained her goodwill by extracting the grub of an Oestrus fly from her back, and thus cured her of a painful tumour. She was decidedly the best-humoured and, to all appearance, the kindest-hearted specimen of her race I had yet seen. She was tall and very stout; in colour much lighter than the ordinary Indian tint, and her ways altogether were more like those of a careless, laughing country wench, such as might be met with any day amongst the labouring class in villages in our own country, than a cannibal. I heard this artless maiden relate, in the coolest manner possible, how she ate a portion of the bodies of the young men whom her tribe had roasted.

However, Harriet wanted to move the conversation on from cannibalism. 'Nowadays, of course, we've even taught them money,' she said. 'First, we gave them clothes, taught them the values of items for barter, then we progressed . . .'

Half an hour later, I had heard a lot about the 'progress' of the Matsés, but still I was not much the wiser about the reception they'd give me: they might either be money-grabbing missionary Matsés who didn't have a clue about the forest or, on the Brazilian side, Indians who did know the forest but who were nervous wrecks. I asked if there was anything else I should know.

Yes. There was a strain of malaria that was untreatable. 'Plus, a lot of venomous snakes. But what season are you going in?'

'Next week.'

I could see her stifling an urge to comment on this. 'Oh?' she said, as lightly as she could. 'So soon?' She went on, 'Coming up to the wet season, then. It's a problem: snakes don't hear your vibrations.'

She was forgetting I was six foot four. Everything in the forest heard *my* vibrations. 'You haven't mentioned problems with terrorists, though. Thank heaven for that.'

'I do like to keep my passport with me in case I need to escape into Brazil. But about the snakes: we've worked out a special electric shock treatment for some types. We rig up a contraption from a car battery. Or you could use a rape gun.' Another glimmer of a smile came from out of that grey face. 'Though I don't suppose you carry one of those.'

'Never have been attacked for my body, that's one thing.'

To my surprise, Harriet was suddenly suppressing a giggle. 'Touch wood!'

But I was seated at the plastic computer console and I suppose somehow I must have failed to do so.

\*     \*     \*

91

Let's face it, I thought, the mission hasn't been very inspiring, and for a while I put off my departure to the Matsés. I sauntered about Iquitos waiting for my ribs to get better. I made friends, moving into a policeman's house, and I talked to anthropologists, missionaries and odd-bods and composed essays on the Real Amazon: already I was getting the picture, I felt. The Indian had never been the unsullied, pristine figure that was depicted in travel books. Had an anthropologist got out his notebook at random on any major tributary even two centuries ago he'd probably have found himself observing not reddish Indians but brownish *mestizos*, already well ensconced in the forest, breeding their own ideas, interbreeding their children. Take the Mayorunas – as far back as 1654 some Mayorunas traded for iron tools near the mission of Santa María on the Huallaga river, west of the Ucayali. A chief of the missionized Cocamilla tribe became a lay preacher to a group and afterwards Father Raimundo de la Cruz baptized among them. Finally, some Mayorunas came voluntarily to the mission – others came not quite so voluntarily. Many of the arrivals almost immediately died of an epidemic that swept the mission in 1655.

For a hundred years the Mayorunas disppeared, evading the Europeans until 1755 when a group was taken to the Mission of San Joaquín de los Omaguas. They soon escaped.

Through friendship with the Omaguas, the tribe that had so entranced the *conquistador* Orellana with their finely glazed pottery, the Mayorunas were drawn into the mission once more, and the Omagua girls taught the roaming, all but possessionless 'Jaguar People' to weave, and the boys to use spear throwers and canoes. While other Mayorunas were brought in to another mission in 1762, the vast majority stayed in the forests, gleaning non-jaguar skills from other more acculturated tribes. For 300 more years, their semi-nomadic existence thwarted all hope of conversion, but at the end of the last century the rubber tappers and *patrónes* were about to make their mark where the evangelists failed.

It was true that there were other, more remote tribes than the Mayorunas – nearby in Peru, the 'uncontacted' Cogapacori, who used bone needles and were busily being sought by the Summer Institute, and in Brazil, on the Ituí, the relatives of the Mayorunas called the Matís, who were being sought busily by other Protestants, these from the New Tribes Mission. Even at this moment, two of their members were sitting at Atalaya, on the lower Javari, awaiting permission from the government to evangelize. But every tribe in the Amazon was well aware of us; every one of them had been in retreat for 400 years.

So I spent each day writing notes on the modern occupants of the basin, the 'Real Amazonians', starting – on a controversial note I liked to think – with the prostitutes in the plaza. I studied these Amazon warriors as they moved benches all day to keep in the shade of the palms.

Then I at last got hold of Jita on the phone, and she told me to get a move on.

'But what about my ribs? I'm not stepping back into the forest in this state.'

There was a sharp intake of breath. '*What* state?'

'Nothing, nothing!'

'Just be brave,' she said. 'And get back as quickly as you can.' Slowly, reluctantly, I began gathering information on Phase Two, finding the Matsés of the River Javari and enlisting their help.

With the tourist trade in ruins because of the Shining Path guerrillas, Iquitos had a surfeit of jungle guides.* The airport swarmed with them. They were smooth operators of various degrees of disreputability who pounced at the passengers as they edged dazed into the tropical sunlight, straight from Miami or Lima. Even the toughest beggars were hoiked aside in the desperate bid for trade. As for me, I didn't even have to make a trip to the airport to find them – these people were trained to spot the weak and vulnerable.

They chased me down the street, flashing their Jungle Trip brochures. They offered trips to fish for piranhas, trips to see naked Indians, witch doctors – whatever your particular Amazon fantasy. One of them, who looked Chinese, had a calling card with someone else's name Tipp-exed out, and his own written in: 'Louis', spelt

* In the past month Abimael Guzmán Reynoso, the cult leader of the twelve-year guerrilla campaign, had been enjoying his last days of freedom. In September he was tracked down to his hideaway and seized by security forces. However, his organization, though now headless, was still alive and kicking. See Michael S. Serrill, *Time International*, September 1992.

the American way. On the first occasion, he ran after me calling in German. '*Guten Tag, guten Tag . . .*' The second time round, I was more impressed. 'English, right? And you are trying to reach the Mayorunas, the Jaguar People.' He had done his homework, and now he was speaking fluent English, with barely a trace of an American accent. I allowed myself to be waylaid – he was after all a representative Amazonian. Like so many other traders, his family had been attracted to the Amazon by opportunities to be had not in the forest but in its spreading towns. Louis' particular trade was serving the needs of foreigners; if this had been Singapore, not the great steamy Amazon, he would have been a subject of a book, Paul Theroux's *Saint Jack*.

As he did his pitch Louis repeatedly divided his hair with his fingers, and petted the neck of the pretty boy with him, his (clearly non-Chinese) 'cousin' Victor. Louis led me to Ari's Burger, an establishment of the McDonald's breed – tasteless decor, tasteless food, selling you the experience rather than the nourishment. There was only one other customer, a camp expatriate. His hair was dyed orange and lay in a page-boy clump. He sobbed to himself as he ate his Ari's Burger Special.

We drew up three of the shiny red chairs. One of the red-aproned waitresses stood over us while we looked at the sterile food depicted in the photographs.

'So, you want to cross to the Javari and then beyond, presumably with the help of the Matsés,' Louis said, twirling a biro over his newspaper. 'The Jaguar People are a tribe I know a lot about – it's really lucky that we've met.' He gave the impression he was genuinely pleased for me. We had something to celebrate. 'The other tour operators have no idea, they really don't. But for me, the Indians are not stupid, I have really learnt a lot from them.'

Louis had been all around the jungle, sometimes flying in on free tickets from the missionaries. 'God's jobs,' he called them. Then there'd been a time working for the Occidental Oil Company as a Spanish translator. They had blown up a lake to get at the oil underneath. A creature was left high and dry when the water went down. It was a black anaconda. 'Forty metres.'

'You mean fourteen,' I corrected him, as an Indian came up, draping his merchandise in front of our eyes. He stood silently dangling his beads and necklaces on one bare foot, placed against his leg like a heron.

Louis waved him away. 'Forty. The Americans measured it, cut it up with a chain saw and took it away in five crates. The Indians there said it had to go in separate crates otherwise it would join itself together again.'

'It can't have been forty metres,' I said. 'The record is eleven metres four and a bit.' But Louis didn't care that I didn't believe him. 'I know it sounds incredible, but it's true.' A lesser liar would have shifted his ground under questioning, moving to where it felt firmer. Louis didn't. He supplemented the tales with more and more outrageous fibs. It made him almost heroic.

'Yeah, another time I was paid to find two American boys. About your age. The father came to Iquitos, and asked around – who around here is qualified for the job, knows the jungle. He was sent to me.' While he was talking, Louis was idly completing a crossword. It was a most impressive display – assuming he wasn't cheating. 'I set off to Colombia – just sensed it was the drug trade. Tracked them down west of Puerto Asis. I joined the drug gang undercover, ran off with the Americans in the night.'

Victor interrupted. 'In the dusk, you mean.' Louis' stories only had any credibility at all because of the resonance Victor gave them, correcting, amplifying. So I wondered whether poor Victor believed in Louis. I said to him, 'And you, Victor. You help Louis, and what else. You have hobbies?'

'I like weightlifting. But I must not use up my energy. If I do, Louis says I will grow weak before I get old.'

Louis concurred. 'This is what I believe. It is why I am an expert in Kung-fu. More efficient use of energy. I carry a card – it helps me explain, if I injure somebody in self defence.'

I decided to move the conversation back to reality. I told them I'd been to see the famous American missionaries, the Two Harriets, and had asked them about Matsés culture. 'Couldn't get anything from them.'

'But do you know why the mission sent two women?' said Victor. He had a soft, Peter Lorre voice. 'It is because the Jaguar People would have killed men. If the Two Harriets had been attacked, the women could have surrendered, just pulled off their dresses and offered up their bodies.' However hard I tried, I couldn't see Harriet the missionary just pulling off her dress and offering up her body.

'I have seen some Matsés,' Louis said. 'You know, I'm a bit of an explorer myself.' He deftly swallowed some pills. They were vitamins. They helped him dream, he said.

We talked on a bit. Mostly, Victor just listened, while looking at himself in the mirrors and checking for pimples – an ordinary teenager, with ordinary teenage problems, being drawn into the slippery smooth and slightly seedy world of Louis.

'What I'd like to suggest is that I arrange everything for the journey to the Javari – food, equipment, guides. A week, ten days' walk. Followed by –'

I stopped Louis. I told him that I wasn't going to do it with fancy equipment. I advanced my usual reasons – it was invasive, exactly what was wrong with western exploration, and besides, machines – even animals – misbehaved in my hands. I told him how, in Peru, a horse had gone mad under me, sensing just that.

Louis plucked at his chest, flipping out his T-shirt for ventilation. 'No outboard motor? You wait until you see this place. It would be crazy!' He battered away at me, using my own language. 'I tell you, I counsel you, *implore* you . . .'

'No.'

'No shotgun even?'

Smoothly, Louis reset his ambitions. 'I could see from the beginning you were not a tourist, and I would never con you. But you must trust me a little. You'll need that outboard in some of the creeks you'll be in. And you'll need a shotgun to hunt. No one knows that forest – you could be stuck there for weeks before you found the Matsés.'

Victor said, 'You do need help.'

I did realize I needed help. You only needed to look at me walking lop-sided down the street. And why else would I have been sitting here talking to a dodgy operator like Louis?

'Look. Don't take my word for it. See what you feel when you've asked a Matsés for yourself. Antonio – ask him. He's a Matsés living just off the Ucayali. He'll tell you more. Maybe even get you there.'

'He's amenable? Speaks Spanish?'

Louis turned to Victor, deftly avoiding both questions. 'He'll get Benedict there, don't you think?'

After an impressively long moment to consider, Victor said, yes, Antonio would get Benedict there.

Louis said, 'Antonio is your man.'

Getting to Antonio was a ferry ride, followed by a canoe ride. It would be a nice little outing, and cheap for me because he'd share the cost with an Irish tourist he was looking after. 'He's going to be out of this world when he hears he's going to meet a Jaguar Man.'

Louis arranged a meeting time for tomorrow and then quickly left. 'Business,' he said, snatching up the crossword before I could see whether he had cheated.

No sooner had the two gone when the waitress came up. '*Cuidado!* Watch out!' She let the word drop vertically from a tight mouth, rather like a secret agent delivering a code. Then she scuttled off. Next the shoe-shine boy ran up. 'That man is a crook! How much money did you hand over? He's a crook!'

'Of course he is. But he's interesting. He's an unstudied Amazonian.'

'Keep away from him! Keep away!'

'Look, if I do eventually go to the jungle with his help, he'll save me money in the markets. And he's not coming with me on my expedition, don't you worry.' The boy violently snatched the calling card. 'Look!' He was scratching a grubby fingernail at the Tipp-ex.

I promised I would take care, and eventually he dropped the subject and got on with business. 'Shoe-shine?' He was already beginning on my right foot.


I had just met Louis Chala, pirate extraordinaire, debonair high-wayman, cheat in fifteen languages. He was one of the Amazon's greatest criminal minds. Soon he would lead me to Fidencio, one of the Amazon's weakest.

At six in the morning, beside the marshy, half-floating slums of Belén, the riverside market was in full swing. Children squatted in rows, scraping the glassy scales off fish; an old Chinese woman stirred splinters of grubby ice into the fruit juices; dugout canoes heaped with manioc, plantains and fish eased quietly towards the river bank through silver and gold mist; larger trading boats swung in the water restlessly, as youths ran down gangplanks with banana branches on their backs. At the second-hand American clothes stall, waifs dug deeply into the piles of stained shirts, then wafted away the smell of American body odour.

Louis led Patrick the tourist through the crowds, slapping away the hands of potential pickpockets as he went. I followed behind and Victor brought up the rear, on his shoulders a huge sack of tinned food for the journey. By the waterside banana market we zigzagged through hawkers, slid on rotten fruit and skipped over mooring ropes, finally swinging ourselves down into one of the low wooden ferries. It was a planked bus which seemed as dark as a ship's hold, and it was seething with passengers.

Within moments the craft, its creaking planks audible even above the market hubbub, was nudging its way out into the river, edging through the simple rafts that were drifting to the quay, loaded with more bananas.

'Anyone seen any lifejackets?' Patrick asked Louis, looking around the semi-darkness. But our two retainers were busy having an argument – Victor had forgotten Louis' comb. Patrick shrugged his shoulders. 'And how did you get involved with this Louis?' he said to me. 'He's a crook if ever I saw one.'

'I was going to ask you the same question.'

Patrick's excuse was that he viewed life with optimism. He found he could take from it all he wanted. 'I reckon 70 years will do me fine.'

We started to talk about Patrick's home in Cork, but found his shorts were attracting attention. The other passengers had never seen anything like them – certainly not on a man. You sometimes saw them on posters of Brazilian beach girls: extremely short denims with frayed edges and all-too-visibly tight around the groin. But Patrick was not a Brazilian playgirl, he was a very thin Irishman trying to get a tan in a dark boat full of *mestizos*, peasants. Everyone else was in their Sunday best, showing the world they could afford the expense of dressing up for town.

Patrick's blue eyes were twinkling at his audience. 'You've travelled a bit,' he said to me. 'What do you think of my chances of pulling the birds?'

'If you're after the girls, I would forget the shorts, quite honestly. This is a Catholic country. To be absolutely frank – and you did ask my opinion – they must think you are outrageous. If I were you –'

However Patrick was already talking to a girl beside him. She didn't understand a word of English but she was entranced as he shone his blue eyes at her and yarned on. Before long his fingers were walking over the girl's hand. If I'd done that, I would have been slapped.

I looked out to the river banks, which were covered with thick, coarse grasses that would be inundated by the rains of the end of the year. Louis joined us and spread his hand along the view, passing it along the white egrets poised in the shallows, the scarlet ibises in the trees. He said he owned the whole stretch.

'Pull the other one,' said Patrick, not taking his eyes off his girl.

Louis said, 'I'm looking for an investor. There's no risk – minimum capital outlay.'

Patrick lovingly fingered the girl's hand, saying into her eyes, 'Well, Louis, you know where you can shove that idea, mate.'

Soon the girl's hand was responding with little twitches of delight and there might have been further progress had the time not come for us to transfer to a larger ferry, the *Atena de Ucayali*.

This was a rusty hulk which stank of oil fumes and appeared to have come from Iquitos anyway. From its support posts and water pipes hung row after row of hammocks, one of which was soon appropriated by Patrick. This time it was the girl who did all the talking, not caring that he didn't understand a word. 'Sometimes you wonder what the fook they're going on about,' he said into her eyes, and, when the girl's mother sent him away, 'I only wanted to say you've got a great pair of tits.'

Early in the morning we came to the village of Jenaro Herrera and disembarked, wrestling through the hawkers. Then Louis located one of his contacts, a villainous *mestizo* called Fernando, and hired him to take us onward in his canoe, a large, motorized dugout.

We slipped up a nearby easterly tributary, the Supay, following the curves of the quiet river. Patrick stripped off to embellish his tan and Louis hid his head under a bag. He explained that he couldn't wear a hat because it made you bald.

Now the forest edged in closer from the sides, and sometimes leaned over to embrace us from above. Fish jumped from the water and skated along the surface, chased by something bigger and nastier sweeping through the waters. An ash grey capuchin monkey scampered along a branch, and then was lost to the forest again. The forest closed in further still when Louis decided to take a short cut across a meander and to everyone's surprise – including his – we found ourselves in the middle of a small lake.

A kingfisher sat hunched on a drowned bush, staring deeply into the water; a duck clattered off, smacking the lake with its wings. Louis pointed to a tree crown, where the leaves were as red as rose petals. 'I was attacked by cannibal monkeys here once – about a dozen of them.'

Neither Patrick nor I said anything. It's difficult to know what to say to someone who's just told you he's been attacked by cannibal monkeys.

'Called burri-burri,' Louis said, authoritatively. 'A type of demon. Prefer human flesh, but of course they eat their own kind when they're running short.'

That was always Louis' downfall. He listened too much to his own stories. He believed in himself, and though this is fine for an upright person, for a conman it is disastrous. For example, at present we were lost and he didn't even know it.

Finally we found our way out of the lake. We rounded a river bend to see a small field and a line of palm-roofed houses around it, typical shacks of *mestizo* smallholders. Children stopped kicking a deflated football around and flooded down the bank to gawp at us. 'Aucayacu,' Louis said.

Patrick said, 'This is it? Home of Benedict's Jaguar Man?'

It was.

'And who's the creep?'

He was looking up at a veranda and a *mestizo* with a shiny face and yellow bandana. I could see what Patrick meant – a sleazy face and slippery eyes. 'Luis!' the man called, starting to come our way.

Even at this distance, his voice was butter smooth, as if he was after something. 'Louis,' he said again, this time remembering to use the American pronunciation Louis preferred.

'Fidencio!' called back Louis.

'Louis! Louis!'

'Fidencio! Fidencio!'

Patrick said, 'For God's sake . . .'

The children – all ten of them – followed us into the cool of Fidencio's veranda. It took me a while to realize that these were not village children, they all belonged to him.

'Take a seat, Benedito!' Fidencio sang out. 'My wife will make coffee. Oh, Benedito, Patrick, I'm pleased to meet you!'

Patrick said, 'Lays it on a bit thick, doesn't he?'

He certainly did. Fidencio exclaimed, rather than talked, treating us like long-lost friends. His children, by contrast, appeared honest and down-to-earth, as if they'd overcome their father's influence by sheer weight of numbers. While Fidencio talked away, they settled down quietly. The eldest son, Dexta, fixed nets that hung up around the veranda like veils. Younger sons played Casino, a simple card game which completely foxed me. Another son, Charo, was outside in the sun, stretching peccary skins over sticks to sweat out their fat.

After coffee, Louis said we'd better go and see Antonio. Victor would stay here and guard the bags.

'What sort of dump is this where you have to guard the bags?' Patrick said as we went round the back of the hamlet to a house that stood apart. It didn't have a veranda, nor any windows of any size. Effectively it was a *maloca*, the closed, circular Indian family house, but in western, rectangular form.

Outside, Louis called, 'Antonio?' He sounded hesitant, as if he hadn't actually ever met the man.

'*Aquí, no más!*' said a small, determined voice. 'No further.'

Then the door opened as if by itself, and Louis stepped in.

The house was very dark, and divided in two, a fireplace at one side of a damp mud floor which had hammocks swung across it, and a raised area of rough planks for sitting around on. Two women were standing by the fire, watching us from behind a slender post. Two toddlers were in the hammock, chewing a thigh-sized disc of alligator tail.

Antonio was small, and he looked it – not like a man bred to hunt like a jaguar, but someone with the hunched shoulders of a nervous office boy. We followed him to the raised portion of the house, where he sat down and watched us.

'So,' said Louis.

'So,' said Patrick. 'This must be the Jaguar Man.' But Patrick wasn't mocking. He began taking off his shoes as a token of respect and when he looked up at the arrows hanging vertically from the thatch, flights made from feathers of a monkey eagle, he sighed, reverently. 'Jesus . . .'

'Well, this is Antonio,' Louis said. 'And as you see he has tattoos across his face.' Louis indicated a line from one ear to the other, a track across Antonio's upper lip. 'And when he's hunting he puts thin spindles in his lips.' Antonio watched Louis' fingers as they skipped around his face. 'The women' – Louis pointed over to the fire and the two characters silently peering at us – 'put palm leaf stem whiskers in their noses.' Patrick and I shyly looked at the Matsés and they shyly looked at us. None of us wanted to stare, but all of us were intensely curious about each other. For my part I was drawn to the tattoos – they were, after all, there to be seen, the badge of his people. Along with the palm spindle 'whiskers' they were a statement that he had affiliation with cats, top predators of the forest. This man who looked so cramped here, faced with strangers led by *loco* Louis, belonged to a semi-nomadic people who traditionally, like the jaguar, that 130-kilo, two-metre killer, wandered great distances in search of food. They too frequented the marshy habitats, and like the jaguar – it seemed a reasonable guess – were silent and lithe stalkers of the undergrowth.

Louis tried an opening gambit. 'They are both your wives, Antonio?'

'*Sí*,' said Antonio.

'And I expect you visit the Matsés in the Upper Javari from time to time, don't you?'

'*Sí*.'

'When you are out foraging, hunting and gathering . . .'

'*Sí*.'

Louis turned to us. 'With strangers, it takes some time for him to relax. But you know I have a lot of respect for these people. I have learnt so many things from them about the forest. Half, maybe more of my knowledge is from the Matsés.'

I said, 'You know I'm not sure Antonio understood a word you were saying.'

'Why don't you speak in his language?' Patrick said to Louis. 'Give the poor bloke some dignity in his home, won't you?'

'Different dialect, you see,' Louis said. 'Go ahead yourself, Benedict, ask him what you want to know in Spanish.'

'How many days is it from here to the Matsés of the Upper Javari?' I asked.

'*Sí*,' said Antonio.

'Holy Jesus,' Patrick said. 'This is a farce.'

The meeting disintegrated further: a tarantula, hitherto secreted in the sticky black ceiling, lost its grip and came hurtling down from the cobwebs to land square on Louis' fat lap. Louis was on his feet and plunging for the door. I got up and squashed the spider into the ground with Patrick's shoe. For the first time, Antonio smiled. He called the two women over for a closer look at us.

They came over, letting out gentle swooping cries, and continuing a sighing, sing-song conversation, punctuated with long shrieks of exclamation each time they joked about Louis' flight. 'Eeeeeeeeeeee!' As Louis stalked back indoors I got out some postcards of Piccadilly Circus and the royal family. The women sighed enviously at the Queen's crown, and crumpled up the postcard as they had a closer look at the jewels. '*Bueno*,' the older one said. So someone here did speak a little Spanish.

After a while the women retreated to their hammocks, but from now on we were objects of amusement and they swung there happily, still reliving how Louis had run from the spider. 'Heeeeeee . . .'

Soon, through the older wife, we tried to begin conversation about my journey. 'I want to visit the Matsés of Brazil,' I explained.

My statement had the effect of immediately killing all conversation.

'Woooo-ah!' she said, abruptly stopping the swing of her hammock. It sounded like an expression of horror. After I'd parted with postcards, needles and thread, fishing line, and finally the photo with the Queen's crown, we learned more. She said, in quite good

Spanish, that three young Matsés were hiding from us round the back of the house. 'They can go.'

'What about Antonio?' Louis said. 'He could take Benedito.'

'The three men are foolish. They are not afraid of the Remo-aucas.' After this word, 'Remo-aucers,' both women began hooting dramatically. It was that word again. 'Wooooo-ah!'

I said, 'Louis, what are the Remo-aucas?'

The very word set the women off again. 'Woooah!' they called. 'Woooooooagh!'

Antonio joined in, and, using his forefinger, pretended to slash his throat. 'Remo-aucas!'

'Woooooooagh!' said both women, hearing the word again.

'This is very interesting,' said Louis. 'They are referring to the Remos, of course – who are meant to be extinct.'

I knew a bit about the Remos. Like the Matsés they avoided the main rivers and were regarded by anthropologists as a hinterland tribe; also like the Matsés they spent much of their time hiding from the dominant members of the Panoan group, the Shipibos and the Conibos. By the 1800s most were staying safely away from the main Ucayali, but in 1859 some supposedly missionized Shipibos uprooted and left to go and attack the Remos. In 1862 the Remos left their hidden-away homelands on the Cayaria tributary, situated above the Javari source, attracted by the idea of the sanctuary provided by a mission downriver. It was a temptation the Conibo could not resist: before very long they had attacked the mission and robbed the Remos of their women and children. When the rubber boom arrived, the white men also took their toll, wiping out most of those who were not yet enslaved or dead.

I said, 'You would have thought the dwindling Matsés would get on better with the Remos nowadays. They are both in the same boat.'

'Not a bit of it. They hate each other. More than the Marúbos and the Matís. The Remo-auca are really the Matsés' most traditional enemies.'

'The Matsés seem to be traditional enemies of everyone,' Patrick observed.

Louis said, 'Getting back to the Remos, there's been no official sighting of them for years. But the Matsés claim to have seen warning signs left in the forest – a bent twig, or a marked branch – letting the Matsés know they are nearby. It's the Remo-auca way of keeping them from sleeping at night. Still, it's probably all nonsense.'

We went to have a chat with Fidencio. He knew more about both the Matsés and Remo-aucas than anyone, Louis said.

While Victor unravelled his picnic of tinned meats, Fidencio sat us down and began talking to us in loud but silky tones, slipping into clear, town Spanish that was easy for me to understand. He said that one day he would be the *conquistador* of the Remo-aucas, and I could believe it. He had an alligator's glint; his eyes were always smiling, charming us, easing his way forward.

He told us how he had been to the Javari before the Two Harriets settled on the river with their tent. Just like any other *mestizo*, he had, as a child, accompanied his father on expeditions, trying to help the family make ends meet. Fishing, trapping, hunting, they had at first kept the feared Matsés at bay with presents. Over time, there had gradually developed a mutual trust. For in those days there were other people for everyone to worry about – the Remo-aucas, the Boca Negras, 'Black Mouths', and the Grimas, the 'crickets', who rolled and jumped through the forest. He taught his wife to defend herself by shooting at tapir skulls, round the back of their little hut, and they kept the Matsés at bay with gifts.

We listened as Fidencio talked. He was so loud and forceful, I wanted to back into the shadow. Yet I was also fascinated by a quality in him; perhaps it was his strength of will or energy – charisma, I suppose. And I wasn't the only one. Louis, Victor, we all sat there around him, feeling like transfixed rabbits.

Only Patrick, unable to understand a word of Spanish, seemed able to gather himself to leave. But when he did stand up, Fidencio softly took his shirt sleeve, and pulled him back down. 'Benedito, tell your friend here I'll take him off hunting one day. He wants to see snakes? Any time. Wild cats? Pigs? Dozens of them.' He let go of Patrick's shirt, but now Patrick was staying of his own accord. Fidencio had something about him.

Fidencio told us his history into the hot night, coaxing us with tales, and touching us sometimes, guiding us with his fingertips to where he wanted us – which was in a circle around him in the lamplight. We sat squinting, batting away the insects drawn to the light, wishing we had the will to slink away. Patrick after a while occupied himself with Arelli, a daughter of about fourteen, who came to sit opposite him. She looked soft and delicate in the paraffin light, hands around her smooth face, and issuing a sensuous smell, like a nectar-oozing scarlet lily.

'She is always playing like this,' Louis whispered, when Fidencio broke off to fetch some coffee for us. 'You had better warn him.'

I said, 'I don't think Patrick needs warning.' I watched the pale, thin, Irish hand advance. 'But maybe she does.'

Fidencio returned with the coffee and handed round mugs. I noticed that when he wasn't performing for us, he had an occasional look of sourness, his lips seemed to thin and eyes harden. But now he was back in the lamplight, and he was the smooth, forceful man we had seen before.

Patrick said, 'What about these Remo characters, then. Benedict's going to run into those?'

Good point. *Was* I going to run into these Remo characters?

Fidencio said, 'Woooaaagh!' He seemed to have picked the habit up from the Matsés. 'Wooooaaaagh! The Remo-aucas are *bravo*.' He mopped his brow, but a fresh gleam of perspiration immediately reappeared. '*Bravo!*' he repeated. Wild. Maybe eight years ago they came just near here to fight the Matsés with clubs. The Matsés later said they'd worn paint, long hair with fringes, tattoos on their chests, and a stick through their upper ear.* He himself had seen a Remo-auca *maloca* from a plane when he was flying into Angamos, a settlement on the middle Javari.

I still hadn't been told whether I would bump into the Remo-aucas, but next Louis brought out a home-made map and asked Fidencio to help him fill in the blanks. There were a lot of blanks. They extended all the way along my route for Phase Two. I'd need to continue east from where we were now, overland to a little river

---

* A story going around at the time was that, a couple of years previously on the Mirim, a western tributary of the Lower Javari, some oil prospectors in a motor-boat encountered three riverside 'Remo' Indians with bows and arrows. They wore shorts and – unlike the Mayorunas – wooden discs in their ears and black paint on their faces. The oilmen chucked a knife to the Indians and while they were scrabbling to pick it up, the oilmen sped off.

called the Matanza, which flowed into the Lobo, which led into the Galvez, which led to the Javari.

Louis got out a pencil from a schoolboy's case and marked all this in, followed by the indigenous population: the Matsés, along the Galvez tributary and upper Javari. And then the Remo-aucas, on this side of the Middle Javari. 'HOSTILE INDIANS' he wrote with a flourish.

'That's a funny coincidence,' I said, looking at the first objective, the Matanza. '*Matanza* also means "slaughter".'

'Benedito . . .' Fidencio took me by the sleeve, drawing me closer. In 1963, he said, a party of three trappers went out into the forest. They had a fight, and two were killed. Their bodies were discovered in the undergrowth. A giant tortoise was eating their toes. 'Well, well,' Louis said. 'And I always thought it was called Matanza because of all the jaguar attacks.'

Patrick said, 'I'm beginning to see why they want you to take a gun.'

'You know, Benedito,' Fidencio said, bringing the paraffin light into my face as if to study me, 'you'll need to take a fully equipped expedition, you can't hope to walk in there like an Indian.'

'That's what I keep telling him,' said Louis. 'He's even got broken ribs.'

Fidencio said, 'Look, I know this place. Want to know how far I'd put *my* chances of survival? Eighty–twenty. That's where I'd put them.'

Coming from an acknowledged expert, this was less than reassuring. He said it wasn't danger of violence from the Matsés, who hadn't killed 'anyone much' since 1965.

'Construction workers, poor fellows,' Louis chipped in. 'Someone should have told them.' I filled in the pieces of the story. In the previous decades clashes with the Indians had gone unrecorded – who in the outside world cared? Whether collecting rubber, hunting or trapping, the invading *mestizos* shot down those Matsés they came across. The Matsés for their part raided the advancing *mestizo* huts for women. However, an Indian attack in response to a road, albeit one running right through their land, was viewed altogether more seriously by the authorities. This was a matter of national security. The armed forces were brought in to bomb the Matsés.

Four years later, when Harriet Fields made contact, the Indians were still in a state of shock.

'Snakes,' Fidencio was saying. '*They* are your chief danger, not Matsés.' He took a night beetle that was batting against the glass of his lamp. 'And they give you a lot more of a bite than this.' He pincered the beetle between two fingernails and flicked the two halves into the night. 'Snakes, that's the problem. They are all over the place. Ask the mad Harriets – they will tell you.'

'They did.'

'And people get lost in this forest. It's the old trails from rubber tappers.'

As for the Matsés, though they wouldn't attack, even on the Galvez tributary where they were more missionized they still did not trust anyone. 'If they feel like it – they have a bit of a chill, or they feel bored – they will abandon you. You, me, anyone.'

'But you yourself get on well with the Matsés.'

'Benedito . . .' Fidencio smiled, slowly. 'I am their father. *Papá de los Matsés.*'

'What's the sleaze-bag saying now?' Patrick asked, his eyes still fixed on Arelli's soft petal face.

'I'll tell you later,' I said. 'You concentrate on what you're doing. So, Fidencio, what is the situation all in all?'

He leaned towards me, crowding me. 'The problems are just as I've told you, Benedito. Getting lost, the snakes, the Matsés leaving you. Then the wild Matsés of Brazil. But I think you would be all right if I guided you. Better than eighty–twenty chance of coming out, probably. I could take you to Tumi, beyond the Javari, in Brazil. He speaks a bit of Spanish and Portuguese. He'll take you onward, he'll know paths into Brazil.'

Louis took me aside. 'You see how much Fidencio knows? Antonio cannot go, so go with Fidencio. He'll get you to Tumi.'

'But he's like an alligator!'

'You are being unreasonable,' Louis said. 'Fidencio knows the forest this side of the Javari better than any other outsider. Better than those three young Matsés even. He can make the Matsés do anything just by talking with them – they would walk a hundred miles with him, if he asked. He is like a magic man with the Indians.'

'God knows who Tumi is. And hasn't it struck you there's a very good reason for Antonio not wanting to risk going? I don't want to go anywhere with Fidencio.'

Patrick agreed. 'Jesus, you only have to take one look at his eyes.'

However, it had to be faced that Antonio, my only other option, was scared off by the Remo-aucas – a hazard not even mentioned on Fidencio's comprehensive-sounding list. And Antonio was living in isolation from other Matsés, and was likely to be an outcast. Louis pressed his point home. 'Benedict, you must wake up. These three Matsés are westernized, but even they might desert you. Even with them, you'll need Fidencio's skills every second of the way.'

We broke off the discussion for the evening, and Arelli decided it was bedtime as well. She retracted her sexy lips and slipped out of Patrick's clutches while he was erecting his mosquito net. The next morning she skirted Patrick, going off to school without so much as a glance. He left the breakfast table and stalked her to the classroom, where the teacher had the unhappy task of teaching all age-groups from kindergarten to high school at once and on a single blackboard.

Patrick soon came back, still clutching his coffee mug. 'Hot by night, cold by day,' he said stoically. 'It goes that way sometimes.'

Louis was talking about Fidencio in reverential terms. 'I feel he is a shaman, really. I can feel his energy.'

I too could see that, just like a shaman, Fidencio was a magnetic performer, a manipulator of words and energies and probably a gifted leader. But that was an end to it. His spiritual insight was no more than that of a fruit-machine.

Patrick was more pragmatic. 'He's a villain – and Louis is as well and probably gets a cut of everything Fidencio pulls off. But he knows his Matsés, doesn't he? Maybe he's your only chance.'

'I was hoping you weren't going to say that.'

'Besides, there's a four-fifths chance of survival. That's not bad.'

'My mum will think it is. My girlfriend will.'

'You're an explorer, for God's sake. What do they expect?'

Louis got out his map again and we took it along to Antonio. Although we still had to stand outside a while before being called in, this time there was a much easier atmosphere. Antonio today held his head up as we entered. He was able to stand his ground in his own house.

Patrick bought a bead bracelet from Antonio; a baby Matsés was given the money to play with and for the rest of our visit slowly tore it up. In the meantime, Antonio's wife began trying to persuade me not to go. She said the Marúbo Indians, their enemies on the Brazilian side of the Javari, had a special type of medicine which withered you away, turning your hands into claws. She also put in a plea for the younger woman here, who feared we still wanted to coax away Antonio, her 'Grandfather'. I wrote in my diary: 'Her Grandfather must not go. The Remos: woooogh! And the Marúbos, they hang up their victims, slit their wrists and drink their blood. They leave the flesh for a few days. When there are worms, they are ready to eat. Woooah!'

Fidencio must not go either, they wailed. Only his soul would come floating back. 'Fidencio will haunt us!' But on the whole the Matsés didn't seem quite so worried about Fidencio's fate.

'And what about the threat from Fidencio,' Patrick said, when I explained where we'd got to in the conversation. 'You haven't covered that yet.'

As the woman swung in her hammock, I asked, 'Fidencio is good for me as a guide, or bad?' For this question I didn't want one of those dubious 'yes' answers that Louis found so satisfactory in his dealings with the Matsés.

The woman put out a foot to stop the rocking of her hammock. 'He speaks Matsés. He knows the forest. He can hunt with a gun. So yes, he can take you, if the young Matsés go. And if you have a motor. And much food.' She began swinging again. 'But it is not good for anyone to go without Matsés.'

'A guarded answer, I'd call that,' I said to Louis as we smiled our goodbyes and left.

Louis said, 'You'll be fine. My palms itch – you know, it is a good sign.'

'I told you I didn't want to take a gun or an outboard.'

'You are limited for choices, if you haven't noticed,' Louis said, his patience growing thin at last. 'And you haven't seen Fidencio with Indians. He is like a magician, believe me. He encountered the Matsés three years before the mad Harriets. How many people will you meet who can speak Matsés and Spanish fluently? People who can get you to the Javari? You've still got broken ribs, remember.'

'It's a fair enough point about your ribs,' said Patrick later that morning as he swam in the river, and I as usual nursed myself delicately in the shallows.

Children started jumping gleefully from the tree, making great splashes, and Patrick decided to abandon the swim and to get on with his tanning programme. He lay out on a log. 'Looks like you're stuck with the creep.'

Before we left the waterside a little child of Antonio's modelled a jaguar out of the riverbank clay. It seemed a portentous omen. I went back up to the house and promised Fidencio I'd be back to launch the expedition with him from here, by river and foot to his friend Tumi in Brazil. I was well aware this was not the best time of year – it was still the dry season and the rivers would rise and fall rapidly, affected by every shower – but the three young Matsés would leave for their home on the Galvez if we didn't hurry up. There was nothing we could do about it.

'Still, I would feel happier if Fidencio and Louis weren't *both* crooks,' Patrick said to me as we loaded up the canoe. 'You don't even have a companion to watch your back.'

'It's all right,' I said. 'Wait till you hear my plan.'

# VII

# In the Alligator's Jaw

ON THE WAY BACK TO IQUITOS, Patrick told me exactly what he thought of my plan to control Fidencio. 'Draw up a *contract* between him and Louis? I don't believe I'm hearing this.'

I tried to tell him I'd lived intimately with remote, even 'uncontacted' tribes, survived the jealousies, war dances, the power struggles of clans and innumerable New Guinea factions. Surely I'd survive Louis and Fidencio.

'Louis and Fidencio aren't some tribe of dangerous fuzzy-wuzzies, they're double-dealing crooks.'

'But *before* you were saying that my best option was to trust Fidencio.'

Patrick seemed on the point of tears. 'I didn't mean you to trust a bit of paper.' He closed his eyes and tried to calm himself. 'Jeeesus wept. A contract nominating Louis head of the expedition, Fidencio his number two . . .'

'I play them off each other. Louis, in charge, stays firmly in Iquitos. Fidencio comes with me. As I've already told you, we get it legally witnessed.'

Patrick said to himself, 'I wouldn't mind, only I'm put off the girls for worrying about you.'

On the one hand there was Louis. He saw the Indians as practitioners of simple natural harmony. They were *Naturmenschen*, and he wouldn't have wished them harm. In fact they could usefully help him make a living. The forest was valuable to westerners, and he could understand that – he was an outsider himself, and shared

112

one of our myths: the mysterious forest as an Eden, a repository of our hopes and dreams. At a price, he was in a position to transport us to our dreams.

Fidencio was different: he lived there. And he was that unfair thing, a half-Indian, a *mestizo*, someone with an Indian's lot and a white man's cravings. If I had explained the forest's value as a genetic pool – I had heard that 90 per cent of the most commonly used western medicines were derived from rain forest materials – he would have nodded, understanding. This was his language: the forest as a financial asset. He had said he wanted to be a *conquistador*, as if it was a matter of pride; but when I investigated further at the Loreto District office in Iquitos, I discovered that he stood to gain a lot of money. An American Protestant, Pastor Saunders, was offering $500 for contact with the Remos and the Ministry of Education in Requena even more if he taught them Spanish.

While Patrick packed his bags, Louis and I went to draw up the agreement. The scribes occupied a narrow street off the plaza; they were a line of men whose shirts had seen better days. Each had a portable typewriter on a little table. Louis carefully chose one and the man began bashing away as directed, using two fingers and with a fluency which suggested he did 50 of the same desperate agreements a day.

Louis excelled himself. He composed a powerful document which itemized some of the main items of equipment I was to take – the outboard motor, the shotgun, cartridges. That it would be a criminal act for anyone to divest me of them. That Fidencio had to REACH AGREEMENT WITH BENEDITO over every stage in the planning of the expedition. And he was reminded that it would be a criminal offence if he failed to honour his side of the contract, which was to deliver me to the Javari and a man called Tumi in Brazil.

In a day or two, Fidencio was coming to Iquitos and Louis would get his signature witnessed by the notary. I showed the contract to Patrick when we said our goodbyes and he said he couldn't help but be impressed. So was I: the expedition was wonderful on paper, a precise course of action in a continent of delays and broken promises. It was a magnificent work of art.

Armed with my equipment list, Louis set off around town with

113

Victor, buying supplies and depositing them in his house. The building had no doors, only three walls, but was perfectly safe because of the presence of his father, who was always to be seen inhaling Chinese infusions, as if permanently plumbed into a hookah pipe.

Much of the next three days I seemed to spend being stopped in the street by tour operators who had heard I had been in the forest with Louis. Some believed I had been left to starve out there. Others just wanted to warn me. 'He is amazing, the things he can do.'

'I'm aware of some of the things he *can't* do.'

The American luxury tour operator, Paul Wright, kindly took me aside, swiftly followed by two of his employees.

### FROM MY DIARY

They've been discussing me: 'Jesus! That poor Englishman with *those* two. Jesus!' One of L's tricks – 'just to give you an example' – was to pretend to be a Filipino & ask banks for money. Another was to be a Brazilian, with Portuguese accent. Another was to be a wealthy Peruvian looking for more investment. 'He's clever, no doubt about *that*,' Charlie told me. It was the same phrase Paul Wright used . . .

At this point, a motor-cycle taxi swung round the plaza. In it was L, an outboard motor, and Victor looking at himself in the wing mirror.

'Piranha,' Charlie said, summarizing. 'If he's been straight with you' – incredulous – 'then he'll be waiting for his moment. ZOOM!' He sliced his hands together. 'He'll be in there quick. Some investment idea, some project. Has he told you he's an owner of land yet? Normally does.'

But I'd always known Louis to be a wide boy and I kept to my plan. After all, two-thirds of the expedition supplies had already been bought, including a second-hand outboard motor, petrol, oil, and my contract did seem to be working. I'd been checking the receipts: Louis hadn't cheated me out of a penny so far.

Midway through the week, Fidencio arrived by boat and was taken off by Louis to sign the agreement. That afternoon we had a conference in Ari's Burger. Victor arrived first, and I checked through the equipment list, crossing off items that Louis kept trying to reinstate – he seemed to have an obsession with snake anti-venoms.

Louis brought along two *mestizo* woodcutters who would be helping out on the log-jammed portions of Javari tributaries. One was José, a shy, likeable man with peasant's wide, thick feet protruding from his split boots. The other, Armando, was quite different, with slick hair, a rodent's eyes that glided smoothly from side to side, and a shifty grin.

'You really know how to pick them, don't you, Louis?' I muttered in English as we sat them down.

We finalized the plan. Louis would help manoeuvre the equipment as far as Fidencio's house. From there the two woodcutters, Fidencio and the three Matsés youths in his hamlet would carry on with me by canoe as far as possible, then travel by foot, carrying the outboard and petrol overland until we could find navigable water. All that porterage sounded a nonsense – just the sort of nightmare expedition I had spent ten years in exploration avoiding.

'I think you'll be pleased with my choice of woodcutters,' said Louis, with a touch of pride. 'This one, Armando, knows the Javari backwards. Isn't that right, Armando?'

'Obviously only the main Javari river,' the ratty-eyed man said, taking his time, and with that slight grin still on his face. 'No one knows the smaller tributaries.' He looked at the menu, not caring what we felt about his unhelpful reply. 'Milkshake. And one for José.'

Louis was left to explain that Armando had worked for Victor Braga. I knew of him, a legendary Brazilian logger based in Benjamin Constant at the mouth of the Javari, he had been on the river for eighteen years. Like all the other operators out there, Braga sent out small teams of woodcutters, *mestizos* like these two, to work alone in the forest selecting out good timber, felling it, and dragging it to the river. In the wet season Braga himself would take a boat upriver, and float down all the giant logs.

'Armando, tell Benedito about the route down the Galvez to the Javari. Tell him about the logs across the small tributaries. Tell him what you told me.'

'*Sí*,' he said, bluntly. '*Hay mucho*. There are many.'

Perhaps Armando was just having a bad day, so I asked Louis how things had gone with Fidencio. 'You've told him I'm friends with the police? You've explained that if he robs me, something nasty, lingering and inexplicable will happen to him?'

'He won't dare break the contract.'

The mention of Fidencio's name had a magical effect on Armando. He was suddenly quite ready to speak. 'Fidencio? You didn't tell me Fidencio was coming on this journey.' Then that grin of his deepened into a smirk. He was amusing himself with a private joke. 'Fidencio . . .' he repeated to himself.

The woodcutter José said, 'He isn't coming, is he?'

Louis admitted he was. 'He's leading it.'

Armando sucked his milkshake down with two straws, then left, taking José with him. He was still smiling to himself.

I said, 'I'm rather afraid he thinks he's dealing with a bunch of amateurs.'

'He's only a bloody woodcutter,' said Louis. 'Where's the man's respect?'


There was just time that day to drop in at the police headquarters, to check there were no new terrorists, drugs men or other miscellaneous killers on the east side of the Ucayali. As I stood queuing in the entrance, Louis passed by in a motor taxi, this time holding the stock and barrel of the newly-acquired shotgun.

'That Chinaman,' a policeman asked, coming forward. 'Friend of yours?'

I had already queued for three-quarters of an hour, but my acquaintance with Louis granted me instant attention. In the interview that followed, my passport was confiscated, 'pending investigation'.

'But I'm a friend of Capitán de Souza. I'm living in his house.'

The policeman just shook his head, as if reflecting on the sorry extent of police corruption.

I found Victor in the market and demanded a meeting with Louis. I waited in Ari's Burger. It was early evening on a Friday, around the time when the police collect drinking money for the weekend, trawling for illegal motor cycles and holding them hostage in the back of a large truck.

Louis came up. From his face I saw immediately he had something else on his plate.

'Benedict, can you come along with me and reassure a business acquaintance? People are saying bad things about me. Just say I am honest. It's not much to ask.'

It was quite a lot to ask. But Louis had been straight with me. Take people as you find them, I always say.

Louis explained more as we walked to a hotel on the waterfront. I learned that we were on our way to see Pastor Saunders, who had been working on the Javari for years. The name rang a bell: this was the American who was said to be offering $500 for a first contact with the Remo-aucas.

'Pastor Saunders has been cheated by everyone. All his church leaders are crooks,' Louis said, wagging his head. 'One Christian after another has robbed him. *Christians!* It disgusts me. Now he doesn't know which way to turn. He is a sad man. Yesterday he held a meeting of his crooked pastors. He was in tears. He said, "I'm not going to judge, *God* will judge those here."'

'And where do you come in?' I asked.

'I'm willing to take over his operation. I will be his local co-ordinator. But there are crooks around here. And you know what? They tell people I am a crook! Me!'

'Terrible, terrible,' I mumbled.

The hotel was set on the waterfront. Balustrades looked out over a slow stretch of water where houses were perched on stilts over floating weeds. Open boats with thatched shelters worked to and fro across the giant Amazonas, their motors silent from here, the vessels only wood splinters pushing deeper into silver haze.

It was a plush hotel, the sort frequented by American missionaries. At the reception, Louis buzzed Pastor Saunders's room. The telephone receiver was handed to me. 'What am I meant to say?' I said to Louis. A voice was already answering, '*Hola?*'

'*Buenas tardes,*' I said. '*Puedo hablar con* –'

'Er . . . Pardon me?'

'He doesn't speak Spanish,' Louis said. I stared at the telephone receiver. What sort of missionary was this?

I explained to the American that I was calling on behalf of one Louis Chala, who wanted me to act as a character reference.

'Did you say Louis? Louis? You are prepared to give him a character reference?' Then the missionary seemed to be experiencing difficulty breathing.

I said, 'Well, all I can say is, he's been perfectly –'

'Before you go any further, just let me say something. Am I right in thinking he's standing next to you and you can't speak freely? That's the situation?'

'That's the situation,' I said.

Louis said, 'Tell him how honest I am. Tell him.'

'Okay,' the missionary said. 'Firstly, I think I know who you are. You're the Englishman. I've been following your progress. I heard that you are planning an expedition. So let me give some advice – you could sure do with some.'

Bloomin' cheek, I thought. Bloomin' imperialist missionaries.

But the missionary said, 'You've unwittingly hired a certain Chinese crook. I don't know what he's told you, but he's one of two men who's bled my mission dry. I've lost seven outboard motors, seven boats. I've lost one entire church building – dismantled by him and his crony. And then I can't begin to tell you how many dollars in cash. $400 for fuel, plus $50, no $60. Or was it –'

He argued with himself for a while, but he had been right first time – he couldn't begin to tell me.

He picked himself up. 'The other man responsible for my present predicament is the man you are setting off into the forest with. Fidencio – his business partner. See, you are caught in an alligator's jaw,' he said, graphically. 'The two nastiest teeth in the whole business, and you're stuck between them.'

'Ah,' I thought. Sometimes you get a sinking feeling, knowing it's going to be a long day. I was getting a sinking feeling, knowing it was going to be a long six months.

The missionary said he'd like to meet me for a coffee but he had to fly back to Miami tomorrow. 'So long. And I do hope you get out of this all right.'

I put down the phone. Louis was still standing beside me, hopping up and down like a puppy waiting for its little treat. 'I got the job?' he asked. 'I got it?'

'I think not,' I said.


The day before departure, 15 October, all the supplies were assembled and packed into sacks. Fidencio went ahead with Armando and José, taking the first load, while Louis and Victor spent the day trying to lure a stray dog to join us. 'He'll help you hunt,' Louis told me. However the dog, although starved, in the end preferred to chance it on the streets.

Still I had no passport. It was an emergency, time to produce my letter from 10 Downing Street. At the police station, the officer held the letter up to the light as if it was a banknote. He thought about it, then agreed to get my documents. I waited in the reception. Outside the door were the business-like sentries with slung rifles, white helmets and green combat gear. Beside me the forlorn mothers of Iquitos' criminal children. 'You are from America,' one mother said. It was an accusation, not a comment. 'It's easy for you, you can pay.'

It took time to sink in. Money. I scrambled for my wallet and found only one large denomination note. I rushed to the policeman at the desk and asked if he had change. He did not. Fortunately there was another woman in the queue with a larger bribe to pay. I changed the money with her just as my policeman reappeared.

He signalled for me to follow. We walked off down the road.

'My passport?' I asked, wondering where we were going.

He pointed to his crutch. For a short moment, I really did think some obscene proposition was about to be put to me. Then he stopped, and dug my passport from out of his trousers. I took it. It was warm and sweaty. I quickly produced my money, and placed it into his hand. Unfortunately there was loose change in my pocket, and it spilled noisily into the street.

The policeman hissed, *'Nada más! Nada más!* No more!' We both looked about to see who was watching. When I looked back at the policeman to apologize, he was already running away.


The good ship *Atena de Ucayali* took us away in the night. Flapping away the oily clouds, I watched the lights fade from sight.

I had sent off final letters to Jita – 'all well,' I wrote, lying dreadfully. And to my editor, so that at least someone in the world would know what happened to me: 'broke ribs . . . 80–20 chance of survival.' Really, I hardly dared think what the future held. I had never been in such bad physical shape setting out on an expedition, and never this dependent on a technology so alien to the forest. It could only end in tears.

I slept little. Once I reached from my hammock and dipped into a little basket of pills being plied among the passengers by a young boy – half-courses of antibiotics, soiled aspirins and unlabelled yellow and red pills that rolled about prettily at the bottom. Otherwise I just lay there, musing about how badly the future would unfold.

'The *conquistador* of the Remo-aucas' Fidencio hoped one day to call himself. Back home, you wouldn't exactly call his views fashionable. 'F. does have extraordinary powers of leadership & conmanship,' I consoled myself in the diary. 'I could imagine him smoothing a *mestizo* into doing anything he wanted: just hope loyalty of Matsés holds up.'

I wondered if the woodcutter Armando would help me out of trouble, if this all went wrong. No one could blame him for laughing at this ludicrous expedition.

'I've watched him observing us with his rat eyes,' I wrote. 'Misses little.' I'd do well to befriend Armando, I thought.


In the morning we found Fernando and he took us onward in his large dugout canoe. At Fidencio's village I noticed how low the river level was now. The tree roots were exposed, the mud baking into bricks. If it didn't rain tonight, we were not going to get Fernando's canoe anywhere near the place upriver where the path led off to the Matanza.

Fidencio walked down the bank to greet us, his arms extended.

120

'Oh! Benedito!' He looked as bad as ever – that oily skin, the stretched, beaky face of a frog.

Together we heaved the last sack into the huge pile of supplies on the veranda, then stood staring at them a while. One by one we each picked up the sacks, weighed them and tutted.

'There was no choice,' said Louis. 'You've already made me cut it down far too much.'

We went to meet the three young Matsés. They were behind Antonio's house, and refused to come out. You couldn't blame them. For the rest of the afternoon, I played Casino with Armando, hoping to get to know him. I always seemed to lose, but Louis assured me he wasn't cheating. Concerning Armando, I learned next to nothing. There was a suggestion that he had left a girl with a child in one Amazon backwater, and there was his address in Iquitos – a dirty street in a disreputable quarter. Otherwise, I was none the wiser. He had the habit of silently materializing at your elbow, giving you a start, and he could disappear equally swiftly. He would have made a good assassin.

By twilight, as the daughter called Arelli began to show herself, coming out like a night flower to tantalize Armando as she had Patrick, I conceded that we'd need two more men to help with all the luggage. Louis suggested the two villagers playing football outside, and they certainly looked fit enough. Their bare feet slapped against the deflated ball as they thumped it at each other. When they realized their game was being watched, the competition rose. There were fisticuffs and Louis had to go and separate them.

'We'll have to take Charo,' Louis said, returning to the veranda. 'Fidencio's son. To be quite honest he's a bit young, but – well, there's no one else.' He pointed to a weedy boy on the other side of the field. He was running about on all fours with an animal skin tied over his back, sweeping the long hairy tail behind him. 'He's being a giant ant-eater,' Victor explained.

It was a dry evening, the air still and smelling of the sweet, sickly rottenness of orchards. No rain.

Louis said we had to go tomorrow. The Matsés wouldn't wait even one day longer – at least, not now they'd seen how much luggage we had to take.

That night, Fidencio obtained an itinerant shaman from

somewhere in order to try and bring rain. He was an Indian called Orlando who had a sleepy left eye and also a line in ceremonies involving tobacco, with which we had to supply him in bulk. He set himself up comfortably by the hearth with half my entire expedition supply. After much contemplation, he sent Charo to throw two kilos of my precious expedition salt into the river – this would bring rain without fail, he pronounced. Later, as the dry night rolled on, Orlando muttered, 'Better kill a few frogs as well.'

After a night remarkable only for its aridity, I woke to find myself face to face with seven white sacks. This was my expedition then: hiring Indians, the experts here, to help us carry an outboard motor over dry land, two extra people to cut through logs so that we could make a decent stretch of water in which to use the motor at all, and now an extra person to carry food for all these extra people.

Armando was the only other expedition member up. He was helping himself liberally to our motor engine oil, using it to sleek back his hair.

I did a spot check on our supplies. I found one plastic jug, one saucepan, three tins of tuna and two bags of sugar had been stolen. It had to be Fidencio – no one else had a hiding place. But what sort of criminal stole when he knew all the evidence would point to him? The answer was, a very stupid or a very confident one. Now we were leaving, though. Dexta, the oldest son, was nominated head of household and given last-minute instructions. The other children ran out of school to say goodbye to their father. Charo, the son coming with us, sauntered about, spilling his loose energy, while we got on with loading Fernando's large canoe.

While we shuffled about, water spilling over the canoe sides as we loaded and reloaded, Antonio stood on the riverbank holding a charred monkey tail and watched the chaos. As time went by, more and more of his family came to watch. Finally I insisted that we took along a second, smaller canoe to share the load and also enable us where necessary to scout ahead. The remainder of the cargo was wedged in among us as we boarded – Fernando the driver, who would return with the canoes after dropping us on the Matanza path, then Fidencio and Charo, then the two woodcutters and then, when they could be encouraged out of the shade, the three shy Matsés. They wore short hair, like Antonio, and ragged

T-shirts and shorts. They kept in a tight bunch, and looked as if they were giggling nervously though they weren't making a sound.

Finally, we were waving Louis and Victor out of sight. I was sorry to see them go – Louis had helped me get my expedition back on course, and, it seemed, without ever pulling that final con-trick.

The river took us into the shade. Trees hung further and further over us, gaining confidence, it seemed, as we entered deeper among their kind – and away from our own. My concerns were lost for a while. I was warming to the adventure of the forest, the sense of my world sinking further and further out of reach. Now, at last, I would see the forest for myself. Soon we were beyond the last palm house, the last banana garden. The Matsés brought out a spike-headed fishing spear to have at hand. The shotgun was passed though to Fidencio in the prow. Sometimes the Matsés murmured words towards the river bank, as if to friends. 'Ooooowe . . . Uubeeee,' they seemed to be calling. 'Loooooommke. Tsoooppee.'

Fidencio said, 'Benedito, they are calling to the spirits for rain to raise the river.' Whether this was true or not, the forest that echoed back their voices quietened us all. We were stilled a little by our immersion in this world of breathing greenery. Even Fidencio had a family which loved him, and which was fast slipping out of reach.

Now, where the sun broke through at all, it bore down strongly, the dappled light on the brown water flashing into our eyes. Leaf-cutting ants crossed on the log bridges, their leaf flags waving. Bats dropped from the underside of river-bank tree roots, oily rags streaking silently away from us to latch on to those shadows to be found deeper into the interior.

For a while we progressed smoothly, no logs barring our way. We paused only once, when the Matsés hissed and flapped their hands and pointed at a large viper asleep in a mud recess of the bank. Its diamond head, a dark green and grey flecked with yellow, remained perfectly still until the Matsés lanced it. Then the snake opened its mouth – a huge, wet, pale yellow rat trap – and for a second its thin fangs made to seize at us. Then its head was swinging lifeless from the spear.

We had successfully dealt with the first snake hazard. For all my desire to see the forest for myself and not be swayed by other writers, I found myself remembering a comment about the local snake fraternity in *The Rivers Ran East*. 'It is imperative, life and death to you, that you correct your mistaken ideas that the jungle is not dangerous,' the American explorer Leonard Clark is warned by a Professor Rosell, head of the Sociedad de Geografía, before setting out into this, the Ucayali region. He is shown bottle upon bottle of preserved serpents, thirty poisonous ones from the Ucayali alone. He is told of 'irritable and vindictive' vipers that attack man without provocation, of the short-fanged coral snakes, 'which, like cobras, hang on and chew after striking', the fer-de-lance, 'night-rover, 94% fatal', and another of the same family, 'only three inches long – most deadly of all'.

The medical profession is less impressed. According to John Hatt's *The Tropical Traveller*, more than half the victims of snakebite receive minimal or no poisoning, and the mortality rate even from the most venomous snakebites is estimated to be less than 10 per cent.

Perhaps, as Clark was warned, this was a high risk region. And not just for fun had the Two Harriets knocked up that dangerous-sounding contraption for snake bites. Harriet had explained in matter-of-fact tones how she wired up the car battery, how the wires delivered a charge to the bite. In certain cases they'd found it beneficial: no, they had never had cause to use it themselves, but they happily applied it to the Indians.

Ahead we heard an agitated twitter in the trees, followed by a crash through the foliage. Around the river bend we saw two large, dark brown cats. They were bickering, tussling with each other. For a moment we all thought we were seeing something rare indeed – black jaguar cubs at play. It wasn't the colour that was rare – like the black leopards of the Asian forests, black varieties of jaguar were common in dense, wet forests – but the sight of jaguars. You heard jaguars, or you thought you smelt them, but you did not see them. Nearer, we realized they were jaguarondis, smaller cats that, so I'd thought, favoured more peripheral forest. Powerful swimmers and climbers, they eat animals ranging from monkeys and birds to rodents and reptiles. Only when we were a bare ten paces away did they shake each other off and lollop up the bank, stopping again to glare irritably at us before disappearing. 'As I told you,' Fidencio commented. 'The animals here have no fear of humans.'

In the middle of the afternoon, the sleepy, hushed forest hours when there was only a chain-saw screeching of noon cicadas, we came to a halt. A fallen tree barred the way. Armando was called forward, and handed the axe. He swept his engine-oiled hair out of his eyes and chopped, the axe occasionally appearing to spark as it bit at the hard wood. We sat waiting, listening to the fizz of the forest and the slow rhythm of relentless white man. The water level was still falling, making it harder all the time to progress. Close behind the first fallen log was another, and another. Finally Fidencio pointed to a patch of clear river bank and we stopped for the night.

Before I was ashore, Fidencio had already begun organizing the camp construction, whipping machetes into the hands of José and Armando and dispatching them with gusto to cut palm fronds for a shelter. Now he was turning to the Matsés. '*Jóvenes!* Youngsters!' he called, reserving a softer tone for them. But they had already crept away to make their own sleeping quarters further off.

Next, Fidencio turned his energies on me. '*Jefe*, chief,' he said, beckoning, 'sit and take things easy, like the *patrónes* of the old days.' He set Charo to making a stool of three crossed sticks of wood for me, and produced a little red cassette recorder. Even had acting like a *patrón* been my cup of tea, I knew I couldn't afford to sit back. Fidencio was far too competent a leader. He was in his element, and by all accounts that made him dangerous. I joined in scything away the leaf-litter. Large ants reared at us, and one shrub released a smell like musty cheese. Clearing the leaves was a precaution against snakes, spiders or scorpions, but as we worked we saw only one of these, and that was down by the water, a snake that was pencil-thin and bright green, the length of my arm, absolutely frozen on the river bank, looking vulnerable on the bare, brown mud.

The Matsés were already on to the next stage, deftly laying beds of palm leaves for their mosquito nets. They pitched fronds over their beds so that they had a protective canopy like a giant squirrel tail. Fidencio called softly whenever passing them, 'Oooo. Matseeeeee.' He would fondle them if he could get near enough, as if they were his little children. They would let him briefly, and dip their heads coyly, shrinking away back to their camp in the bushes. But Fidencio was starting to work his magic.

In the morning the air was still as damp on our skin, but the river level had dropped half a metre. Logs over which we might have glided yesterday now lay squarely across our path. By the afternoon, the forest closing in on us further, clouding us with darker shade and mossy cave smells, we had progressed only a couple of river loops. We agreed that the canoe driver, Fernando, had better leave us before he was trapped. Somehow we would have to follow the twisting river course on foot.

We unloaded our supplies, untied our little scout canoe, and stood on the bank, watching the reflection sparkle on the clay waters as the motor faded from earshot. We listened to the sound growing again as the canoe rounded a meander, then fading again. Growing. Then fading. I waited longer than anyone else, still listening, increasingly unhappy with my isolation out here in Fidencio's hands. At last the canoe was out of earshot, and we were alone. The forest seemed to close in further.

Fidencio organized camp, and then, while the rice cooked, I tackled him about how we would get seven sacks of 40 to 50 kilograms through the forest. 'Benedito! You must leave the worrying to me!' It seemed a suitable moment to remind him that I had to be consulted over all expedition plans.

'I want to be kept informed,' I said. 'What do you propose to do?'

'Well, Benedito,' he said, seeing an ant on his sleeve and with one finger rolling it into a crumb. 'You will see what I decide.'

Never mind the contract, out here I was in this man's power. We all were – all of us except the Matsés. They came near us only when necessary. One of them, heavier built and less shy than the others, would slip in to the fireside to fetch all their share of the rice and tinned fish. Later the same Indian would come back with the empty pot – but only when the rest of us were sitting back, quietly drinking coffee, and Fidencio couldn't reach to touch him.

I woke in the morning to find it already light. Even before I was out of my mosquito net I realized something was different. Fidencio was at the fireside, cleaning the gun. Charo was playing his cassette music, Armando was over by the supply sacks, examining a knot. I had the feeling he was waiting to talk to me.

'What's up?' I asked him.

Armando pointed with his chin at our leaf shelter. I realized that José had packed up in the night. 'Gone with two Matsés,' Armando said, and turned his chin to point it at Fidencio.

I walked over to Fidencio. 'Morning, Benedito!' he said, rising for me. 'Charo has made you a special American breakfast. The last eggs!' Charo extended a pan to me. 'Mr Benedito!' he said, and in English: 'How are you do, very well thankyou!'

I thanked him, but I didn't take my eyes off Fidencio. 'We seem to be missing three members of the expedition,' I said to him.

'Is that a problem?' he said.

I stood there, demanding more. Behind me I knew Armando was watching closely, waiting to see how I'd deal with this.

'Benedito, after you went to bed, I decided on a plan.' Fidencio bent to tidy up last night's dirty dishes. 'There's an abandoned canoe – a large one – a short way up the river. We can get it, then wait until the water level rises and then carry on – spreading the weight between that canoe and our scout one. In two days we'll get to the path – the one that leads to the Matanza. From there, two days by river to the Lobo, then two days to the Galvez and Javari.' I was being reminded just how little I knew about the region, how much I was in this man's palm. 'What do you think?' he said.

I didn't know. I said I expected he must be right.

'We can wait here today, while the two Matsés make their way up the river bank with José. Which Matsés would you have kept here with us? We can call them back if you like.'

I could hardly tell them apart. 'The shortest one?' I suggested, unable to keep the questioning tone out of my voice.

'That's what I decided as well. Makes sense.'

I couldn't think of anything to add that would not further emphasize my total ignorance of the region.

At midday I went off for a walk, ostensibly to look for the frogs that yapped like dogs to each other from holes beneath the leaf litter, but in fact hoping for a chance of a word with Armando, who had gone off in the same direction. For a while I picked through the dark, tight, riverside undergrowth. It was hard work, even with a machete. I sat down on a log, got out my diary and wrote: 'Feel need for exercise: not for strength but for agility. Feel v. v. tall – my body unwieldy, gangly and uncontrolled.' I was horribly unprepared for the journey into Brazil.

A little further, I came across the remaining Matsés. He was alone and looking up into the foliage. At first I saw nothing overhead – just the diamonds of light descending to us from the canopy way up above. Then I distinguished a woolly monkey picking slowly through the tree crowns – slow and quiet, as if it might be heard in the still of midday. The sun on its tail showed up the thick black fur. The moment was an intimate one, just between the Matsés and the monkey, as if they were wondering together about something. Then the monkey was gone, and I looked down. The Indian was looking at me.

I went up and squatted at his feet to ask him the names of some of the things around us. '*Como se llama?*' But he just took the fern leaf, the piece of bark, sniffed them, scratched them and then put them carefully on the ground. I waited beside him, close enough to smell his woodsmoke smell, but he said nothing. I realized I'd never actually heard any of the three Matsés talk as such, only whisper.

That's how much this large expedition is working against me, I thought. To this Matsés I'm just another well-laden white man too mean to share out my possessions. All I've given him are these presents of bark and leaves; to him I'm probably as bad as the greasy '*conquistador*' himself. And I need his knowledge to get me through this journey.

Now he was growing impatient. He rubbed one large foot pad against the side of another, flicked a fat fly off his skin. I walked back towards the camp and almost immediately bumped into Armando. 'Ah, Benedito,' he said, a smile spreading. 'Lost, and so near the camp.'

I said I was just going for a walk.

'A walk,' he said. I could see his mind working: he wants to go walking now, when we might have to walk for two weeks to get out of here . . .

'Just around,' I said. 'To learn.'

He took my machete to see the condition of the blade but I felt he was actually studying me – again that look of private amusement I'd seen in Ari's Burger. 'You want to learn,' he repeated.

'Learn from the Matsés, eventually. To be able to do my journey just lightly. But at present, well – my ribs.'

'So you have to put yourself in Fidencio's hands.' Armando enjoyed this thought for a second. 'I can see now.' He accompanied me down the path, stopping sometimes, pointing out objects of interest – a tuber, said to be used against cancer, and *palo sangre*, a heavy wood with bloody veins.

I asked if he had heard of this Tumi to whom Fidencio was taking me.

'They all seem to be called Tumi. It's one of the commonest names. An Inca name, too.'

He raised a flattened hand in the air, a signal to stop and listen. I heard a single, long note – plaintive, lonely. A far-off bird call. The sound was from a jungle fowl, and a call I knew. It was said to be good luck to hear it, perhaps because its presence meant there were no jaguars around. But it was an immensely lonely tune, a gentleman stalking by himself, whistling bravely, his hands in his pockets.

'He's called a perdees,' Armando said, and again, amused by something, smiled to himself. He walked on. 'He's alone out here, like you.'

'Something I've been wondering,' I said, stopping him on the path before we were too near the camp. 'Why did Fidencio keep the shorter Matsés here? He said it made sense.'

'The short one – Weeki, Fidencio calls him – is a bit younger. The others will come back for him. And only one of them speaks any Spanish – so he had to go with José. Also, he's more reliable. Been in the army – though he ran off in due course.' I noticed for the first time that Armando had very few teeth. He only ever smiled with that ironic smirk, so that his teeth were very rarely missed. 'As you must know, the other Matsés will wander off, if they are given the chance. Especially when we get near to the Remo-auca settlements.'

'You mean the Matsés settlements,' I corrected him, gently. I watched a gliding butterfly which had lacy, transparent wings, only a tag of mottled blue painted on it.

'The Remo-auca settlements. The settlements of the baddies.'

Armando saw that I was in a state of confusion, hearing this. He nodded to himself, 'So you don't know, then.' I saw him make up his mind to tell me some painful news. I braced myself. 'Look, I think you should know that Fidencio has a document saying he's on his way to find them. The Remo-aucas.'

'He has?'

'A contract between him and the Chinaman.'

'You mean Louis?'

'I'm not sure,' Armando said. 'The man you chose to help you. The swindler.'

Louis.

Armando conceded that perhaps he had misread. 'I didn't have long to read it – it was hidden in his bags.' Before I had found out why he was going through Fidencio's luggage, Armando delivered more bad news. 'I also overheard Fidencio tell Louis that he could have you killed by the Matsés, any time he wanted.'

'He said that?'

'One word and they'd do it, he said. But I don't think he necessarily meant he would.'

I would have liked to discuss the possibility of my forthcoming execution further, but I spotted Fidencio coming to see what we were up to.

'Talking so much together, my friends,' he said. 'Come back to the camp and eat something with us.'

However, once Armando had walked off, Fidencio stayed to give me an impromptu botany lesson of his own. He indicated a little epiphyte making its way up a tree trunk, and stroked it with the blade of the machete. It had the leaves of a pennywort and the manner of a clinging fern. The tree had a flaky bark, a tactic against creepers. None the less, against all the odds, it had inched its way up the tree.

Whack! Fidencio chopped it off. He took it in his hand and let it dangle like a frail little insect. 'Many people believe it makes people fall in love with you. You put it in your love's clothes. My wife believes in this. She puts it in my washing.'

130

He dropped the poor little shoot. I said, 'About this man Tumi, the Matsés man you are taking me to in Brazil . . .'

Fidencio didn't say anything but just made a fresh cut in another tree and see-sawed the blade backwards and forwards. Red resin oozed out to gum up any invading insects – one tree's defence tactic in a fast and furious forest.

'I don't know much about this man Tumi,' I went on. 'I know nothing, actually.'

'Benedito,' he said. 'There are two weeks to talk.' He walked off ahead of me down the path.

'I'd like to know more, Fidencio.' My voice sounded weak and rather tight – I realized I was pleading. I tried again, trying for a harder edge. 'More *now*.'

Fidencio stopped and turned. He was smiling but his eyes had sharpened. He was monitoring me again. Then he laughed, bending to take a twig out of his rubber boots. 'Benedito, you do not trust me!' I laughed this off good-naturedly, at the same time noticing that those boots weren't his, they were from my bag of presents for 'Tumi'.

From that moment on I felt a complete absence of power. The expedition had its own force, and I was being carried along by it.

# VIII

# The Bird that Walked by Itself

AT NIGHT I SAT looking into the fire, hoping the situation wasn't quite as bad as it seemed. Fidencio tried to jolly me along. 'Benedito, you've heard about the hermit? Charo, tell Benedito the story.'

'Benedito, on the Ucayali is a hermit – a woman! I mean, well she looks like a girl, but she must be a woman. She's about fifteen, you'd have thought, looking at her. But she has seven children! *Sí o no*, Armando?'

'I don't know,' said Armando. 'It is only a story.'

'Seven,' said Charo.

Fidencio stepped in to recover the tale. 'Eight. Four girls, four boys. But she lives alone – she has no husband, and no sisters or brothers. She has no fear of the forest, or of the snakes. Benedito, you are wondering who built her house? And who looks after the children when she's finding food? The answer is, no one knows.'

'Maybe she's clever,' Armando said. 'She has the children several years apart. They look after themselves.'

'Good point,' I said. I was more than happy to ruin Fidencio's story.

Charo said, 'Let me tell Benedito the most interesting thing, *papá*. Not only does this woman look like a girl. But do you know the most interesting thing? She came out of the forest once –'

Fidencio said, 'The most interesting thing was, she had to go into hospital in Requena – a woman's problem.'

Charo was sitting up, even Armando and I were sitting up. We knew an ending was coming.

Fidencio waited for the silence. 'The doctor found that she was a virgin.'

'It's true, Benedito!'

'Had never known a man,' Fidencio concluded. 'No doubt about it.'

I went to bed early, thinking of the girl alone in the forest, never ageing but like a goddess producing children. I wanted to believe in her, this angel, this semi-divine creature, a fountain of life and hope. This evening I'd seen that Fidencio also had the machete from the bag labelled 'Gifts for Tumi'.

'You are quiet, Benedito,' Fidencio called out from the camp fire. 'Just something on your mind, perhaps.'

Later I was woken by Armando. 'Take this,' he said.

I propped myself up. Frogs were croaking and cracking around me in the trees and leaves. I must have slept for an hour, perhaps. Everyone else had only recently gone to bed, it seemed, because Charo was still humming to himself.

'Take it, idiot – before the mosquitoes finish me off.'

'What is it?'

Armando had the expedition torch. He flashed it at some paper in his hand. I opened the mosquito net, and examined it. Armando said, 'You've got five minutes before I come back and collect it.'

It was Fidencio's copy of the contract between Louis and himself. Or rather it wasn't. Our whole itinerary had changed. Of the Matsés there was virtually no mention at all.

'Louis Chala of . . .' it gave the address. 'And Fidencio Suarez Artigas of . . .' it gave his. 'Agreement, this day . . .' I read on, my eyes darting over the words. 'Will pursue and track down the Remo-aucas. If they meet with no success, they shall proceed to the Boca Negras, the Grillos . . .' There was also mentioned a group I had never heard of, with long beards.

'For each group he will find, Fidencio Suarez Artigas will keep all monies promised by the educational authorities, while Louis Chala will have full rights to bringing in missionaries, anthropologists, press, adventurers to the said tribal groups.'

The next day I said nothing, but mulled the information over, watching Fidencio polish the gun as if it was his, his son pull apart the torch, as if it was his. I listened to the lone whistle of jungle fowl in the dusk and wondering whether like the creature, I was destined to walk by myself.

The third day, and still no sign of the scout party. The forest was starting to take us into itself. Termites, enjoying the undisposable nature of our plastic floursacks, were cementing them down, and the Matsés, Weeki, told Fidencio that in the night a large cat had prowled around his shelter. He had got up in the dark and seen its prints. We all went over to inspect them, but the marks were already gone, melted away in the night rain. Fidencio gave the Matsés the gun and four cartridges, and told him to go off and have a look around. It was probably only an ocelot.

We all knew very well it was not. The ocelot, black spotted on a golden yellow pelt, was only a small cat. It ran its prey down rather than ambushing them, and preferred more open forest. Of the other small cats, there was the solitary margay and the tiger cat – both too shy to come near a camp. That only left the powerful jaguarondi, the plain, dusky-coated type of cat that we had seen fighting a few days before. And, of course, the almighty jaguar. Was it right here among us, the largest and fiercest South American carnivore, said, even in scientific accounts, to be a cat which has little fear of humans? The cat whose name is derived from an Indian word *jaguara*, 'animal that overcomes its prey in a single bound'. I grew excited, not scared. I thought ahead to the Matsés, the Jaguar People with whom I was going to live. I remembered childhood stories of jaguars – *el tigre*, lying in wait, then dropping silently on to the back of Amazon explorers. The third largest cat in the world – only slightly smaller than the true tiger and lion – the jaguars were, in reality, too heavy to be able climbers. However, there was no doubting their strength and intelligence: in other tales *el tigre* lay by the riverside, lazily flicking their tails in the water to attract the curiosity of fish, then scooping them up with their paws. They were good swimmers, often lurking by rivers and preying on aquatic tortoises, caymans and night animals, rodents like agoutis that came to drink. Best of all they liked wild pigs, the white-lipped peccary which moved in noisy herds of up to a hundred. The herds roamed leaderless, slowly through the forests, sniffing out edible roots and shoots, and, when alerted by sentries, charging en masse towards any predator which came too near. The jaguar haunted the margins of these herds, picking out a straggler and awaiting the chance to pounce.

Before long, we heard four shots. It didn't sound like a lone Indian with a single-barrelled shotgun, it sounded like a gun battle. The Matsés came running back, grinning shyly. He had a pig, a white-lipped peccary, trussed up on his shoulders. '*Cuatro*,' he said, managing the Spanish for four. He enthusiastically plucked up a sapling and rammed it down the gun barrel to clean it.

Fidencio took the Matsés by the shoulder and hugged him. 'Is this your pussy cat?' he teased him in Spanish, 'Is this your pussy cat?' Weeki turned away, blushing, his yellow skin becoming brassy red as Fidencio squeezed him. Everybody laughed, and as I was the amateur here I decided I could forget about how the jaguar liked, best of all, to live with peccaries. I laughed along too.

Armando collected two more corpses and gutted them by the river, and Charo and I began cooking them in great chunks. It was the Matsés who went to collect the fourth pig, and while he was still out in the forest he let out a yelp. It was the noise of someone taken by surprise, but the silence after it was just as bad. Fidencio grabbed the shotgun. 'Charo!' he barked. 'Stay here!' He was walking forward and listening, the gun aimed forward, braced against his shoulder. Next we heard Weeki making a fearful creeing sound, a moan of a wailing woman. He was coming our way. Fidencio lowered the gun and Weeki tore through the undergrowth totally breathless, running up to Fidencio like a child who has had a nightmare.

We gathered around as he told Fidencio what had happened. Weeki had gone up to the dead pig without looking properly. He had bent down to pick it up – only to find it wasn't there. He saw it had been dragged along the ground and he was just wondering what animal was big enough to do this when he found himself looking into the golden eyes of a jaguar. They both froze: the jaguar stared at him, and he at the jaguar. Then the Indian bolted. He ran screaming, expecting any second to feel the weight of the cat on his shoulders – the fat paws thumping him to the ground, the teeth sinking into his neck. But nothing . . .

We settled down again. Armando cured the meat on the fire, and sliced up the last onion. I'd already learnt not to offer Armando help; I offended his sense of craftsmanship. He liked his onions cut as neatly as his logs.

However, before we could eat there was further mayhem. An animal came ripping through the bushes right into our camp. It was only a piglet, looking for its mother, but by the time we saw that we were diving for cover and Charo was screaming. The piglet had no fear of us at all. It stood panting at our feet, wondering why we had stopped running away. As it considered who to charge first, Armando picked it up. He gave it to Charo to hold while he constructed a little pen between two tree root buttresses. 'Better the jaguar goes for him. Which he will do, given the choice.'

While we waited for dark, the hour of the jaguar, I tried to get to know the furious peccary – I was fascinated by the piglet's aggression, its spirit. The peccary often killed and even ate snakes – it was always comforting for a traveller when a herd had been through, clearing the undergrowth. They were even said to be immune to the venom of the bushmaster, which, at up to four metres, was the largest poisonous snake in South America, and apparently something of a legend in these parts. Weeki moved his mosquito net into our camp for safety. The rest of us stood around the fire taking it in turns to borrow the torch and point it at the darkness to pick out those burning eyes.

Fidencio said he himself had been attacked when coming through this forest with his wife. 'I shot that *tigre* two times,' he said. 'It's still out here somewhere.'

'Probably just over there,' I said. We all stared into the dark again.

At dawn the piglet gave a squeal of panic. We were immediately awake, and scrabbling to get out of our mosquito nets. The piglet had already escaped and we wanted to escape, too. Then we saw why the piglet had run. The two creatures stood above us, watching – black, sinister vulture figures with bright yellow collars.

'They have a nest in the clouds, Benedito,' Charo said as we gazed up. 'That's where they've come from.' I wanted to share his vision of a bird that had soared down from the Andes, but later discovered that these were not the mighty gliders of the Andean range, but a related, smaller species. Here they were, perched above us in the forest, somehow drawn from the sky by the smell of the fresh kill. As we watched, a third bird settled on a branch, coming to land with a great whooshing of its jet-black wings.

Rain came in a rush soon after. First we heard the frogs, so many of them yipping and yapping that we could hardly talk above the noise. Next, as the wind gathered, way up above us in the treetops, leaves descended to us down here in the thick, still air. Then the rain itself, torrents of it that came down all day, raising the river and opening up our passage further into the interior. The scouts arrived with the hunters' canoe at dusk. They were so tired and hungry from three days' heaving it over river logs they stood a while in silence by the fire before saying hello.

We left by canoe early the next morning, every few hundred yards stopping to chop through logs blocking our way. After the rain the damp air had a fresh smack to it, and sometimes now I saw a tree frog, lying like a melted plastic blob on a leaf or a fallen slab of tree bark.

So far so good, I thought. We seemed to be heading to the Matanza as planned, and if we did go off course to the Remo-aucas, Fidencio must know that the Matsés would abandon us. Only he seemed to have the bit between his teeth now. His mind was focused on something ahead, and he had gone quiet on us, even on his son Charo. He had dispensed with the charm and I noticed that sour look on him more often. Sometimes, now, he wasn't even bothering to hide it. Perhaps we were dispensable, because now only the Matsés, the people who could get us out of any trouble, still received the full treatment, his hugging and wooing.

The Matsés had their different world and some of it seemed to be a world that went on at night, when we outsiders were asleep. Once or twice I woke up, hearing mice clattering among our cooking pots, and I'd catch sight of the Matsés then. They had crept out to play, just like the mice, but it was only the mice that made a clatter. Mostly the Matsés seemed to want just to stand by the fire and get warm, and only once was there any clue that they, like the other night creatures, had rustled through our bags. Charo one day got out his little red tape recorder, pressed the PLAY button and instead of hearing Los Chiches, a Peruvian pop group of the moment, he found himself hearing a recording of excited whispering and giggling, the Matsés playing with the dials and switches.

To speed our progress, two Matsés went on ahead in the small scout canoe with Armando and the axe. Sometimes we heard them in front, sometimes behind, as the river wound through the forest. The little craft returned to us from time to time, like a child to a mother, and the Matsés came back with palm leaf bands around their arms and waists. I saw that Fidencio took careful note of this – the Matsés decorating themselves. It bothered him. Once, when Weeki came back wearing a simple leaf crown, I noticed Fidencio inch nearer the Matsés to eavesdrop.

'It's a protection for them,' Armando told me, quietly. 'I've seen the Matsés with these leaf bands on the Javari. They're from the palm they call *poró*.'

'I'm more interested in what it means. Mainly because it's worrying Fidencio.'

'It means they are preparing to go deep into the forest – with or without us.'

There had been no rain for two days; the water levels were dropping in front of our eyes. Now we found ourselves caught between two log barriers. A day later, and still no rain. Fidencio ordered Charo to chuck salt in the river, according to the *mestizo* superstition. 'More!' he suddenly snapped, scaring his son. But that didn't work either. We waited a day more, then another.

And the change in Fidencio became all the greater. I remembered how, when we left his home, he had had a burnished look of vigour on his face. But that all seemed a long time ago now. Nowadays, only a week later, he was pale – not drawn and tired, but with a grey look of anger.

The Matsés were now murmuring to themselves and they had lost interest in our tinned fish and rice. They asked for a machete each. They asked for the shotgun to go hunting with. Fidencio gave them machetes, and made promises about other presents, and tugged their arms boyishly and rubbed their shoulders, but he wouldn't surrender the gun. He pretended not to hear when they asked and stood looking into the flames, cooing, 'Ooooo, Matseeeeeeee!'

We waited for the rains. While José, Armando and I played Casino, the Matsés stood in their group by the fire to keep warm, their arms folded across their chests, hands in their armpits. We hardly dared speak to Fidencio any more. He prowled around, tidying the camp and keeping busy sharpening machete blades. His fast, noisy movements made the Matsés nervous, but Fidencio didn't seem able to help himself now. He would increasingly lose his temper even with his son. 'Don't use the pan lid as a plate!' he'd bark. 'Hygiene!' And the Matsés would duck down.

That evening, after dark, there was a booming noise, as if some-one far away was lost and thumping his foot against a tree buttress to call for help. The noise made the Matsés silent, the same silence they gave off when they sensed Fidencio was angry. They were scared.

'Remo-aucas?' I ventured.

'They call him Mai-yan,' Armando said. 'A ghost or something. Try asking the lunatic. Ask Fidencio.'

'You try asking him.'

Fidencio was in any case busy dealing with a crisis. He was talking to the Matsés softly, whooping a bit with them around the camp fire. He was doing his magic, this thing that had made him a legend, this thing that had made me employ him, against all reason. It seemed to be all physical – how he pulled them in around the camp fire with him, touching them, making himself one of their number, but always showing that he was stronger, unafraid. He was suddenly someone they could lean on. Then, to my surprise, Fidencio called me into the circle too. He began showing me off. He importantly read the long, typed agreement between Louis and him – the original one. He spoke to the Matsés in Spanish, not their own language, and with all the authoritarian tones of a *patrón*. The Matsés suffered in silence, hearing about the common duty to deliver the white man, how we must pull together. They slowly gave up hope of leaving. Fidencio threw the agreement aside, as if he hated this beastly job himself, and went back to fondling the Matsés. As always they shied away and cringed, and when they backed off he reached after them. They tried to bring a serious, admonishing tone, saying urgently, 'Fidencio . . .' But they followed it up with nothing, uncertain how to continue. Or, when he began a new speech, they just said the word, 'Fidencio,' seeming to enjoy the certainty of his name, the only hold they had ever had on him.

Crisis over.

'Ghosts?' I asked Fidencio, for his triumph with the Matsés had put him in a better mood; he was much like his old, slick self.

'No, ghosts are people that they haven't eaten. Once, I saw a body way up in a tree, put there on display. For some reason it hadn't been consumed – an enemy perhaps. That dead man would be a ghost by now.'

'And this? I'd have said thunder, but then the Matsés would obviously know the difference.'

'*La madre de la selva*,' Fidencio said definitively. The mother of the forest, a devilish spirit sometimes known affectionately as 'Odd Foot'. She sometimes took the form of a friend, and led you off into the forest. You could tell her because she had too many toes on one foot.

As the Matsés drifted off back into the dark and their own camp, I heard Charo say to his father, 'Papa, they'll stay with us?'

Fidencio lay back and began flicking the expedition knife about. 'They'll stay with us if we keep moving. We *must* have rain tonight. If not, we abandon the canoes and walk.'

'*Walk*, papa? But the Matsés won't stay if they have to carry this weight.'

'They will stay if we keep moving. We walk along the river banks, we walk in circles if necessary. They are nomads, and that's what they like. We just keep walking.'


Rain did come in the night. It ripped through the forest, stripping off leaves, slashing foliage. We woke to these violent sounds, each of us lying there in the dark knowing that we would not be abandoned by the Matsés. Not for a while. We were on the move.

That same day, we made it to the track that cut through to the Matanza, the tributary that would lead us, eventually, to the Javari. Early the next morning we divided the loads and made rucksacks from palm leaves, with bark-string headstraps to take the weight. Armando, the surest on his feet, took our 40-kilo sack of *farinha*, the baked manioc which is the staple of the Brazilian Amazon, José took the petrol, which didn't weigh much less, and Fidencio strapped the outboard motor to his back. Because of my rib injury I could only take 20 kilos, the same as Charo.

We started out, whooping to keep within earshot of each other.

I stayed with the cluster of Matsés, following behind, waiting for an opportunity to befriend them. When they stopped for a break I helped their packs from their shoulders. I offered to lighten their loads, taking more weight myself. I gave them gifts of fishing hooks and line. None of this did any good. It just confused them, made them wonder where the trick was. They did give me things to carry, but were not grateful. Soon they were expecting these services, and handed me things as if I was the butler.

Were these people at all like the Araraibo, whom the traveller Georg Seitz described in 1960 as 'our simple friends who, cut off by lonely forests . . . accept what few gifts Nature has offered them in quiet gratitude'? They didn't seem very simple. Nor had they yet revealed themselves either as 'buried alive in their barbarism' – or, for that matter, as 'Jaguar People'. Time would tell what the jaguar meant to these people who chose to share its wetland forests, but already it seemed to me a purely practical arrangement, a survival strategy. Every animal and plant in the competitive forest had its own niche, its own slot in the system – even each of the different cats. And the Mayorunas, finding themselves competing with the jaguar for deer and peccaries, couldn't do better than emulate its efficient methods.

Glancing around, it was only too obvious how difficult it would be to live off this forest without sharpened senses. Consider the fate of the forest-hardened Percy Fawcett. His last message, dated 29 May 1925, suggested he was intending to gain the help of Indians to the north, ten days' walk away, but would he have managed even a week's march in the forest that was around me now? We know that the foot of Raleigh Rimell, his son's friend, was already inflamed from an infected tick bite.

To keep my mind off my own fate as I trudged along, I thought about Fawcett's. Far from being impenetrable, as one is led to believe, most forest floors like this one have only sparse vegetation. Away from the rivers, there simply isn't enough light – most of the forest biomass is up out of sight in the hundred-foot-high tree canopy. Few large ground-dwelling mammals risk moving by daylight in this place of predators – the tapir, deer and peccary are rare exceptions – and other obvious food sources tend to be restricted to rivers. Thrown on your own resources, your best chance is to stick to rivers, and attempt to spear fish, lizards and turtles.

Even with a rifle the task confronting Fawcett would have been immense – and all the more so because he was on the move, unable to set traps. Walking through forest myself, I could see it all too clearly: within a week of their departure, the party straying from their intended route. Wandering off, in an increasingly desperate search for game; the wandering continuing for some days, the forest-seasoned Fawcett faring better than his two young companions. But gradually, perhaps weakened further by fever, the humidity sapping their energy, the men lost heart; one by one they gave up washing, they gave up pitching their mosquito nets, and then, pallid, covered in insect bites, they gave up the struggle altogether. They collapsed in a pitiful daze – unable to summon the strength even to brush off the feeding ants and mosquitoes.

And I thought of Fawcett as I plodded on, now so much sweat in my own eyes I could hardly see the animals around me, only the ones that moved. Sometimes there was a snake, turning away, or a whistling oriole. A bird flashed by with a scarlet crest and black wings; in front of my eye, a dragonfly with only a circle of yellow on its transparent lace wings. The Matsés' bare feet rose and fell in front of me, aged feet on young bodies. The Indians danced as we came through an ant column, and they veered off the path to clobber birds they'd spotted in the ground scrub – often the scrawny fowl they called *kwé-vu*.

I grew no closer to the three Matsés. It was actually dangerous to walk with them. They were more interested in looking for meat than in our expedition and if I ever fell behind, clutching at my ribcage, they carried on out of sight. Once I looked up and found myself alone. I called out. They didn't answer. I tried again. No reply. I looked around, fighting to calm myself. I made the mistake of moving, and for a long while I lost their tracks. The forest was a barrage all around me. Standing alone in that forest I suddenly remembered Colonel Fawcett again. Once more, I was sure: he wasn't eaten by Indians, he was eaten by scavenger birds and worms, lost in the forest and already dead from starvation.

At the end of another day, Fidencio lay pinned to the ground by his own load, the outboard motor and all our oil. Like the rest of us he was dazed from the walk. His bleary eyes were focused as usual on the Matsés. They had thrown down their little loads, already erected their camp and were ripping open a bird they had caught on the march. Our supper, when we eventually got around to it, was to be tuna, levered out of tins.

The next morning Fidencio went faster, not slower, and left us all straggling behind, cutting away from our track and now blazing a new trail. He sped on, head down. Nothing seemed to deter him, not even the fear of getting lost. A pale brown scorpion got into his boot, stinging him repeatedly. He chucked it out, and walked on. A thorn caught his head and he left the scratch untreated. 'The flies can eat it clean,' he said, and kept walking.

The end of the third day's march, and we still hadn't reached the Matanza. And, though it was difficult even to see the sun through the shelves of leaves overhead, it was as if we were heading north, exactly the wrong way. The Matsés sunk down in a sorry heap with their packs on their backs, and stayed there, murmuring to each other. Fidencio spent much of the evening with them, cajoling them –'Oooooooh Matseeeeee!' – but he came away in a brooding silence and told Armando that tomorrow we'd all be taking a greater share of the Matsés' baggage.

The next morning, Armando, José and Fidencio made up their loads to perhaps 50 kilos each, and I took 30 kilos. We had to hoist each other to our feet, like ancient knights in armour.

We staggered off through the forest, Fidencio pausing only whenever Charo showed signs of imminent collapse. Only once, after four hours, did I manage to catch a word with Armando in private. I found him resting ahead of me on the trail. He was leaning back on a log, eyes fixed unfocused on the canopy, the log taking the weight of his pack. It hardly seemed to matter where we were heading any more. After a moment to get my breath back, I had the energy to wipe the sweat from my eyes. 'Seems . . .' I panted. 'Seems . . . a funny sort of route.'

'Not ... not if we're going to the Remo-aucas,' Armando wheezed. 'If we're going to the Remo-aucas ... it's probably a very sensible route.' He tilted his head to listen for the others. 'Mustn't stop too long.'

'You really think he's going to the Remo-aucas?' That morning I had written in my diary, 'Keep turning to Armando to sort out my problems. I admire his craftsmanlike ways: cuts-through, re-aligns, cuts again, constructing something useful out of the tangles I get into.'

'He thinks he's a genius,' Armando said, taking the weight on his legs, preparing them for more agony. 'Thinks he can get the Matsés to do anything.'

'And what do you think?'

'I think he is a genius,' Armando said, leading away up the obscure track. 'But he's also a cheap crook. And that makes him dangerous.'

Now each step I took was sending a jab of pain up from my ribs. I felt like crying. When I saw Weeki toss out some of his load I walked right over it, not caring what vital thing we were losing. I hated this expedition that was distancing me from the Matsés, not drawing me to them.

I called forward to Armando, 'Let's threaten to leave Fidencio. He needs us now that the Matsés are rebellious. How about it?'

'I can't leave José. And José will stay with Fidencio.'

It didn't seem likely that anyone would willingly spend more time than necessary staggering along like this, but José was coming up the path and I asked him myself.

José stopped to hear me out, bending to prop his hands on his knees, and take the weight off his shoulders. 'My job is to get Fidencio to his destination. I won't let him down.'

'If he goes on like this he's going to get us killed.'

'I will follow the agreement. He is the *jefe*. The boss.'

'Hold on. Fidencio is just an employee of mine – and he changed the agreement. What about you sticking by me?'

'I am not going to leave him.' He crossed his hands, miming as if he were shackled – tied to Fidencio's service by a promise. Then he walked on, lugging his load, a huge plastic petrol container. I watched him disappear through the leaves – José, my hope of

144

recovering the expedition. He was a person bound by feudal honour. It was enough in his life just to follow.

'Not your day, is it, Benedito?' Armando commented.

'It hasn't been my day for weeks.' We carried on walking.

Fidencio was now rarely seen by us at the back. We just heard him calling us onward through the trees, making sure we were still in earshot. He was out in front, charging ahead, his face, if we ever saw it, an unhealthy russet colour. His headstrap bit into his fore-head as he buffeted on through the undergrowth, clearing a path with a machete, and with the outboard motor on his back. Charo ran after him, trying to keep up. Sometimes I was sure he was crying.

Neither Armando nor José knew where we were, and the Matsés, our 'scouts', trailed at the back with us. We walked on, none of us wanting to and all of us doing it anyway. We marched behind this man, tied to him by something disturbing and touching, José's blind devotion to a *patrón*. We walked until the dark began to fall. And there was still no sign we were going to stop.

Armando and I paused for breath again. 'I can see it now,' I gasped. 'Fidencio has had this idea for years. He saw the *maloca* from the air. My expedition has given him a chance to track it down.'

'That's just about it,' Armando croaked.

We walked on towards the Remos, and I was now wondering if I had drifted into the plot of a third-rate novel. I had to rein in my fears – fears of Fidencio, but also fears of getting an arrow in my chest. The Matsés, who knew this forest backwards, were scared of the Remos – they weren't just a figment of a crazed explorer's imagination. The Matsés saw the Remos much as, almost laughably, the Ucayali missionary of Smyth and Lowe's 1836 book saw his potential Indian converts. 'When a Cashibo is pursuing the chase in the woods, and hears another hunter imitating the cry of an animal he is in pursuit of, he immediately makes the same cry, for the purpose of enticing the other within his reach and, if he is of another tribe [e.g. Mayoruna], kills him if he can, and eats him.'

Fidencio forged on, still with those sickly eyes, the ones haunted by his vision, his need to conquer the Remo-aucas. He did stop to talk quietly to Charo sometimes, offering him *sheebé*, a mix of *farinha*, sugar and water, to perk him up. But what sort of father brought his son on an expedition that might kill him?

'You're not tired,' he said to José, who was lagging with the petrol container on his back. 'My son is half your age. Are you saying you're tired?'

José hadn't said anything. He was too tired to speak. He could only groan a little. He picked himself up, the reek of petrol in a cloud around him, and plodded onward. Fidencio stood to the side, counting us off as we went by. 'When Charo is tired, then you've got a right to be tired.'

Charo, though, was on his last legs. Sweat was flying out behind, springing out of his pores. His face was red, like raw meat, and under his eyes he was blue and puffed up, as if someone had socked him in the face.

Daylight was failing and there was no time to find palm leaves and running water, the two necessary ingredients for a camp site. We did the best we could, pitching our camp in a swamp, and splashing petrol over dank wood for a fire. Charo was the only person able to voice his frustration to Fidencio – he was the only person Fidencio could hear. 'How far, papa?' he asked feebly, still strapped into his pack. I'd lifted his load once, and thought it light, but then I'd lifted up Charo himself and he had seemed the same weight.

'Two days.'

'But every day you say two days, papa.'

'Because you walk too slow.'

However, the scouts were up all night, decorated with leaf bands again and shifting like ghouls against the firelight. We all knew they were not going to go a step further. In the end the Matsés had given us no warning at all – no sullen glances, no defiant declarations. These people didn't need any of us, this forest was their home. They could wander off whenever they pleased, and it pleased them right now.

The next morning Fidencio made no immediate attempt to get them strapped into their packs. He knew he had pushed them too far. They kept their distance when he did try to approach, backing away as if still scolded by his smell of anger. They skulked around him, taking avoiding action each time he ventured near. 'All right, all right,' he said at last, with a half laugh, 'No harm done. We'll go to the Matanza and down to Galvez and Javari.'

I sensed my moment. 'You'll take me to Tumi, then.'

'Everything is as planned,' he said. But he still had that look in his eye.

I was sure he was now intending to reach the Remo-aucas not from the south, but by circling round to come in on them from somewhere north-east of here, on the Javari. He would revert to the original expedition plan to get east to the main river, but instead of continuing eastward into Brazil and to 'Tumi' he would go north down the Javari then cut west overland to the Remo-aucas. But our scouts would only stick with us as far as their home on the Galvez. And what was he intending to do with me? On the main Javari was a settlement called Angamos. Was he so blind as not to worry that I'd inform the police?

I pondered this for the one and a half days it took us to cut through the forest, back south towards the Matanza. We didn't talk, we just trailed behind this man who – no one could deny it – had the genius to deliver us where he wanted. 'Chicos, in a few days we will be out of here. We'll be on the Javari.' That was meant to be our reward. Getting out of the place he had bullied us into.

In my diary I raged about Fidencio, how I wanted to boil and skin him, but I never had any doubt that he could get us back to the Matanza. He made his way, cutting straight through the forest, rarely slowing to pick about for signs of old trails. At last we came to an old camp. There was a tapir hip-bone from a forgotten feast, and a discarded heap of palm nuts that were now sprouting roots. A sluggish river was visible through the trees. We threw down our packs and fell asleep without putting up a leaf shelter. This was the Matanza, where the two men had been murdered and then had their toes eaten by a giant tortoise.

For a while we were back on course. And we were grateful. We could follow this man. We willingly fell in line – even I, who knew now that I had no expedition, no way out of here into Brazil. The plan remained unspoken: we'd descend to the Javari via the Matanza, then the Lobo, then the Galvez as planned. He'd lose the Matsés somewhere near their home with other acculturated Indians. Somewhere too, he'd lose me.

That was all right. I'd get out of here, somehow – many mission-ized Peruvian Matsés spoke Spanish. But continuing my Amazon journey was a different matter. I needed the Matsés' help: I was still that lonely old bird that walked by itself.

At dawn we woke as a distant troop of howler monkeys gave out the sound of a great wind. As we broke up the camp, Armando discovered that the petrol container had split. José's load had seeped away into the leaf litter. All his loyalty, all his sweat on behalf of the *patrón*, for nothing.

We cut palm trees for a raft, first testing chips of the wood for buoyancy, then driving pegs into the trunks and sliding them through the forest towards the water. For a while Fidencio was more like the relentlessly oozing man of the old days, and smoothed us through this gruelling work, 'Quicker we move, *chicos*, the quicker we'll be there.' And, '*El hombre más ocupado es el más feliz.*' The busiest person is the happiest.

We worked quickly and quietly, following Fidencio's orders with-out hesitation and distracted only by a five-foot viper that eased out at us from a tree root, unwinding length upon length of black, white and brown jagged bands. Then, in a muddy side-stream, we encountered a grey electric eel the length of my leg. The muscle banks lining its sides could discharge 500 volts and even when the Matsés sliced it to bits, it gulped in the water, shifting loudly, as if trying to join itself sufficiently to electrocute us.

Then off we drifted downstream, Armando, José and Fidencio in front cutting at vines that snagged the raft, the Matsés, Charo and me at the back as a counterweight. The vessel surged as Armando swung the axe and groaned, hacking at logs as tough as iron. Water ran over the timbers, and the ants and other accidental travellers scrambled up our legs to escape the waves.

'Your best plan is to head for Angamos,' Armando said later, as we drifted on. That I was abandoning my own expedition didn't seem to be in doubt, though this was the first time the subject had been aired. 'It's near the mouth of the Galvez, anyway. They even have planes sometimes. Get out that way.'

'You're telling me to give up? Not to go into Brazil?'

'There's a lot of forest out there, and you've seen how unlikely the Matsés are to guide you.' He was looking at our scouts. They sat in their group by themselves – just passengers, like the beetles and hoppers that twitched and watched. 'No one makes friends with the Matsés, not real friends. Someone should have told you that.'

To be fair, Louis had told me that. It was why I had resorted to bringing Fidencio, and all this equipment. I told Armando that he'd forgotten about the Two Harriets who'd sat on the river bank in their tent. They had made friends with the Matsés.

Armando said, 'There are whole villages on the Galvez founded just by escapees from that mission.'

Fidencio was expecting me to abandon all this equipment, be content to get away with my own pack and a few gifts for the Matsés, calculating I'd not feel strongly enough to bring the law down on him. It was a stupid risk, but it had also been a stupid risk to steal kitchen supplies before we set off, and a stupid risk to push the Matsés towards the Remo-aucas. The odd thing was, I was more than happy to comply. I was better off without all this equipment. Perhaps Fidencio even knew that.

Sometimes in faster currents we used what little petrol we did have to motor out of trouble. Usually we drifted, poling our way, and feeling the hidden animals around us, scratching, itching, chewing, as we went on by. We had to duck as branches tried to scrape us off the raft. Occasionally we whacked at the scorpions and large spiders that were to be found between the creaking timbers under our feet.

Slowly, the river widened, the trees drew back and revealed pieces of sky. The sun cut through, and dried our shirts and the fungus spores that had settled over us. In these quiet times, our raft curling with the water flow, we saw the larger creatures. A spider monkey fished for fruit with one long, spindly black hand, the other arm in mid-air as balance. Another watched us go, fingering its little, coconut-sized head, marvelling at us with eyes that were alert to opportunity. Small caymans, cousins to the true crocodiles and alligators, lay slumped grimly on the mud, or simply suspended in the water, legs splayed. On a log the skin of a discarded hairy caterpillar, scraps left by a bird, and after dusk the scratchings of an armadillo digging worms, the eyes of the small, compact plant-eating mammals that could run through the undergrowth – the agouti, a long-legged rodent which for ever stored its food in caches, the paca which by day was in its burrow, the entrances safely blocked up. We spun along lazily, watching the darkness that was watching us.

And the next morning, tucked in behind a river bend, a tapir. A distant relative of the rhinoceros but with no armour, it was a generally solitary, shy animal, a river browser. This one stood square on the bank, chewing, lost in its tapir thoughts. Its solid, rounded body made it a slow forest animal but a strong one, and its only two forest predators, the jaguar and cayman, preferred smaller riverside prey. Smelling us at last, the tapir instinctively charged for the safety of the river, plunging in like a frolicking middle-aged bather, its short trunk up as it wondered when it would be safe to come out. Finally, it decided that our creaking, spinning raft was more menacing than the forest, and surged out into the trees. The Matsés took the gun, leapt overboard without getting it wet, and fired two shots. We quartered the tapir, and, our raft trailing blood, were on our way again, a string of hopeful piranhas swimming behind.

The truth about the Amazon's piranhas? The most aggressive species, such as the red piranha, threshed a bit when you gutted fish into the river, and could cut your fishing line without a tug, but unless you were bleeding and they were starved, trapped in a dry season pool, they nearly always left you alone. That was the simple truth of it, and the snakes of the Amazon were much the same – overrated. We saw them daily, and once I saw three within minutes. But that was by standing still, not searching around. They were all about us, but only watching peaceably as we drifted on downriver.

The Matanza turned into the Lobo, and, as our raft showed signs that it was slowly sinking, we began to see abandoned Indian gardens – now thick stands of weed creepers and cutting grasses. Our scouts sat up as we fully emerged into the bright sunlight, whispering and pointing.

Fidencio said that the village was destroyed after a boy was attacked there by a jaguar in broad daylight. Another man who tried to beat the animal off was also bitten. The boy died. A jaguar as bold as this was sometimes believed to be the restless spirit of a bewitched man. A party hunted it down and built a huge bonfire to burn it away to nothing. Next, they fired off burning arrows at their own *malocas*. Leaving their homes and all their possessions still smouldering, they walked off into the forest with their families to start again somewhere else.

Dolphins lifted into the air and slipped down into the clouded waters again. Night-time once more and a chunky cayman as long as a man slid into the water. Frogs in the trees interrupted our thoughts with an 'Aark!' In the distance a roar, frogs calling that more rain was on the way. Finally, the Galvez, the tributary with the missionized Matsés. Our scouts waited for the first village to come into sight.

Fidencio was showing me more attention now. I knew he was monitoring me, wondering how I'd react when the moment came for me to be dumped. But I didn't care. The sooner I was away from the expedition the better.

Armando said, 'Fidencio, you're just going to leave Benedito?'

'They've got a school and church. I'm not leaving him with savages.' Fidencio twisted round to speak to me. 'I'm not leaving you with savages, you know, Benedito. Don't tell anyone that.'

'You're not leaving me with Tumi, either,' I said. Armando looked at me, wondering if I would at last put up a fight. But no, I was well out of it.

We began to see the first Matsés of the Galvez. First a dugout canoe with a woman in it, scraping scales off a fish. She was pale, just like the Mayoruna 'wench' that the naturalist Bates had taken on to clean his hearth fires. Fidencio sang a greeting across the water, then rifled through one of our sacks and threw her a mirror. She caught it up, losing the fish overboard in her excitement. Her husband, squatting as still as a piece of clay on the bank, was flung a reel of fishing line.

Another canoe, a family with an assortment of little boys. Again, Fidencio tossed them presents. Crayons to the children, razor blades and hairbands for the parents. The boys took them slowly, wondering whether they should, but the adults snatched them up, and held their hands out for more.

151

'Fidencio's got a lot of friends,' I said to Armando.

'Or a lot of enemies.'

We heard a peculiar sound around the bend. It sounded like a huge wild beast – and we were about to meet it head on. But it was a canoe that came into view. It seemed to be marooned. Closer, we saw five or six men paddling rather hopelessly. They were town men, with hats and long-sleeved office shirts, and they were singing as they tried their best to paddle, making lots of splashes.

'*Evangelistas*,' Armando said. Like the Putumayo river boat passengers, he used the word as if it explained everything.

The evangelists were waving, calling us nearer. Perhaps they needed assistance – it certainly looked like it. The five men, of town, Spanish stock, had beaming, blank smiles, as if they were slightly drunk. One of them was holding a hardback book. As we drifted nearer, he called, 'Have you got time to talk about the Bible?' Had I heard that correctly? We were in the middle of a tropical river, drifting out of the forest on a sinking raft, and they were floundering in a canoe with a broken motor with no potential converts for miles. But they didn't want to be rescued, they wanted to talk about the Bible.

'The *evangelistas* will look after you, Benedito,' Fidencio said. 'I'll let you off with them.'

I looked at the missionaries as they waved inanely at us. 'I'd prefer to chance it in the jungle,' I said to myself.

However we couldn't escape that quickly – catching lost people was these people's speciality. Right here, pressed against a curve in the river, the evangelists got out a recording which they had made in the two main Brazilian Matsés settlements, Lobo and Trinta e um. While they rewound the tape they told us they'd been lucky to escape at all. And the same Matsés had recently raided the Two Harriets' mission. It was a wife-hunting raid and they had actually picked girls out of their hammocks.

'The Americans are safe?' The Two Harriets might have been carried off over some jubilant Indian's shoulder. They might at this very moment be naked and tattooed, dutifully conceiving half-Matsés children as third or fourth wives to some victorious headman.

The chief evangelist said the raid was a month or more ago, 'so

I can put your fears at rest'. We listened to the recording. Instead of traditional incantations, there was a ranting man. He wasn't speaking clearly but it was very clear what he was saying – all the important words were not in his language, but Spanish and Portuguese. It was a shopping list: clothes, machetes, beads, more clothes.

'We had to run,' the evangelists said. 'Our presents weren't enough.'

The tape was to raise money in the States. 'We believe,' the preacher said, 'America is the future. They are rich, but you know, nine-tenths of people go to church.'

I said that I had heard this myself.

'This forest is dangerous,' he said. 'We shall make it safe. We shall make it like the States.'

Did he know how many people were shot in America each year? 20,000. Discounting cowboys like Fidencio, it probably made the modern Amazon a comparatively safe place. About 2,000 people were shot in New York each year, and another 200 died just getting caught in the crossfire. In the western world, jungle wasn't a problem, the people were.

But I must hold back, I thought. I must see more of the Amazon myself before judging. The fact that all my problems so far had come from westerners – the video-recorder (broken ribs), the cocaine dealers (attempted murder), Fidencio (the rest) – might just be unlucky.


The presence of the evangelists told us we were nearly at the first village, but now our petrol ran out. We travelled on, paddling the raft with a plate each, while José steered with a bamboo pole.

At last the village, Bien Peru. Tin roofs flashed from rectangular houses on a high bank and soon maybe a hundred children were running along the high bank to look at us, this strange raft of palm trees coming out of the forest propelled by plastic plates.

'Where are we tying up?' Armando asked, as we manoeuvred the semi-submerged raft.

Fidencio said, 'We don't tie up.' He was sorting out a little package from the supplies – presents for the Matsés guides. He handed the sack to Weeki, who took it but seemed more interested in positioning himself to leap for the shore.

'We have to tie up,' Armando said. 'The raft isn't stable. We've got to let the Matsés and Benedito off.'

I said, 'And I want to sort out how much I'm taking.'

But Fidencio didn't hear. He was frowning against the light, looking up at the children on the river bank, as if searching for someone.

'We don't tie up.'

It wasn't what he said, it was the change in his voice. Fidencio, the man of all-conquering smoothness, the man who could walk us through that forest and talk the Matsés through their fears, had a high, nervous quaver in his voice. When, back in the forest, Weeki had cried out, seeing the jaguar, Fidencio had walked towards the problem, not away. He had strutted out towards the danger, towards the scared cries of the Indian, oozing that smell of confidence, that chemical, that pheromone of power. But now, no.

Armando said, 'We can't expect Benedito to jump.'

I said, 'And as I've said, I've got to sort out my bags. What things I'm taking.'

'Okay, we stop, we stop. But not here.'

Now, as we were brushing against a pontoon moored for washer-women, we heard something that made us look up. It was an angry yell, not coming from the children, but from further behind, the village out of sight. It came again, louder, nearer – someone beside himself with emotion. The word might have been Spanish. It sounded like, '*Ladrón! Ladrón!* Robber! Robber!'

We could see the man now. He was on the edge of the bank, hopping up and down. And where, a second ago, there had been children, there were suddenly men. '*Ladrón!*' At least three had machetes, two old men had bows and arrows.

Two of our three scouts leapt ashore, getting out of harm's way. '*Ladrón!*' The men were flooding down the steep bank. It was a real war party.

I gaped, unable to believe what I was seeing.

I heard Charo breathe, 'Papa!' and was aware of him pressing himself against his father. Water was surging over the raft as the last Matsés jumped. Behind me, Armando was fighting to get some life out of the engine.

Then I knew I wasn't in danger. The crowd seemed to know exactly who they wanted, and it wasn't the woodcutters or the white man. Fidencio began a few cheery calls of Matsés welcome, and gestured at our supplies. I recognized a Spanish word. *'Regalos!* Gifts!'

The crowd was still jostling and gibing on the river bank. Fidencio began one of his speeches, and the Matsés began barracking him. Charo was trying to interrupt as well. 'Papa,' he said. 'Why are they saying *ladrón*, papa?'

Fidencio gave his son a sort of broken smile, then quickly looked away at the crowd. Suddenly I had forgotten about the mob and was watching the boy trying to catch his father's darting eyes – this quiet, tragic drama. It was a terrible thing to see a child witnessing his father being exposed as a cheap crook.

An old man pushed through to the front line and drew a bow. He must have had difficulty getting here – he was breathless and late – but he had the strength to hold the string back. He stood there, braced against the bow, tottering, while Fidencio, infinitely alone in the universe, desperately began paddling his plate to get the raft away. Then, abruptly, he changed his mind. He jumped ashore into the crowd. He opened his arms, and shouted back at the crowd, throwing down the expedition pocket-knife, an indignant gesture which suggested his honour had been called into question. He was quite brilliant. The crowd took a pace backward. They had lost the initiative – a crowd on their own territory against one man.

As arguments broke out among the Matsés as to what they should do next, Fidencio ordered José to open up his bag and get the document from the Ministry of Education. He read it out – the same trick that had worked so well with our scouts. Spanish, with its resonance of colonial power, Spanish, the language of the conquerors. Fidencio pronounced that he had been authorized to lead an expedition to find the Remo-aucas. The *'Ministerio de Educación'* didn't seem to register with the Matsés, but 'Remo-aucas' did.

Fidencio, sensing the direction he must lead his speech, said he was off to the Remo-aucas, traditional enemies of the Matsés. He was their *conquistador*. Again he said it: *'Conquistador'*, taking time to enjoy the weight of the syllables. Probably no one knew the word here, probably they didn't even know they had been defeated by *conquistadores* such as Fidencio and the Two Harriets, but Fidencio set great store by the word, and his confidence showed. The crowd paused, absolutely still. The old man at the front was still waving his bow about, but his grip looked wobbly now. His arrow could shoot off anywhere. I kept down, hoping it wouldn't come my particular way.

Fidencio took one sack at random, and spilled it open at the crowd's feet. As the young men began sorting through lipsticks, fishing lines and mirrors, he scrambled aboard, kicking us off into the river flow. 'I will be back to inspect the school,' he yelled.

His speech had been so bold, and performed with such indifference to the wavering crowd, the Matsés took his lead and nodded dutifully in agreement. We spun on downriver in silence. So accustomed were we to following Fidencio's lead, we, the remaining members of the expedition, sat there not doing anything while he gathered himself. It took a while to realize he was not going to be gathering himself. Charo was holding his father and looking him over. Fidencio was in a state of shock. He had pulled it off, but only just.

Slowly it dawned on me that I had recovered charge. I said, 'Armando? We'd better head for Angamos. Take stock.'

We took up our little plates to paddle – and immediately realized we still needed help from the Matsés, even to get away from them. It took us half an hour even to reach the neighbouring settlement, Remo-yacca. Fidencio refused to go ashore for help – he refused even to answer us. I wondered if he had had a minor heart attack. He avoided Charo's eyes and looked cramped, like a captured animal that hates being watched. Even after all he had done, I felt sorry for him then.

We drifted downriver under the sun, burning slowly as we spun with the currents, overtaken by fish. Once a canoe came by with only Indian children on board. They slowed to have a closer look, and then paddled swiftly away. We were castaways, adrift on a raft in the middle of water.

When dark came we camped on the bank – still not a word from the diminished Fidencio. Next morning we were about to get on our way again when a Matsés drew up in a large, motorized canoe. With him was a Matsés woman, with a longish, freckled face. The man addressed us quietly. We had to stop loading the raft in order to hear him. He spoke formally, as if he was practising to be a white man. First he carefully asked after our health, and then told us who he was – Filipe. He added, 'I have eight mothers.' He was from Remo-yacca, he said. He didn't ask where we had come from. He knew already.

He said, 'I transport you to Angamos if you like. I save you.'

Armando, who'd had dealings with the missionized Matsés before, was suspicious. 'In exchange for what?'

'Nothing. *Un regalo.*' A gift – again that suspect Spanish word.

'But it's too far for you to bother,' Armando protested. 'It's very kind, but you can't spend that much petrol on us.'

It was my turn to protest. 'I don't see why he can't if he wants,' I said. Another day in the sun was too much to contemplate.

'It's over five hours' journey for you,' Armando persisted, considerately. I wanted to throttle him.

Filipe was confused. 'You do not accept?'

'We accept,' I said, before Armando could raise any more objections.

As we transferred our stores into the large canoe, Filipe said, 'I remember the wife of Fidencio. She bent my wife's hair with a stick. She bent it until her hair was beautiful.'

We all turned to look at Filipe's wife. She was yanking his sleeve, admonishing her husband for embarrassing her.

Fidencio suddenly spoke. 'Hair curlers,' he said limply. 'My wife borrowed them from Pastor Saunders.'

As we went on our way, I said, 'Pastor Saunders uses hair curlers?'

Armando just said, 'I don't mind if his dog does, let's get out of here.'

# IX

# The Outpost

THAT WAS HOW the great expedition reached the River Javari, and the frontier to Brazil – on the strength of Pastor Saunders's stolen hair curlers.

In Filipe's motorized dugout we sped downriver from the Galvez to the main Javari, Brazil on our right, Peru still on our left. In a moment we would be at the outpost of Angamos, on the Peruvian side, where I'd be rid of Fidencio and ready to plan my next move. For the moment he was still in a daze, unable to snap out of it. He was sitting hunched up on himself, a defenceless creature.

The sun rose on the simple, thatched roofs of the Peruvian border community. But before the forlorn civilian settlement came the forlorn military camp – low barracks and, at the water's edge, a watchtower and a corporal with a squad of soldiers who were washing their socks. The corporal had the job of monitoring the few river craft that went by. Most were Indian canoes, whose occupants couldn't understand a word of Spanish. These were ignored. More rarely there were *mestizos* who came up the river to hunt or to extract timber. Many of these were drinking companions of the soldiers, and also ignored. But we were a new category: people who came from nowhere.

The corporal took one look at us. Whereas only recently we had been gaunt from more than two weeks of forest, as pallid from its darkness as deep-water fish, now, after days exposed in the sun, we were blackened and burnt. He got to his feet. He tucked his trousers properly into his boots and waved us in to the river bank for an inspection. '*Gringo*,' breathed one of the riflemen, pointing me out as he kicked his feet into his boots.

The corporal said, '*De dónde?* From where?'

It all took some explaining.

We were told to climb ashore. We did as we were told, all of us except for Filipe and his wife. The Matsés didn't seem to count. Two soldiers came aboard to pick through the luggage. There wasn't much left now – clothes, three machetes, mosquito nets, waterproof sheeting, a few kitchen things, some gifts, and a sack containing a scattering of *farinha*.

Eventually the inspection was finished, and we pulled away and carried on to the civilian quarter of the settlement, with instructions to return on foot to see *el comandante*. The corporal watched us go. He was looking more worried than when we arrived, not less. He hadn't found drugs, so what were we up to?

The civilian settlement was a whimsical assortment of timber houses. 'Welcome!' called a man from the bottom of the mud street that ended at the river. He was calling to me, not Fidencio. I could see he already knew all about Fidencio.

This was the man in charge, *el gobernador*, who had somehow been alerted to our arrival. He looked like a *mestizo*, but he wouldn't have thanked you for telling him. I could see he felt he hadn't deserved to be posted to Angamos. He was above all this – the mosquitoes, the silt. Coming towards me he looked apologetic. Behind him, children walked through the mud back from school and the teachers, imported from Iquitos, looked in our direction with renewed interest in life.

'You've come from?'

And I went through it all again.

The governor was horrified at our overland crossing, as was the *mestizo* with him. However this man, Hugo, went on to describe the infrequent plane flights here and they didn't sound any safer. If the pilot decided that conditions favoured a successful landing, which meant dropping out of the sky to the slot of mud between the trees, then passengers prayed together, parents crossing themselves and their heirs.

Hugo, who had the physique of a Roman centurion – a long, straight nose, huge muscular belly, the cheek muscles of Charlton Heston, lived in the timber house overlooking the river. He said we could stay with him and pointed to a narrow, slanting pole that served as steps to the door.

159

The governor said, 'Report to me formally after –' he paused, seeing the state of our clothes as we climbed ashore '– after introducing yourself to *el comandante*. But stay as long as you like, Mister Benedito.' He targeted a shrewd glance in Fidencio's direction. 'And how long were you intending to stay for?'

Fidencio looked away from us, and mumbled that he didn't know. He was that cornered creature that we'd seen back at Bien Peru – yet now he was among his own kind, and that looked worse. It was only at this moment that I realized that now was the time to ruin Fidencio, issue a *denunciación*, as they say in Peru. He had failed to fulfil the contract, imperilled a foreigner. The government would gladly lock him away. But what good would that do? He had almost a dozen dependants.

I told the governor none of us quite knew what we were doing yet. We'd be discussing it when we had washed and rested.

Filipe and his wife quietly stepped ashore and vanished. Armando, José and I brought in all the remaining supplies and then discovered that Hugo was related by marriage to Fidencio, who would also be staying in the house. One of us was going to have to stay to guard our bags.

That wasn't all the bad news. We would soon be joined by the '*hermanos*', the brothers. Not more relatives, but the evangelists we'd seen splashing about in the canoe upriver.

The other occupants of the house were Hugo's wife, who gamely began preparing a meal for us, a little boy called Edward who had a smoker's crackly voice, a mentally retarded woman who was his playmate – they sat in the corner, making a little house with imaginary characters, bits of grass from the surrounding jungle – and finally there was Hugo's daughter, who had limp hair, her father's straight nose and – though she was only thirteen – her mother's extensive bosom. She took a load of our clothes off to the river for a scrubbing, and was immediately followed by Armando. Her mother watched them from the veranda, proudly gazing upon them as if this was a match of some years' standing. 'She is hardworking and dutiful,' she said with satisfaction.

We all walked up the steep mud street, which resembled a river bed, then over the rickety footbridge to the army barracks to pay my respects to *el comandante*, the army major. At a distance he looked friendly, his eyes open and kind, but as he marched closer, perhaps because he recognized Fidencio, he began ferociously working his moustache. He addressed us as if we were under suspicion of some crime, and we decided to leave quickly, finding ourselves sharing the path with his wife, a splendid woman who strutted like a flamenco dancer, terrifying the conscripts.

The governor was sitting proudly in his little office, a shed with a typewriter, spare paper, one rubber stamp and an IN tray – empty. He pointed out of the window to show me the sights of Angamos. They consisted in their entirety of a new plaza. It was the settlement's bold step towards western civilization.

The governor offered his office as a hiding-place for my expedition supplies. He showed me a little sketch map of the Matsés settlements, and I began to piece together the geography of the remaining part of Phase Two, continuing east through Brazil to the Juruá river. I would have to go up to the Batã tributary of the upper Javari, and walk through the Brazilian forests to the town of Cruzeiro do Sul, on the Juruá itself. 'But not with the *Matsés*,' the governor said. 'They don't go anywhere up there on the Brazil side because of the *seringueiros* – rubber tappers. Too much trouble between them.'

It was a devastating blow. Not only had I been hoping to travel with the Matsés, the 'Jaguar People', experts of the forest, but I was relying on learning enough from them to travel through the Brazilian forests beyond the Juruá, in Phase Three.

'So you are saying I have to travel with *mestizos*,' I said glumly.

'Not with them, either,' the governor said. 'There is a story going around of a murder up there. And of robberies. No one will go near the place, just now.'

'Who, then?'

'I think between the Indians and the *mestizos* you've covered everybody.'

'The army?'

'But they never set foot in the forest,' the governor said, goggling at my naïvety. 'Scared stiff of it.' He advised me to go to the Brazilian military base of Palmeiras, an hour downriver, and find out for myself.

'First let me show you around.' We walked over the mud to the plaza. He introduced me to Carlos, the radio operator, who could be heard right across the settlement, screaming into the radio transmitter as he tried to communicate with Iquitos. The rest of the walk circled the cement monument. He said he was glad to hear that I wasn't an anthropologist hoping to study the Matsés culture. 'They don't have any, of course.'

None?

'Don't make anything, don't even fish. Just put poison in the stream. And you think they're good conservationists? I can't stop them cutting down trees.'

I reminded myself that Harriet had agreed with me: the less cultural extras the Matsés carried around, the better hunters they'd be. 'A thousand generations the Indians have been living in the forests,' I said, 'they must be expert at their environment. They must be. Aren't they?'

'Wouldn't put my life on it,' the governor said with horrible simplicity. 'Not like you.'

Sometimes as we sat in the plaza I saw Matsés walking stiffly backwards and forwards as if on urgent business. They had boys' haircuts, and hung around the stores like lost children, waiting with little eager eyes. Earlier, on the way to the governor, I'd given one of them two bars of soap. 'Three!' he'd said indignantly.

We went to see the communal dwelling built for Matsés visiting the settlement, people like Filipe and his wife. No one was home, but I looked around. The Indians had been built bunk beds, and these were used as shelves to store paddles, bits of root crop, coils of rope. The room was a cross between an orphanage of Victorian sparseness and a fruit and tortoise market. The tortoises were placed upside down to send them to sleep and each had carrying handles, made of strands of forest vine.

Sitting in the plaza again, I mused that it was interesting how tribal people often placed emphasis on 'man-making' rituals, yet more than anything they struck us westerners as child-like.

'Childish,' was all the governor said. 'Hopeless.' We sat on the bench, wondering what to talk about next. The plaza was a desolate place; the *mestizo* community hadn't yet got the hang of its purpose – courting, strolling. Those teenagers passing us were old enough to have lost their teeth through decay, but not old enough to afford

162

dentures. They were like graduates of a testing ritual of Aboriginal manhood, their incisors knocked out.

An army welfare officer went by. He was doing his rounds, stopping at houses to type out fictitious sick-notes, to help people on to the next flight out of here.

Suddenly the governor said, 'Ever heard of the Remos?'

'More than enough.'

'They're an interest of mine.' It seemed that collecting stories had become something of a hobby for the governor, just as a prisoner, bored out of his mind in his cement cell, might have studied the feeding patterns of itinerant centipedes.

He'd heard numerous reports of Remo-auca *malocas* seen by people flying in to Angamos. 'You don't want to make history and go and find this tribe do you?'

'No.'

'Pity.'

The governor said he had to leave. 'Things to do.' This seemed unlikely. 'We've had a delivery of oil,' he explained. 'A supply vessel has made it all the way up here, and the rainy season hasn't even begun! We'll have electricity tomorrow night. We'll have a fiesta.' He was getting excited, just imagining it. Some sort of rum was being mixed in buckets by the council men, they were pooling cassettes from the villagers, and they were rigging up loudspeakers. 'Electricity!' the governor sighed.

I was meant to be impressed, so I said, 'Great.'

'Yes,' the governor said, departing, 'that's the third time this year!'

'Second,' someone said sadly, as he passed.

Armando came by, carrying a brace of pineapples. 'Gift,' he explained. We walked off to see the mud streets together – there were only the two of them – and soon found ourselves at the plaza again. Once more we set off.

All the way, passers-by nodded amiably at Armando. Apparently he was still remembered from his time working under Victor Braga, the Brazilian logger. Old ladies shrieked with pleasure out of their windows, girls with babies riding on their hips proffered more pineapples. The teachers were more professionally flirtatious with Armando, doing it while fielding volleyballs and while dancing to songs in their heads. He was even stopped by a Matsés, a forty-year-old with a timid schoolchild's face. 'Armando . . .' he breathed softly. That was all. He walked off, saying again, 'Armando . . .'

Armando was regarded as a sort of national treasure. Everyone wanted to be his friend. And it wasn't as if Armando smiled warmly back. He passed on by, evading all their claims to him, only ever enjoying a quiet grin to himself. Most of us weren't even calling him by his true name. For although he was Armando to us, here he was also Raimundo, Normando and Gilberto.

Whoever Armando really was, everyone adored him. What was it about him: his ratty face? His missing teeth? That off-hand manner? Perhaps that was it. The governor had already warned me that in Angamos there were many men just like Fidencio, charmers who called you 'amigo', then stabbed you in the back. Armando played things straight. I knew I couldn't afford to lose him yet.

That evening, while Hugo's wife cooked up a woolly monkey and Armando lay in my hammock tweaking the daughter's bottom with his toe, I conducted a strained conversation around the paraffin light with Fidencio, who was proffering me information on the Matsés, angling for an amnesty and – outrageously – the same bonus I'd just given José. While we were talking it through, there was a crash at the door and the evangelists from Iquitos arrived. We retreated to the kitchen, but they came and sat down with us as we concluded our delicate negotiations. They were poised, smiling, waiting for the chance to break into the conversation.

Fidencio and I came to an agreement. In exchange for more information on the Matsés, I would help equip him, José and Charo to return home. When he was ready to set off, Filipe would transport him from here to a Galvez village called San Juan, where they would be left to walk the path to the Ucayali. Armando would stay on to assist me.

Supper was ready and we arranged the log seats in a circle by the fireplace. The evangelists cracked hearty jokes and only after an interminably long grace did they allow us to sink into the monkey's beefy flesh. 'They have pleasant affable smiles that aren't directed at anyone,' I noted in my diary, after I'd retired to my hammock to watch from a safe distance. 'Vacuous.' They were also very loud. Later, having given up all hope of sleep, I wrote, 'Preacher has head too big for short body. Gilt-edged teeth, also possibly one of those plastic fill-in sections.' Later still, 'Seems to enjoy stroking his penis under his big boring sack-brown trousers (belted, always). Likes to sit up straight on his log and tell us stories. Thankfully not religious tales – just encounters with piranhas etc. – but all the same even his friends lose interest long before the stories end.'

I did doze off, but late into the night, every quarter of an hour or so, the sentries in the army camp called to each other to keep themselves awake. It was a nightbird's call: *'Viva Perú!' 'Viva!'*, a haunting refrain of loneliness in this outpost, still in the pocket of the forest. The next moment it was dawn, and the evangelists were again loudly whispering their prayers.

I walked down to the shimmering waterfront, and looked across at Brazil, the hazy, virgin vegetation opposite, off which bounced the sounds of Angamos. I had forgotten what it was like to wake up in a human community – children under the houses, snooping about after chickens' eggs, the warm hubbub of other people getting their day together. After being so vulnerable in the forest, it was a relief to be here among my kind, as if I had discovered the existence of a Victim Support group.

Armando and I bought some petrol from Angel, the store owner, who had a private supply. We sped away downriver in Filipe's canoe, with Filipe and three other Matsés who came for the ride. An hour later we drew up at the Brazilian side of the river and a very serious-looking military camp. Armando and I fumbled a few words of Portuguese to the sentry and he marched us off past immaculate barracks and into a neat wooden office where soldiers were lounging, watching TV. No one noticed us – they were all glued to Xuxa, a blonde Brazilian singer, dancer, entertainer and all-pervasive television idol.

The Matsés refused to come in, and stood in a huddle outside gazing around them, fascinated enough by the insect netting on the windows. Just like the soldiers, Armando and I were soon glued to the TV. Xuxa, adored by the nation in just the way that, back in Britain, the Mustard Dog had been, was singing amidst a throng of star-struck children. The programme ended as it did every time, with Xuxa applying lipstick and planting her lips on the cheek of a guest celebrity – who, like everyone else, had a giant crush on her. Then, all too soon, she was once again blasting off through fake smoke in a tinselled rocket. And she was gone from us, back to her heavenly paradise.

But then the Brazilian commandant strolled into the room, with a towel around his neck and holding his shaving kit. All the soldiers jumped to their feet. He looked as ill-tempered as his Peruvian counterpart, but he had fair hair and a moustache instead of black hair and a moustache. He took me outside and I asked what he knew of the Batã.

'The what?'

'The Batã. It's a tributary on the Upper Javari with a path leading into Brazil. The rubber tappers live up there.'

'The who?'

The commandant, when we did get him talking, talked about the forest as if it was miles away, not around us on all sides. He instructed his lieutenant to take down our names and details, then left, swatting a mosquito on his arm and examining it as if it was something strange and novel.

'Must be new out here,' I said.

Armando said, 'Been out here three years.'

'Time he went home, then.'

The lieutenant took down our names, starting with the four Matsés, for whom he simply wrote 'X, X, X, X'. He said if we wanted to learn more we should talk to the *caboclos*, the 'peasants'. He pointed towards the trees.

We found some palm houses on the forest edge. A group of men sitting around outside them said that no one would accompany me into Brazil from the Batã tributary, though I would need someone to guide me through all the old trails. People were saying that some *seringueiros* had killed two of the loggers, and there seemed to be a spate of robberies just now. 'Try again next year,' said a man with an axe in his hands. He had mittens made out of rubber tyre inners, to save his hands from thorns.

'What about going with the Matsés,' I said. 'Maybe another route.'

'Not a hope.' I walked back to the canoe, feeling the world had ended for me.

It was an ironic twist of history. Once it had been the 'cannibal' Matsés whom the *seringueiros* had feared; nowadays the Matsés wouldn't budge because of the threat posed by ruthless frontiersmen down the ages. Although they had successfully evaded the Jesuits, that first generation of missionaries, nothing could have prepared them for the rubber boom. For as it happened, the area beyond the headwaters of the Javari, what was then the Bolivian territory of Acre, was probably richer in rubber trees than anywhere in Amazonia. As the rubber price soared, 18,000 Brazilians and Peruvians flooded in.*

The liquidation of Indians by the rubber tappers was on an ad hoc basis – a rape here, a massacre there – and not well documented.** More recently, although the pressure on Indians was lifted with the collapse in the rubber market and the subsequent departure of nearly all the *seringueiros*, the skirmishes between the encroaching hunters and other frontiersmen in all the years since had been enough to put the Matsés off going anywhere very far.***

---

\* While the Indians shrank away or were shot and/or raped, the rubber tappers organized themselves into a semi-autonomous state and rebelled against paying Bolivian taxes. The territory was conceded to Brazil in the 1903 Treaty of Petró- polis, which gave Bolivia a cash sum and a promise to help remote Bolivia enjoy the rewards of the rubber boom by completing the Madeira–Mamoré railway, which would lead from the mid-Amazon town of Pôrto Velho south to Riberalta, Bolivia.

\*\* In *Amazon Frontier*, Hemming mentions an American traveller, Algot Lange, who claimed to have witnessed one skirmish. A dozen Mayorunas, heavily decked with macaw and egret feathers, ambushed a gang of Peruvian rubber prospectors on the Ituí using clubs studded with jaguar teeth, three-pronged poisoned spears, huge bows and arrows, and blow-guns. The Mayorunas lost four men to rifle bullets, but all twenty Peruvians died – Lange noted with relish the sickening thud of the big black clubs falling on the *mestizo* skulls, the jaguar teeth piercing their brains.

\*\*\* After yet more localized conflict, this with petroleum explorers, in 1973 the Peruvian Ministry of Agriculture designated the forests between the Upper Javari and Galvez a reserve. For the present, this seemed to be safeguarding the Peruvian Matsés and their immediate resources. There had also been talk for many years of various types of *Parque Indígena do Vale do Javari* on the Brazil side. Timber extraction was the greatest potential threat here, the river providing easy access to the Brazilian towns of the main Amazon. As yet forests were not clear-felled, trees being removed selectively and on a comparatively small scale, away from Matsés habitation, from operations based in Tabatinga and Benjamin Constant in the Javari river mouth.

'Well, that's that,' Armando said. 'Pity you've come so far, really.'

'You don't think I could get the Matsés to teach me enough to try it alone?'

'No I do not,' Armando said, flatly. 'Not you.'

Well thank you very much for your show of confidence, I thought.

Rain came down as we walked back to the canoe. Armando paused to watch a girl playing volleyball. Under the downpour, she had pulled off her shirt and was carrying on in her bra. 'Brazilian girls . . .' was all Armando said.

We tracked down the Matsés, who were wandering in a tight group in and out of the married quarters, staring in through the windows. On the way in the canoe, Armando did ask Filipe if he'd help me, but Filipe didn't seem interested in trying to teach a gangling white man enough to get out of there alone. All the way back to Angamos he just smiled pleasantly, pretending not to hear.

The only enthusiasm he showed was when he spotted a kitchen knife sticking out of my bag. By brand name a 'Kitchen Devil', it in fact belonged to my mother; I'd accidentally included it in my luggage during my frantic last night of packing. The three Matsés scouts had already much admired the Kitchen Devil on our way here through the forest, testing the blade on their fingernails, and buffing it so they could see their reflections. I handed it over to Filipe, and he looked at the serrated blade lovingly. However, when I brought up the subject of him possibly teaching me about the forest his face became expressionless again, like clay. As soon as we drew up at Angamos, he disappeared, leaving the Kitchen Devil behind.

In the afternoon I went to have a quieter word with him in the Indian hut. I found only the preacher alone with a half-wit, a skinny Matsés boy who was adorned with the full jaguar tattoos, like a lucky mascot. The preacher preached on, oblivious of me and also of the boy, who was playing with himself.

The Matsés had left for upriver. They had just picked themselves up and gone, scared off, apparently, by children who had been firing toy guns.

\*　　　\*　　　\*

That afternoon everyone was milling about excitedly, preparing themselves for the great fiesta. As the engineers fiddled with the generator, Hugo's wife brought a nylon dress down from the timbers and black plastic shoes from where they hung from nails in the bark wall. Armando shampooed his hair in the river, then spread a generous dollop of engine oil in it. I washed with him and then, because I slipped in the street mud coming back, in the kitchen washing-up bowl. This I had to share with a turtle, an armour-plated fish, and a normal fish. The armour-plated fish ate my soap.

Girls repaired hemlines and stitched hairbands. They fluttered from their palm houses each like a different species of butterfly, soft and quivering after emergence from a dull chrysalis. They showed themselves off to each other, displaying the lacy dresses that in England might have been bridesmaids' outfits, and ran back indoors to share each other's lipsticks. When the music began the population of Angamos drifted to the council room and started shuffling timidly around the edge of the cement floor. Then a contingent of Brazilian girls arrived from Palmeiras. Their mascara and dance-floor sophistication made them look like prostitutes here in Angamos, but everyone stood back gratefully to learn from their dance steps.

Fidencio and Charo stayed at home with the evangelists but Armando, José and I went to join in. We stood awkwardly in our jungle boots on the edge of the dance floor, along with the army conscripts. Women and girls good-naturedly passed themselves down the queues of men waiting to dance, and Armando began drinking heavily and was soon on the floor in the corner.

Later, Matsés too were drawn in from the dark like moths, and watched from the safety of the plaza. By ten o'clock the party was well under way. The buckets of booze were empty, and the soldiers were dancing together. The Matsés looked on, silently goggling at the sight of the men sharing round the women dance partners. Some time in the late hours I noticed a small figure, perhaps a child, creep in through the crowd. He was wearing only shorts, and was dripping wet, leaving a trail of water. When I followed the trail I discovered it wasn't a boy but a small Indian who must have fallen in the river. He had red greasepaint smeared across his chest and his shorts had been yanked up too high. While I watched, he was moving along the benches, finishing off the drinks of dancers while they weren't looking. Seeing him, men stepped back, giving the Indian space. Their female partners froze.

I disentangled Armando from the arms of a soldier. 'Who's the Indian?'

But, as in all the best stories, the mysterious figure was already gone.

Next morning this same short man had left a story in his wake. Washing women on the foreshore reported having found his shorts out in the mud and soon people were saying that he had swum the river and disappeared naked into the forest. There was not much evidence to support the story, but that didn't matter to me. 'Pablito', as he was called by everyone here, was a man who had the confidence to span two worlds – his world of the trees and jaguars, and ours of the plazas and smooth cement. It made him extraordinary, someone who inspired legends. At lunchtime, when Armando at last woke up, I told him we should try to speak to this man. He was clearly very special.

'I've never heard of him,' Armando groaned from his hammock. He looked yellow and was sweating, as if he needed to run to be sick.

'Wake up, Armando. The short Indian we saw last night.'

'He stole my drink.'

'We'll ask him to go hunting with us,' I said. 'Get him away from everyone. This man can be my teacher, perhaps. Worth a go.' Armando was already asleep again.

I went about the town to find out more.

Information is an important commodity on any frontier, and often the only asset of poor people. The citizens of Angamos gave more than generously.

'Saw him up on the Lobo river once,' said the municipal officer, gravely recalling a sight that had left him profoundly shocked. 'Naked. With a young girl. She had black paint over her . . . her breasts. A child.'

'What does that symbolize? A ritual?'

The municipal officer looked at me strangely. 'You know what the Matsés are like . . . Probably he was decorating his latest wife.'

Angel, the owner of the little store, said that Pablito's wife wasn't young at all. She was a wise old hag who lived deep in the forest.

Only Angel's father came close to the truth. He had been one of the first settlers here and had witnessed Pablito's comings and goings over the years. Pablito had three wives, and they were spread up and down the Galvez. The nearest was the youngest, a pleasant woman who loved to wear clothes. She was his launchpad for Angamos. The middle wife, further upriver, was a shy woman who was afraid of Angamos but was seen fishing on occasion. The furthest woman was his oldest wife and she lived unseen, deep in the interior. Pablito moved between them, choosing a more or less westernized one as it suited him.

'It's amazing, don't you see?' I told Armando, when he came to the plaza, still holding his head. He sat down shakily. He still wasn't sharing my enthusiasm about visiting Pablito. The governor sat at the other side of the plaza in his yellow T-shirt, picking up insects, pulling off their wings, and putting them down again. He too had a hangover. 'Don't you see,' I talked on. 'It's as if he has the wives placed up and down the river just so that he can slip in and out of our world at will, just disappear and become like a jaguar.'

Armando said drily, 'And you want me to come and help you find him, this man who can "disappear and become like a jaguar" . . .'

'I wish you'd act a bit more enthusiastically. It's not my fault you can't hold your drink.'

Armando said, 'If you want to know, I've got a very good head for drink, actually. I just can't see how you think you are going to learn anything from a man who everyone agrees is more difficult to pin down even than normal Matsés *and* who stole my drink *and* he doesn't speak a word of Spanish *and you've only got one chance in hell and that's to get help from Fidencio who's a crook but he also happens to be a genius* and I'm going back to bed.'

Brazil's trees were feathery silhouettes in the dawn mist, and the sounds of the Peruvian river bank shimmered across the water to them and back, a whispering of the shadows.

This morning to the usual sounds were added the sounds of me assembling some basic equipment – *farinha*, mosquito nets, machete, axe – while Matsés crowded round hoping for free handouts. We had already bought an old dug-out, blocked up its holes with clay, and lashed my outboard motor on to it.

We put together a package of gifts for Pablito: beads – much prized by mothers for decorating their babies – an axe, washing-up bowl, knives, fishing line. I promised Charo and José we'd be back in a few days. The last passenger aboard was the flawed genius himself, Fidencio.

Armando steered us upriver towards the first of Pablito's homes at Anushi. I was on the edge of my seat, waiting to meet this man who could move between my world and his, and maybe had the power to take me with him. He lived rather like a jaguar – that is, like a bit of the forest itself. He travelled through the forest as every western explorer had failed to do, not as an outsider but as a small part of what was there.

I had my pen and paper out, ready to record his forest fresh on the page.

# X

# Fidencio's Revenge

## BASED ON MY DIARY

6 NOVEMBER · *Canoe journey up the Galvez tributary in search of Pablito. First stop Anushi, home of his third wife.*

Is Armando laughing at me, or is he just squinting into the light? God knows, there's enough to laugh about. But bringing the old crook back into my employment was his idea and he'd better accept some of the blame if/when this all goes wrong.

Fidencio's job is to introduce me to Pablito, explain I'm here to learn. After that, it'll be up to me. I should be excited – this is the one thing I'm meant to have a talent at – 'integrating with tribal people'. But I have only a matter of weeks to learn in. At the moment I just wish I was a Polar explorer.

The governor tried to lend me a hand by threatening Fidencio – 'Until you return with Benedito, your I.D. card will remain in my office.' He managed to make it sound like he was commuting a death sentence, rather than just chucking a bit of laminated cardboard in his empty IN tray. But Fidencio sort of chuckled – he's more or less i/c [in charge of this new expedition] and has begun to light up again. Power is what charges him.

My up-to-now imperturbable stomach has been rendered unserviceable by dried pig (with mould on) sold by Indians. Fidencio got Charo to ask me to buy this in Angamos. Hope it gives him hell as well.

Even more severe diarrhoea has now taken hold . . . Even worse news: it doesn't seem to have affected Fidencio.

∗    ∗    ∗

Fidencio has said only one thing so far on our way upriver. 'A cayman lives here.' He pointed at a sandbank on the inside of a bend. 'Five metres or more. It took three Matsés once,' he said. And, turning to look me in the eye, 'Better watch out – he might get you.' Not said with a great deal of sympathy.

He feels he's in the ascendant. Danger?!

## At Anushi, a village on the lower Galvez

Took only a couple of hours to get here – or would have done without Fidencio's Revenge. Anushi means 'paca' or some similar nocturnal rodent.

We saw Pablito alone on the forested slope below the village, hacking at a giant dug-out [canoe]. As we approached, Pablito didn't look up. He didn't need to – he must have seen us miles away. Fidencio called out softly, 'Matseeeee . . .' He wove his magic spell.

Fidencio started just by singing soft Matsés sounds, and Pablito smiled but said nothing – he didn't want to get involved. He kept his axe in his hand and he kept looking down at his canoe, as if at a friend. He wanted to get on with his chopping. (I'm pleased: he isn't a soft touch; he sees what I saw in Fidencio when I first met him.) Fidencio flagged Armando to steer the canoe ashore, and sang more of the Matsés' conversational song. He must have been explaining about me wanting to learn about the forest because Pablito looked over at me, inspected my white legs, and looked puzzled.

He began walking away up the slope, but Fidencio turned to me and said it was all right, Pablito had invited us indoors because in a moment it would rain.

Fidencio followed Pablito, still singing Matsés words and trying to get near enough to cuddle him – the usual technique. But Pablito was too quick for him.

Rain arrived before Armando and I were moored up. It came in torrents, rattling the leaves. The path became a drain.

Three or four boys and girls in shorts and skirts came running through the foliage high up on the bank. They ran up the tree and perched like birds. They had come to see us try to climb the river bank. It was now a waterfall – running water, running mud.

I went first, striking out through the cascade. I lost my footing half-way up, pulling Armando with me. We shot on our stomachs back down to the riverside. Armando was very angry with me. The children were bouncing in the branches, almost falling out as they laughed.

We stood for a while like Laurel and Hardy, as mud spread over our feet. The rain was loud around us, but we could easily hear the children tittering.

Eventually, we made it up the bank by going through the trees, gripping our toes around the roots. Rain stopped just as we achieved the ridge – by then we were feeling like Himalayan mountaineers. The children hopped down the trees like frogs, and were gone.

Where to? The palm houses were rectangular, but with few windows and no locks. I opened the door to the first house and at first saw only darkness. Then I made out an open mud floor, a smoky fire, and a string hammock in which was a snoozing woman. A naked toddler was dangling a stick over her, about to ram it into her ear.

I closed the door and heard the woman scream – the stick in her ear.

The next house also had all the gloom of a *maloca*: the dark, the children everywhere, lolling from hammocks. There was a stir when we opened the door. Children parted, disappearing further back into the dark. Pablito was sitting on a block of wood along the wall, eating steaming manioc with Fidencio. Around the edges of the house were females of various stages of physical development. Some, one or two, might have been his wives, but most must have been cousins, aunts and daughters – all trained into his service, it looked like.

Pablito was being talked to by Fidencio. He wasn't listening, but *that* didn't bother Fidencio. For now, he would just let Pablito get used to his voice. Fidencio was now where he wanted to be: back in charge. While he talked, Pablito gave me a carefree smile. He pointed at a pot on the clay floor and invited us to eat. 'Buen,' he said.

'He means "*bueno*" I suppose,' Armando muttered. 'Probably his Spanish is better than yours, Benedito.' I'm afraid he's still angry with me for pulling him into the mud.

A series of women bustled over to the fireplace, and then, giggling, made dashes towards us to deposit pans of steaming manioc.

Armando was picking through his portion, pulling out all the stringy bits. 'Least it's not *chicha* – that stuff the women spit into to help fermentation.' Hearing the word *chicha* the women kindly brought [the manioc drink] forward. Armando said, 'Looks freshly spat into.'

From the roof hung arrows, which had simply been jabbed there. A little boy [later known to me as Roberto] was sitting on a plank along the wall, sharpening one arrow-tip with the tooth of a paca. In the gloom I made out some wall decorations – obsolete banknotes of unbelievably high denominations, hung limply beside a poster showing you, in a series of explicit cartoons, how to put on your condom.

'Wife?' Fidencio asked Pablito, teasing. He was indicating a little girl of nine or ten: clear, cream face with nose freckles.

The girl [who was referred to by the Christian mission name of Lucy] ran to the shadows and the women laughed. She giggled, twisting as if she was being tickled.

To indicate his wife Pablito called a woman over; she came forward to a housepost, stood hugging it, then quickly went back to her hammock, making a bubbling laugh with her fingers in her mouth. She must be the third wife, the youngest – perhaps twenty-five or thirty years old. She has a pair of twins with her in the hammock.

I asked Fidencio to ask Pablito how many children he had. Thirty, he said. It sounded like an estimate.

Fidencio opened the sack of presents at Pablito's feet. Saucepan, knives and other metal things spilled on to the clay. He wasn't interested, which impressed me enormously. Good for him. The women, however, swooped in and snatched the bright things like birds.

Fidencio began taking his usual liberties – stroking the Matsés, teasing them outrageously. It was amusing, it broke the ice. He strolled about, making theatre, squeezing and plucking the noses of the women here – it's the impudent (it seems to me) charm he uses with all of us.

It worked. The first wife now giggled and, half hiding behind the fireplace, where pig bits and pieces were drying on a rack, asked Fidencio if I was married. There were shrieks of laughter when I said no. Fidencio said in Matsés that as it happened I was looking for a wife. This was met by absolute quiet, and some horrified whispers. Then Fidencio said, 'But Benedito is waiting to find a *tall* Mayoruna!'

'Heeeeeeeee!' they laughed. 'The Mayorunas are *not* the right height, for he is very tall!' the wife said in Matsés.

Fidencio squeezed the wife by her elbow. 'He is too tall for Mayorunas, and he is too tall even for the trees!' This was how Fidencio worked it, flirtatiously.

Had to go outside soon after that – ill with Fidencio's Revenge. I went off down the jungle path but had to cut short my visit to the loo because the children were creeping up the path, stalking me.

When I walked back, the children ran away. One of them, determined to be brave, tagged along behind me. Back at the house, I asked his name and Pablito had a quick think and said 'Roberto'.

'Roberto' is, I suspect, just a name given for us outsiders to use – like 'Lucy' and 'Helena', the names of his sisters. They keep their real names safely to themselves and label themselves with these, words picked up from the missionaries. 'Roberto' has a balding flat top to his head, like his father. A stern face, tinged with aggressive fear that breaks into a great smile at a whim.

Mid-afternoon now, and Pablito is looking bored. He's wondering to himself when we are going away. I told Fidencio we are overstaying our welcome and that he'd better tell Pablito why I'm here – to learn enough to get out of here alone through the forest.

*Later*

Pablito has listened to Fidencio again, and – to my surprise – perked up. 'Cass? Cass?' he said. *Cazar*. 'Hunt? Hunt?'

'With Benedito,' Fidencio had to keep saying. '*With* Benedito.

Mustn't leave him.' (Fidencio's skill is such that he talks in both Spanish and Matsés as he goes along.) Pablito announced to his wife that he was going hunting. He stood up, ready to go.

Fidencio: '*With* Benedito. Teach him. Don't leave him. More presents if you don't leave him.' Finally, 'You are happy to teach Benedito to be like a Matsés – for a month or more?' Pablito said yes, but Fidencio kept repeating the question until Pablito had said for himself, '*Mirambó Beneee.*' This is Matsés for 'Teach Benedict.' And then, using his favourite faulty Spanish word, Pablito said, 'Buen,' *bueno*, good.

It's the best we'll get.

Fidencio, all is forgiven. He's set for departure tomorrow. (Let's dump the creep as soon as possible.) Armando will take him back to Angamos. Then Pablito and I will go hunting. Fidencio suggested to Pablito that we go to visit his second wife up the Galvez, then the first, further away still. Fidencio says the forest up there is 'crawling with wildlife' – I do hope it's not crawling too much.

One more thing has happened to consolidate my relationship with Pablito.

'Water?' I asked Pablito – I indicated with my hands that I wanted to wash. He got up and escorted me outside. We headed down a footpath, followed by a trail of children, and came to barely disturbed forest. I felt proud to be alone with the legendary man – I had a feeling about him. He's not shy one bit – a shaman? We came to a little stream.

Pablito retreated and I was then overtaken by the children, who ran into the water and splashed and screamed, and ran back to the house. A young boy burst into tears at being left behind with me.

Now there was a rare bit of privacy. I pulled off my trousers and immediately realized I had nothing to cover myself with. (To counter fungus infections, I don't wear underpants in the forest – not that I've yet dared tell my mother this.)

Did it matter if the women saw me bathing naked? I supposed not – the Matsés are hardly churchgoers. At least, not yet. But I tried to make it quick, before I was disturbed.

Within seconds the children had crept back to watch from the bushes. They didn't notice I was naked, but watched me casually, while they played with a lizard, letting it bite hold of their fingers and hang from them. Roberto then ran down into the water with another child and they swung from a pole bridge. I splashed them, wanting to play. At this they ran off screaming and in tears.

That wasn't all. Just as I was about to get out of the water a young mother appeared with a baby to wash. Roberto was hiding behind her. I decided it best to give her privacy – though she had decided I didn't need any.

Still naked, I couldn't very well stride manfully out of the water in front of her, so I sank a little into the water, and slowly drifted off, rather like a jellyfish. At a short distance I stopped and tried to busy myself washing.

She must have thought I had shorts on, and that I was just staying in the water to flirt with her. She exclaimed, 'Heeee!' in mock crossness and looked at Roberto and muttered something that must have meant, 'Well *really*.' I felt blood surge to my cheeks. I knew my neck had come out in red blotches.

The teenager doused her baby in a business-like manner and called Roberto to hold it while she bathed. Unencumbered, she squatted down into the water, rubbing under her arms and over her breasts, and then sprang out, dripping. She yanked the baby up on to her chest, and marched off up the path. As they disappeared from view, I heard her pause with Roberto, and sigh, mischievously, 'Eeeeeeee!'

When I came back to the house, the women let out a joyful shriek. They knew about the incident.

Fidencio said, 'What did *you* get up to?'

Clearly, the girl had told them the whole story (to cover herself?) and gone off out of sight to a little partitioned-off area.

'You went bathing with Helena!' Fidencio said in Spanish and Matsés. 'But she has a husband already!' Hoots of laughter from everyone, led by Pablito.

Now the women are teasing her, trying to coax her out of hiding with pretend offers of food. What makes this so funny to everyone is that – so Fidencio says – Matsés make love in the water. I'm interested by their association with water. Traditionally, they avoided the main rivers because these were the passageways of the predatory tribes like the Conibos, and travelled across them only briefly, on simple *palo de balsa* rafts. Although they occasionally took turtles by means of harpoon arrows, they rarely dared spend much time fishing on the main rivers for fear of exposing themselves to enemies. And yet the Mayorunas traded with their enemies.* If rivers always meant danger to the Mayorunas, perhaps that's why it is said that their most feared of animal spirits is a monstrous water snake.

At this moment there was an interruption. A bat was heard squeaking in the roof, and the women began trying to reach it with one of the arrows. Armando got up and helped them, stabbing it to death. 'It isn't a vampire bat, but they said it can bite,' Fidencio said simply. The poor thing looked harmless to me.

More manioc presented for supper. We'll sleep here.

I'm writing my diary now, before dark. Helena, the young woman, has just appeared at last – couldn't hold out for food any longer. She scuttled by, making her 'heeeeeee!' noise to the other women, and taking cover among them. Her humour is dry – she smiles wryly in my direction. She has thin but expressive lips, and her high cheeks are hidden in part under a long, low fringe.

Fidencio fished her out. 'Helena . . .'

'*Fidencio* . . .' she rebuked him. She was stern – determined not to be the butt of a joke.

'Benedito wants to sleep "*al lado*", at your side.'

More laughter. Helena skilfully deflected the humour by slipping behind Lucy, the pale-skinned younger sister who is perhaps ten years old. 'Wife!' Helena said, and propelled her across the clay floor towards me.

'Yaaagh!' the girl screeched, and veered off and out of the door. Didn't come back till after dark.

I have just found out that all this time there was a boy swaddled in blankets in one of the hammocks. He barely looked at the presents – they hardly mattered to him. Same reaction as Pablito, who *isn't*

---

* The anthropologist Steward quotes a description of the Mayorunas emerging from the forest at rivers, and blowing shell or bamboo trumpets to signal to Indians on the opposite side. The enemies canoed over and, without landing, held out articles for exchange on the points of their spears. The Mayorunas swopped hammocks woven of wild cotton, parrots and feather headdresses for knives and other metal tools. The traders then separated, shooting arrows at each other.

sick. This has set me worrying. I haven't given him anything he really wants. Maybe he will help me, but I need a lot of help – I mean, not just a quick hunting trip. I need to survive alone.


7 NOVEMBER

Fidencio is gone. Relief. But the Matsés look uncertain – wondering, what next? Armando back tonight. I will stay quietly here.

On reflection, Fidencio was a sort of shaman, just as Louis said. I now feel the power vacuum in the Matsés house. Pablito hasn't filled it – worrying. I overestimated him? Or he works in more subtle ways?

From Fidencio's questioning, we think there are no paths through to the Ituí [the Javari tributary east of here]. It's looking like I do have to go up to the Batã, cutting through the forest alone if and when necessary.

From experience, I know there are ten phrases more important than any others [for learning from indigenous people]. Fidencio has given me the Matsés for them: *bírambu*, good; *isambó*, bad; *ayee*, yes; *parghee*, no; *eesme*, teach me; *mirambó*, show me (place etc), also, demonstrate for me; *korásé*, give me; *boo-nék*, I like; *pi-ombee*, thank you; *wee ma burobee*, I'm tired (carrying etc).

Saying goodbye, Fidencio and I tried to be hearty, and pretend we cared about each other. 'Happy memories,' we both said, lying outrageously. 'You have any last-minute advice?' I asked.

The women crowded round, swinging their babies from side to side and watching, waiting to be amused by Fidencio.

He didn't let them down. An old trooper, he is. 'The Matsés hug very tight!' he said. And: 'If you want to sleep with a girl, you signal by pinching her!' *Vereské*, he said, 'Pinch!' in Matsés.

'Wooah,' the women screamed, and they padded off. Goodbyes are not much part of nomadic society.

Lucy, the pale little girl, went with him: someone [in fact it was Hugo] has offered her a seat in a plane to Iquitos, and to look after her once she's in the town.

This morning she was in the forest, with Roberto as he hunted lizards. Now she's off to a noisy grey place of cars. It will be the first time Lucy has been to the outside world, and it will mean an absence of three months. Yet she didn't even turn to say goodbye to her family. Just went a bit quiet.

This morning I went pottering about the forest, hoping Pablito would come out to join me. Didn't. But the children, as I'd expected, tracked me. I'd hoped they'd start showing me things, if I asked about animals and plants. But now they simply look at me as if I'm a spy.

Deep down, they really don't trust me at all, here. And it's not just the children. I'm so scared by the size of the task ahead . . .

However, down by the water, I did again bump into Helena. (You'd have thought she'd learned her lesson.) She put her baby high on the clay bank with Roberto, prior to washing herself. She really doesn't mind being seen with me. Trust? Or are Matsés as 'liberal' as the *mestizos* believe, sharing their wives on occasion?

Didn't speak to Helena except to say 'Good afternoon', keeping it formal so as to avoid misunderstandings. I *must* blend, but not with her. I'm very wary of problems arising from relationships in these tight communities. As always, the way to be invited into the community is to get to know the very young – they are excited, curious, proud to be your tutor. Or to get to know the very old who will adopt me in place of their own teenagers, who nowadays can't be bothered with tradition.

*Later, after Armando's return from Angamos*

Unlike me, Armando is relaxed about my chances of getting absorbed into the family. Basically, he doesn't think I stand a chance. 'Just lie back and have a holiday, like me.' How lovely for him – and all on my money.

I did make some progress with the family today, but it's all oh so slow. While Pablito was thumping away on his canoe Roberto, the little boy, let me play with his toy bow and arrow. He'd snatched it from his little brother and put it in my hands. It is strung, I notice, with a bootlace of mine.

We weren't aiming at targets, but my incompetence showed anyway. The rain then came – the arrows were left behind without any care, and the eagle feathers [of the arrow flights] were ruined – but it's a start.

This evening, Armando sat with me indoors, dreading being offered more *chicha*.

'How's your Mayorunita?' he asked.

This is how he refers to Helena – my 'Mayorunita', my little Mayoruna [Matsés] girl.

My little Mayoruna girl is doing fine, thank you. Actually I'm avoiding her. She's too sure of herself by half – heaven knows what dangers lie her way.

An American I met in Iquitos said the only bosoms he ever saw as a boy were in the *National Geographic*. That's how he learnt the facts of life – 'That's how *everyone* learns the facts of life in the Midwest. Benedict, do please promise me you'll send photos of those Indians in to the magazine. You will, won't you? If you were an American, I'd say it was your duty to your country.'

As I'm not an American, I'm let off the hook, perhaps. For the record, though: her breasts are tubular from being sucked by, and loaded for, a baby which has a spotty, unhealthy scalp. Is Helena so lovely because of that long, straight fringe – the frame it gives to her eyes? Her humour suddenly shows in an otherwise serious face. There are faded black ink lines across her cheeks, from some previous phase of adornment.

Wonder where her husband is.

The women keep filling up my cup, and trying to top up Armando's. His *chicha* hasn't been touched. The women are calmer now, as they walk up, pour, walk away. But they never talk to us. 'It's going very slowly, isn't it?' I said to Armando.

He said, rather bluntly, 'Looks like without Fidencio's powers, you're sunk.' Should I retreat to Angamos already? The plaza is like the set of *Waiting for Godot*. Everyone waits, and Godot – in this case the plane from Iquitos – never comes. Each time they have faith that it will come, as promised, and each time it fails them. And then, once again, it's time for the medical officer to begin his rounds, issuing fresh sick-notes for passengers to jump the queue out of there.

We sat listening to the sound of Pablito, still down by the water, chopping his canoe. He came in, dripping with water from a bathe, dropped an axe on the floor and stood by the fire, drying off. Then he went to his hammock and slept.

This is the key moment I've recognized from so many other expeditions: that point at which it is decided whether I'm going to be invited into a community or not.

8 NOVEMBER

Earlier this morning I was in the forest, hanging around with the children, trying to get them to play with me. I felt like a dirty old man, loitering there. At last I got Roberto to show me what was in his little hand. A big cicada. Reluctantly, he gave me another go on his bow. Trying to impress him I broke one of his arrows. Luckily the poor lad seemed more fascinated with my inability than worried about his equipment.

Pablito came out, perhaps feeling a bit guilty about not having lifted a finger to help my forest education. He walked down the path towards me. But then he stopped. He had heard something. He let out a barking croak, 'Graaagh!' It was a frog or toad noise. A creature answered back from the leaves. 'Graaaagh!' Then Pablito walked back up the path – he'd forgotten why he came.

We've had a quiet evening in the firelight. Also some slapstick with the women again – jokes about me being single, and Helena's husband being away. I suddenly have an urgent desire to get to the heart of Pablito, get below these silly jokes and superficialities. Should I play up to Helena? Use her as a 'way in'? She's intent on using *me* some way, I'm sure.

9 NOVEMBER

Pablito was sitting with me when I wrote the above, smiling as the women joked at my expense. Once or twice Pablito did try to talk to us, but he got nowhere and gave up, and his eyes glazed over.

Armando and I sat trying to work out what he had meant. 'Poof! Manny-anna!'

Then his wife went to our bags and tapped one of them with her foot. She was indicating something. This was the bag with the shotgun hidden in it, disassembled. (NB How did she know the shotgun was in there?)

We worked it out. 'Poof! Manny-anna!' = 'Bang bang, *mañana*' = 'Let's go hunting tomorrow.'

I said to Armando, 'See? He's going to help.'

Armando: 'He's just stringing you along. His heart isn't in it.'

'We'll take it slowly. Visit his second wife, then remotest wife. After that we'll go off even further.'

Armando muttered, 'To the moon, maybe.' He thinks I'm beyond learning anything. He's a craftsman, like Stew [my brother]: to him it's clear that, compared to Fidencio, I just haven't got it. I must believe that I have. 'We,' I said to Pablito, gesturing, 'go a long way. Long, long way. *Lejos*, far.'

'Poof!' said Pablito.

'I think he's making fun of us,' Armando said, and he went to bed, stretching out a mosquito net on the floor, and I soon erected mine alongside.

What's so irritating is that Armando isn't even trying to help – but that's just him. Puts little into life. [An unfair comment, this, but one accurately reflecting our frustration with each other at the time.]

I lay in the dark hearing the chirruping and sighing of the women, a domestic sound that sent me into a deep sleep.

This morning we got up excitedly. 'We're off!' I thought. But there was no movement from Pablito's hammock. We loaded the canoe, but Pablito, when he got up, said, *'Parghee'*, the Matsés word for no. He didn't even look apologetic.

Armando walked back to the canoe with a superior look on his face, like a schoolboy with his tongue out. 'Told you!'

At this rate I'll have to sack Pablito, and learn from his 30 offspring. This morning, I brought out my camera for the first time. Roberto is fascinated by the flash, which makes him blink repeatedly afterwards. Also, the irritating noise of its automatic wind-on mechanism. He copies it. 'Cling-cleng,' he sings, like a bird. I've realized he learns by imitation like this. 'Cling-cleng.' His little brother copies from him in the same way – like jaguar cubs, I can't help thinking.

*Cling-cleng!* After the excitement of the camera, Roberto showed me a toy pitfall trap he'd made. It's a very simple device, the Tarzan variety for catching lions but this one is small, only 2 foot deep. He's put little bamboo stakes at the bottom, camouflaged with A4-sized leaves. If I'd wandered over this I would have given myself a nasty injury. Can't be permissible to have these around the village, can it? How many more of Roberto's little deathtraps are there out here waiting for me?

## 10 NOVEMBER

The expedition is a shambles again. Late last night I woke needing to go to the loo. Fidencio's Revenge. I tiptoed out, ducking the strings of the mosquito netting, all the time waiting for the moment the dogs would wake and savage me. At last I was outside, no dogs alerted – remarkable feat.

I headed back to my mosquito net – or what I took to be my mosquito net. As I plunged in there was a frightened yelp. I froze, knowing the owner of the mosquito net was doing the same. I thought: Please don't scream. Please don't!

She didn't scream, but she let out a lowish chattering series of exclamations. A baby started crying. Just my luck: it was *her*. My 'Mayorunita', little Mayoruna. I backed off, not knowing where to go – if this wasn't where my net was, where was it? I was still half asleep. I stood totally disorientated, holding my little towel around me, and everyone waking up. A woman called out, crossly, and Helena yipped and yapped back to her. Armando's torch went on. Only Pablito carried on snoring.

You would have thought Armando might have seen the funny side of this. He didn't. 'You come here saying you want to learn from the Indians, but you just want to exploit them.' He was on his feet, and shining his torch in my eyes. 'I like girls – all right, I admit it. Some of them are young.' *Very* young, would have been more accurate. 'But you, Benedito –'

'A mistake.' Besides, whoever heard of Indians sleeping on the ground. Where's her hammock, for heaven's sake?

Armando said slowly, 'You can't even be honest. And you know what, Benedito? I don't feel sorry for you, I *pity* you.'

He switched off his torch. His last words were: 'And you'll get us killed, with this sort of behaviour.' I was left standing there with my little towel. And I still wasn't sure where my mosquito net was.

The rest of the night went very slowly. The baby was awake, the dogs barking fitfully, Pablito snoring.

This morning, I was too ashamed to get out of my mosquito net. But the world had to be faced. I ran past the women and straight outside to try and find Pablito and apologize – shake his hand or something. It was cool outside, misty rain filling the sky. Pablito was bent down, apparently in conversation with a dog.

'*Champee!*' he said brightly. I knew this word by now. Girl. '*Champee* buen? Girl good?'

Back indoors, Armando said, 'Made your peace with him?'

I said I didn't think there was a problem.

'Then you must remind him of his favourite wife-hunting raids.'

The women seem to have forgiven me, which is amazing since white men almost wiped these people out, something even the Remo-aucas' didn't manage.

Armando brought out our little bag of presents. 'The least we can do is mend feelings a bit.' (Does he still seriously believe we might have been executed?) He began handing out gifts meant for my whole stay. Pablito was only interested in the knives. He inspected each one with care, testing the blade on the leather of his fingers, before passing them on. His wife ran off with each in turn, and the other women inspected them carefully.

I said, weakly, as the assets for the remainder of the journey were distributed, 'But these are all I've got.'

Armando gave me a long, hard stare, and carried on handing them out until they were finished. I took my punishment.

'My Mayorunita' came in with a baby riding her hip. The women cooed, teasing her. 'Helenaaaa!' Except they used a different word – not this western name that we'd been fobbed off with. The girl smiled kind of slyly, wrapping up her mosquito net with one foot as she held the baby.

Soon she was deftly tweaking at an outside pocket of my shoulderbag, using her toes. She had spotted my Kitchen Devil.

I said, as I looked at the knife, 'It's my mum's really.' Another hard stare from Armando. 'But I suppose she won't mind.'

I handed it over at arm's length, a gesture of decorum. She took it, and there was another 'coooo' from the women. They studied the glimmering blade and sighed aloud, as women tried it out in turn, sawing at the houseposts. 'It'll be handy around the kitchen,' I said to Armando.

Armando said to himself, 'I should think *she*'s handy round the kitchen.'

Our raft, now old and grey, has appeared in front of the village. It has been used by various Matsés to float down here. 'A fitting monument' one Matsés called it – referring to the raft's colossal size and weight, I suspect.

The man spoke Spanish and we went to considerable lengths to get him to translate a remark Helena made earlier today. It had sent everyone into near hysteria, no matter how many times it was repeated. The translation of Helena's words: 'I can marry Bennee now! I can kill my man with Bennee's very sharp knife!'

We still haven't left yet. Mid-morning. All the luggage is in the canoe but Pablito's wife refuses to come. Pablito seems to insist on having a female with him. Each man always seems to hunt with a woman. The wife is a stout-hearted old stick but she collapsed back into her hammock, laughing the idea of travelling off. 'Whoooooo!' Too far, too difficult.

She doesn't even know where we are going yet. At least, I don't.

Lucy, supposedly on her way to the bright lights of Iquitos, has turned up. The plane didn't arrive. She's not going to be thrown into that huge, alien, tarmac world any more, but looks neither happy nor sad about what she missed. She has the women's stoic acceptance of life, even at that age.

I've made an important discovery: she can speak a little Spanish, when she feels inclined. Armando overheard her practising little phrases to herself.

10 NOVEMBER CONTD · *En route up the Galvez river*

We are off! With me is my sidekick Armando, also Pablito, Lucy and Roberto. Also (wait for it) Helena.

I asked for Pablito. The rest stepped into the canoe as we left. When Helena decided to come too there were *no* giggles. Why not? Is this the beginning of something more complicated – it's therefore not a teasing matter any more? Where's her husband?

I keep asking Armando for reassurance, but he just says, 'It's probably all right.' We both make jokes about it, but we both know enough about tribal life to know jealousies can flare from nowhere. The sorry result: ten expeditions and I've never had a relationship with a girl. And God knows they've tried their best to have their ways: the Iban maiden of perfectly fluted neck, the Papuan of burning black eyes . . . I have evaded them all – countless slinky limbs and polished mahogany torsos. And now there's a woman with all the powers of heaven mustered under one skin, and I'll be staying away from her as well. At least, I intend to try. On a more sober note: I now recall Harriet saying that, when she first got to talk to the Mayoruna women, she found that almost half of them were considered of inferior status to other Mayoruna wives – the reason? They had been captured from other clans or groups. Almost *half* of them. For their own protection, therefore, the women and older female children were never left alone, even inside their own homes. Bearing this in mind, is Pablito really going to be prepared to trust me with his family?

On this journey up the Galvez I've got to gain Pablito's co-operation. Then help. I'll give myself a month, then I must enter Brazil, whether I know enough or not. The countdown is on . . .

We are proceeding upriver, Pablito established comfortably in the prow of the canoe. His wife has given him a packed lunch – smoked fish in a leaf package.

Things are going wrong already. Pablito left his bow and arrows behind and just now he asked for the shotgun to be passed forward. I tried to say I wanted to learn without relying on a firearm but he put his hand out for cartridges. 'De!'

'Means *dies*,' said Armando. 'Give him ten cartridges.'

I gave him seven. He rubbed his hands with chilli peppers produced from nowhere. It's a preparation – a sort of cleansing ritual.

Within seconds the gun had been fired. A curassow, a black bird the size of a pheasant and this one with a red wedge of horn on its head, dropped into the river. The dead bird kicked its red legs in the water, paddling itself towards our canoe. But before we had picked it up, Pablito had discharged another shot. A second bird fell to the water.

This was only the beginning. We had come only a mile or two, and soon there were seven curassow flapping in the canoe. Tree fruit rolled like pebbles out of the mouths of the dead birds.

'Bastan!' Pablito cried. *Bastante*. Lots! Pablito looked flabbergasted when I didn't hand over more cartridges. Not that there are many more left.

As we sat in the sun, continuing upriver, I examined the sore on my foot.

It needs antiseptic (don't have), sun screen cream (don't have), and anti-fungal cream (don't have). Of all my foot's problems, the fungal one looks worst – there are spreading, itchy roots.

Helena is behind me, having a picnic with Lucy and Roberto. What's going on in that scheming head? She makes me miss Jita. Armando's thoughts on the subject are simply: 'We need to find out if her husband knows.' Useless. Soon we met Fidencio's cayman – this species the largest and most dangerous of all the caymans and this individual the one that had eaten three Matsés.

I have never seen anything quite like this creature. A black cayman. A book I read once said they grow up to four and a half metres. This one must have been brought up on a better diet as a baby. It didn't swim downriver, it floated like a barge, not caring about us.

'No, no, no!!' I called at Pablito. He was on his feet, shouting at it, screaming for permission to shoot. 'Poof! Wooooaaaaaagh! POOOF!'

I reached for the videocamera and filmed a bit, Pablito going berserk though we were twenty or more metres away. The children went absolutely quiet. Bang! Pablito couldn't hold himself back any longer. The animal sunk itself down. 'Does he have to shoot at *everything*,' I said. In hindsight, perhaps I was being mean – it might have eaten his best friends.

'Five and a half metres,' was all Armando could think of saying. 'Fidencio wasn't lying this time.'

A dolphin jumped clean from the water, its pink and grey skin flashing. It's not a very elegant shape – the nose rather long and thin and straight on the end of a bulbous head. Perhaps the inept statue in Iquitos is a bit better than I thought.

We stopped at a bushy shrub overhanging the water, and plucked its fruit – weetão. It's a duff brown kiwi-fruit type of pod [I think a type of genipap] for making black resin face dye.

Piums [biting flies] are bad when we slow down. They are so full of my blood they tumble off me as heavy as beetles.

We've rearranged the seating, so that I'm at the back with Armando, and can watch Lucy and Roberto – and keep a watchful eye on Helena. Pablito is still in front, eyes taking in the forest.

Lucy and Roberto don't talk, but point at every game bird that goes by. A very good habit to get into – it trains the eye. Helena is not so aware of our surroundings – I forgot to mention she has her baby with her.

Lucy must have spent half her few years organizing younger children, and – as long as she doesn't stop to think about it – she also bosses me about softly in Matsés. She was very indignant when I wetted her seat with my big feet.

Just now, Pablito insisted we stopped. I thought he wanted to go to the loo, but when he reappeared out of the trees he had smears of red paint on his face. What's he up to? I see he has brought a few pods of achiote [the red grease] with him. I get the feeling he's knuckling down to a job.

We've just passed a pale green alligator that's longer than me. It sat on the bank with its mouth half ajar. It thrashed into the water as we came by.

[I continued to pay special attention to Lucy, the only Spanish-speaker, looking for chances to make friends with her, but also painfully aware that I must try to take things slowly and not scare her.]

If I address her, Lucy looks into her lap, frowning furiously and blushing. But I must make headway. It's scary to think that my survival could depend on getting to know this child.

She sometimes counts the numbers of toucans or macaws that pass overhead. The numbers are delivered in Spanish – numbers are the language of the *racionales*. Westerners, the 'rational people'.

Helena sometimes silently guides her baby's hand to point at the wildlife, as Lucy and Roberto do. The child is newly born, the baby can hardly focus, but Helena does it anyway.

We've just passed a party of Indians on a sandbank, where they'd been digging for turtles. They also had a tukunaré [a long, yellow and black striped fish] and an arawanis, a two to three foot fish with a trapdoor mouth – inside which it rears its young, a little cloud of olive green fry. How it does this without eating them, I'm not sure. Armando says the mouth is actually more like a protective harbour – the young come and go. Even then, some must get gulped down when there's an emergency.

We gave these Indians half the birds we had shot, and moved on.

Pablito is looking around for other creatures to destroy. Birds – red-legged, and like thin chickens – perch on the high branches almost waiting to be shot. 'Puka konga', he calls one with a red, bald throat. 'Kushú', another with a white crest.

*Dusk*

We've stopped at a little hunters' camp. The children padded into the forest to collect firewood. Pablito wandered off into the forest whistling back at the birds.

Now we are sitting around drinking mugs of stewed bananas. Lucy and Roberto are whispering as they groom each other, looking for lice. Helena has retired to her mosquito net.

So far, Helena seems to be here for Pablito, to cook for him. She is his daughter, after all.

I wonder about these girls I've met on this journey. There was Mari-elena, the Ecuadorean woman on the bus, in whose warm hair I slept, and Francesca the Colombian who threw litter out so beautifully, and now Helena. They are South American substitutes for Jita, a composite female that I seek out to keep me going. As I travel along my attention drifts from one to another, homing in as they come within range – gaining comfort from them, then losing them, as my expedition moves me on.

11 NOVEMBER · *Still at the hunters' camp, Galvez river*

Last night Armando had a bad dream. It was about tortoises and water turtles. He wasn't any more specific than that, except that he says they signify bad luck on travels. Normally imperturbable, Armando is clearly shaken. The first thing he asked, on waking, was: 'Pablito, are you here?'

I also had a bad dream, though I never normally dream at all. It concerned the danger which I will be putting myself through – how the risks I take hurt everyone back home. [In my dream] I arrived home and my mother had an expression on her face of something dreadful having happened. 'What?' I asked. 'Jita is suicidal with worry,' was all she said.

I feel a desperate desire to get on with learning, and increase my chances of survival. So difficult to be patient. But *mustn't* push too hard too quickly. I've been looking to Lucy as a bridge to Pablito, but even Lucy could teach me enough to get out of this forest.

It's as if we are moving back in time. This journey back upriver is a journey back into Pablito's youth, the time when he evaded all white men. Then it was just the forest and his type of people.

Because of the language problem, Pablito has to take the lead on this expedition, which is what I want. Now he's walked off into the forest, and Roberto and the rest are following. Think we are meant to go too.

*Later that day*

Armando waited back in the camp; I went off in my shorts and bare feet, behind Pablito. 'Tshi-i,' he said, listening – the name of a monkey which I couldn't even hear.

A frog cried out: Pablito pouted, barked a cough back at it.

He cut a young tree into a spear, and used that to poke into the caverns of rotten logs. Among the rest of us, only Roberto had a weapon – his toy bow and arrow. We walked further, through a smell of sweet resin and another of musky fungi. Lucy picked up a harlequin beetle, dabbing its red, yellow and black patterning, and flicking the poor insect's antennae. Once, Pablito shook a liana to get a bird to stand up for a better target for his son. Roberto took aim and fired. He missed, but only just. Little Roberto is a real killer. We think of children as harmless, and we try not to hurt them because they're fragile. Roberto, nine or ten, could exterminate me with one toy arrow.

As we dawdled along Pablito became less aware of me, and more responsive to his family and the forest.

We stopped and Pablito spliced open a palm shoot, handed out the fresh yellow leaves and fashioned them into crowns, armbands, waistbands. As far as Pablito was concerned, I was totally excluded from this – it was a Matsés thing only. I was not of their tribe, and these leaves Harriet said were a protective force, a spiritual clothing. A white man can't even feel their 'spirits', so leaves are hardly useful. But Lucy fashioned a little crown (far too small) for my head. I was a playmate. Such is the childlike way in which I hang back, she didn't think twice about including me.

Helena, coming up the path behind us, produced a few pods of achiote [a tree of which grew in the camp] and put stripes on the palm bands, and dappled Lucy's pale flat chest. Pablito reddened his own forehead, then Roberto's. Next he carefully worked his fingers around Helena's eyes, painting a scarlet mask across her. He also poked a hole into the weetáo fruit, and drew black lines across her cheeks, and along the lines of her lips. She looked fearsome with just the red. Now, with black lipstick, she looks like a Gothic horror. The purpose of this? Adornment, a bonding of people who have little to fall back on but themselves. They have no great tribal initiation cere-monies to bind them, no permanent settlements in which to shelter from the forest. They can only hope to rely on each other.

While I was looking around at the forest, Helena, Lucy and Roberto played a new game. They took it in turns to creep up on me unawares. Each tiptoed up and measured themselves off against my back. They are so quiet, so light on their feet, I only discovered the game when I happened to turn. There was Roberto, a red striped jaguar stalking up on me, caught in the act.

The others laughed, but Roberto jumped away, and was a little scared – that catty fierce look in his eyes. As usual, I found that by smiling hard I could snap a smile out of Roberto. I'm always relieved when I do: I can't stop thinking of his vicious little arrows.

We pottered on for a whole morning, Roberto shooting his arrows off and running with Lucy to go and retrieve them. Helena was fascinated with her own appearance. She stopped to look at her reflection in a black pool. When I watched she carried on looking at herself. So this was the 'careless, laughing, country wench', was it? The 'artless maiden'?

She corrected some lines of paint until she was happy. When I photographed her she flashed her eyes at me from under her fringe. She's very pleased with her decorations.

Her baby has anklets of beads. I now realize that the younger the child is, the more beads it has. I suspect it's a spiritual protection, a more durable version of the leaves.

While walking along, I tried to talk properly to Lucy for the first time, just asking her softly what she imagined Iquitos to be like. But she became selfconscious, went pink, and half concealed herself behind a bush. The Spanish language is a barrier in itself – it is so full of harsh sounds.

'Eesme, eesme,' I keep saying, teach me, teach me, and she likes that. It makes her titter, and that starts Roberto off. However, she's yet to teach me anything.

*Written in the canoe, on the way up the Galvez to the second wife*

We arrived back in camp and Armando looked at Helena – the red across her eyes, and the black paint in a line from cheek to cheek. He said, 'What have *you two* been up to?'

He meant this comment for me, but Helena picked it up. (She understands some Spanish?)

'Ar*man*do!' she said, with a playful gasp of shock. It was impossible to know what she was thinking. She pursed her thin lips, hoiked up her baby, and walked away.

I said, 'I wonder what it means, decorating herself like this?'

'What do you *think* it means?'

'I don't think it means what you are thinking. I mean, she might just be hoping for another Kitchen Devil.'

She might well have been, but this afternoon, in the canoe, Pablito couldn't keep a smile off his face and repeatedly said to me, out of earshot of his daughter, 'Buen *champee*? Good girl?'

'Know what he wants?' Armando called out, as he steered the engine. 'He wants you in his family.'

'Oh I don't think so, you know.'

'He's never asked you for any presents. What else does he want out of you?'

'He's special,' I said, fondly.

*But is he?*

*Evening, at Horichaves, a village on the Galvez, having passed various Matsés settlements*

Pablito's second wife is camped here in a small house with lots of boys in it dissecting a tapir. The wife is chirpy, rather nice. She is missing a front tooth – this is only noticeable because Matsés teeth are so much better than those of the citizens of Angamos. At this moment she is lying back in her hammock, looking at me but pretending not to. Armando is sitting against the bark wall surrounded by dishes of various sorts that he hasn't eaten.

'How are you getting on with your "father-in-law"?' he has just asked me. It's his little joke.

I said, 'Pablito's friendly enough.'

'But you've got to start *learning*.'

'I know. I feel like I'm on Death Row.'

12 NOVEMBER

Something rather dramatic happened in the night.

This morning we found Helena gone. By 'we' I mean Armando and I. Everyone else knew all right.

We don't know quite what happened, which makes it all the more worrying. We do know her husband got here by one means or other and removed her in the dark. Sadly, she accidentally left her Kitchen Devil behind – or her husband decided she wasn't going to be allowed to keep it.

Armando, once regarded by me as a man of cold steel, has been transformed into a neurotic again. He's pacing about: 'Snatched her in the night! Without even waking the dogs! He could have killed us!'

Pablito was very calm. 'Helena, no buen,' he said, simply. Helena, not good. (Not a good person? Not a good choice of girl?)

It has to be said, I can't take her 'abduction' as seriously as Armando does. As in all the other mishaps of this journey, it's accompanied by an element of farce.

Armando is still in a stupor. 'Could have cut my throat . . .' he's musing to himself. 'Could have done it with that idiotic kitchen knife . . .'

I picked up the Kitchen Devil lying forlornly on the pole floor. It's as if the Matsés have now attributed terrible malignant properties to this piece of cutlery – everyone seems to be avoiding it. Still, waste not, want not . . .

There is a young boy in the village, and he's now explained in broken Spanish what happened. 'Helena not good. She married. Better not see her again. She frightened because he fight you, maybe.'

Very sweet of her to be frightened for me, but why am *I* the one he wants to fight?

Anyway, this is no time for chivalry. We're off.*

[We pressed on up the Galvez, still with Roberto and Lucy, now having picked up one of Pablito's sets of bows and arrows and bargained for another set for myself. At last we were above Bien Peru, the highest settlement, where Fidencio had met his come-uppance. Before long we were beyond the mouth of the Lobo,

---

* The husband turned out to be a young teacher at Buenas Lomas, the SIL mission. This Christian influence might have made him more easygoing about his wife's chosen companions. On the other hand, perhaps not.

where we had entered the Galvez on the raft. Way up the Galvez we went, more and more alone with the forest.]

Dolphins keep jiving around us, overtaking, almost nudging us, and blowing air in a way that seems aggressive. Once, Pablito sighed at them, turned to me and waved and smiled. We are entering the depths of the forest, and he's in high spirits.

[As the dolphins left and we moved deeper into the interior, his mood calmed, again reflecting the surroundings.]

Pablito is now very quiet, listening to the forest, absorbed by it. I have that feeling again: of going back in time. That he is no longer aware of me, the motor, or any other thing from the Outside World.

A woolly monkey is watching us. Its smoky brown tail hangs vertically down from a branch like a fat tendril. Roberto is smiling back at it.

Lucy is pulling insects apart, absentmindedly. She has now placed the ochre butterfly wings in Pablito's hair. He smiled at her but his mind is on the forest ahead. I'm glad we have children along on the journey, though; whatever happens, he won't abandon us.

Pablito pointed to the bank and we let him ashore. From time to time there was a frog croak, and Armando and I argued about whether it was Pablito.

'That noise is Pablito?' Armando asked Lucy, using all the charm he has. She leaned forward to me, wanting to exclude Armando, and whispered, '*Parghee*, no.' She wanted to please only me. Rather touching. It also shows me how far I've come: Armando isn't the slightest included in this little Matsés family. But I should also say that it's of Armando's choosing. He's staying apart, just cooking and steering the canoe. I'm grateful to him for not involving himself and complicating things.

While we waited for Pablito to return, I said to Lucy, 'Iquitos, what is Iquitos like?'

She rubbed her finger along the canoe rim, coyly. She murmured, '*Pueblo grande, grande.* Big, big village.'

'What do people eat there?'

She giggled, and put her arms around Roberto, speaking in his ear. Giggled again. 'Those people eat many foods. Food from boxes.

Food from fishes, and from animals – just like we do. They eat worms too.'

Armando later explained that the Matsés believed pasta strands were worms.

Meanwhile, Pablito was still off hunting in the forest. A second later we heard an alarm cry. It was a bird in distress. Then there was a squawk. It was a bird dying a startled death.

Pablito came with a huge bird slung over his shoulder like a jacket. He stopped, answering an animal call. '*Dao-kwedt*,' he said, looking at the noise, then he climbed aboard.

He had more red paint on, vertical crosses on his chest. With all his make-up he looked like a camp actor. But maybe that is half the point. There is drama in this, it's like a play being enacted. He's taking on a role or something.

Pablito said the name of the bird for me, 'Surnú', and held it out to Lucy. Silently she took it between her legs to pluck it as we went on upriver. '*Sur . . . nú*,' she said, not looking up, but knowing by now I write all this stuff down in my [other] notebook.

At last I'm seeing how Pablito manages this shift between two worlds – ours and his – shifting in and out of the forest life between the security of his wives.

*At an upper Galvez riverside camp, while we cooked the bird*

As dusk came on, the birds were flying home across the river. '*Eesme*, teach me,' I said to Lucy, and she did. She named them for me as they clacked and flapped their way over the dark silver water.

Macaws, with their hoarse shrieks: pésá. Térushku, a bird with a gabbling twitter. Sentere was the jungle fowl with the lone whistle that walks alone, like me.

'Thank you,' I said to Lucy. '*Pi-ombee*.' In a small way, I have succeeded in becoming adopted. She treats me like her little brother Roberto, except that I'm considered even younger.

'*Pi-ombee. Boo-nék*. Thank you. I like,' she said.

We are all feeling the effects of this forest we are slipping into. It's as if we're no longer journeying through, but inside. There's a stillness round and about our little group.

Armando really is a special man to be able quietly to detach himself, let me carry on this matter with the Matsés alone. He's trying to improve my chances.

## 13 NOVEMBER

[As we went our way upriver] Now Pablito has put fresh make-up on his face: and something else. He also has whiskers protruding from his lips, made from palm-leaf ribs. This man is undergoing a strange metamorphosis.

After another flex or so of the Galvez I saw two small canoes moored to the bank beside a slit in the forest vegetation. I could smell woodsmoke, and Roberto and Lucy stood up and started hooting excitedly at the trees. We were there, the hidden camp of Pablito's first wife.

As we drew up at the bank, Pablito sprang to the shore. We followed him into the shade, and came to a temporary *maloca* made from loose palms interlaced into a two-metre-high rounded roof. There was Pablito's oldest wife, who had palish skin, and a sickly baby, and another older couple who seemed to be here just to look after them and left almost as soon as we arrived.

The sight of me created a stir in the camp. Everyone rose, and with them the butterflies and other insects that were gathered here. Pablito's wife then went into action, stoking up the camp fire and cooking up the contents of a battered tin pot – all the time snatching glimpses of me and exclaiming 'heeeeeeeeeeee!' When things settled down, and we were all nattering together and eating yucca, a root crop like manioc with which we had resupplied her, I saw she had long spindles from her nose, jaguar whiskers.

What with Roberto and Lucy running about, playing, there is a total absence of tension. A calm has descended on us; this is a family outing.

'I'm leaving,' said Armando, when I went to fetch my bag. He knew that he was an intrusion here. 'I'll wait back down at Angamos. These people will get you downriver.'

It was probably for the best. I told him I didn't know how long

I'd be. I joked, 'If I don't come down after a few months you can call out the National Guard.'

As Armando was untying the mooring rope, he said, 'I can't come. You do know that.' He means he can't come with me into Brazil. He showed no emotion, no regret, he just laid the words out smoothly. But he didn't look me in the eyes.

He thinks I don't stand a chance.


14 NOVEMBER · *First wife's camp, upper Galvez*

I don't blame Armando a bit [for not wanting to go into Brazil] – who in their right mind *would* go into a den of thieves? The future scares me.

This camp is five days' paddle to Angamos, and we are without a large canoe, but I feel no sense of isolation. Pablito has that quality in him.

My entire equipment is as follows: clothes (shorts – being worn – long trousers, a long-sleeved shirt); sleeping gear (towel, mosquito net, a sleeping bag 'inner', hammock); hunting gear (bow and arrows, fishing hooks/line, boots, socks); plus malaria tablets and sponge bag. Also, camera and video equipment and other notebook and pens. And my hat.

Having said I don't feel isolated, I now see that the Matsés *are* vulnerable out here. The baby isn't very healthy, and there's no garden. This is a very temporary camp, and I wonder what use it has for Pablito. Is it just his quiet retreat from the invading world?

Midday. Screeching, rasping insects, frantic ants. I'm sitting here, writing and watching. The fish that is sitting in the cooking pot is trampled over by bees, which come and go in wild dances. Tiredness is enveloping me with each click of the cicadas. But so much to learn . . .

Roberto and Lucy are pottering around. It's hard to have a sense of urgency among these timeless people and their green, timeless drapery.

I've erected my hammock in the *maloca* beside the others, but, testing it with my weight, I almost brought the structure down.

201

15 NOVEMBER

Earlier this morning Pablito led us away through the trees.

I was in bare feet but he very courteously pointed out spines along the route. Lucy and Roberto followed behind, chirruping noisily and screaming as they pinched each other. They ran about blowing trumpets made from the clay ramparts of a worm's house, 'Kweeka-mamang', which were to be found rising in little turrets between the fallen leaves.

I jotted a note to myself: I know I have lots to learn from these children, but I need an intensive survival course. When will the serious hunting begin? i.e. when will I go off just with Pablito?

The wildlife vanishes in front of my eyes – the tail of a monkey draws up and disappears, a rodent patters off through the leaves. Pablito never admonishes his children, and at this rate I'll still be trying to learn the forest when I'm a pensioner.

We stopped for the usual ritual, decorating ourselves for the forest. Pablito peeled open the yellow leafshoots from a mawate palm, and the children ran about as if this was a fancy dress party, excitedly making these into leafbands and carefully striping them with purple dye from a tree leaf, *wakamy-o kaspee*. I was more inter-ested in getting on with hunting, but Lucy ran up and put waist bands and arm bands on me as she had already done with Roberto. It made me feel better. If I could only wear the jaguar whiskers too, I thought, then I could, like them, be a stealthy predator.

Before he left, Pablito pulled off his shorts. Instead he now has more traditional dress – only a bark strip around his waist with which to tuck his penis up out of the way. He is also wearing gym shoes, which Armando accidentally left behind.

I'm wearing my shorts, as always, but the others have a carefree attitude to clothing. They take their clothes off when it rains, and forget to put them on afterwards. Lucy is a little slower to take off her little skirt – she is just becoming aware of herself.

Then Pablito walked off ahead, looking about for timber to reinforce the *maloca* for the weight of my hammock. The three of us followed behind.

The children keep touching the forest – tapping barks, fingering leaves, reminding themselves of species they know. But if only they would apply themselves more to hunting for food. They did find an egg on the ground as they skipped along. Roberto fashioned a little rucksack of leaves – *matchee-mungó* – to put it in, and sauntered on.

They played with lizards, blew leaf whistles. I keep hoping Roberto and Lucy are going to turn back, trot home to the camp.


## Shortly after

Has just dawned on me that the children are not going back. We are going to be out here all day: in Lucy's little palm leaf rucksack are a load of boiled yucca, our lunch.

And it's going to be the same every day here. Pablito has put me in the kindergarten class. But the thing is, I can't afford to start from childhood! Pablito has no sense of the deadline I'm facing.


## Two hours later

I'm resigned to my place behind the two children.

Silence has settled on the forest of the afternoon. I'm squatting with the 'other' children in front of Pablito, who has assembled the bark of a number of trees – white sap, beetroot sap, all sorts of sap, bleeds out. One of them smells like frankincense, another has a smell like Evo-stik [glue]. I'm now utterly confused, assaulted by the species variety. And what *use* do these plants have? They all look like poisons.

One shrub has long, wrinkled leaves of olive green. '*Shi-ta-chit*,' Pablito calls it. Having told me this he let the leaves fall from his hands and dug at the sapling's roots with the tip of his bow. He bit into one root, and passed it on. I was at the end of the line. By the time the root reached me both Roberto and Lucy had chewed it, and it was already horribly wet and warm when I put it in my mouth. It numbed my tongue, and that's how I know it's an anaesthetic.*

Pablito hardly talks out here in the forest. In fact, there's not

---

* An ethnobotanist studying the Chácobo tribe of Bolivia, has estimated that, in a one-hectare forest site, the community made use of 82% of all the species and 95% of the individual trees. See Brian M. Boom, 'Ethnobotany of the Chácobo Indians'.

much talking even back at the camp. The children learn by copying, not asking. Pablito starts a job – now, for example, cutting a bigger bow for Roberto – and passes it on for his little son to help finish. Again, I have this image in my head of jaguar cubs learning through imitation. Copy cats.

And we all watch together as Pablito crouches, motionless, fanning his lips to emit a bird's pensive whistle. Together we hear the unsuspecting bird answer him.

Then we watch him fire an arrow. It thwacks off, and rattles down again, landing on the forest floor with a bird stuck on it.

A feeling of pride – I now have my very own spear, made by Pablito. I say 'made', but he chopped it out of a long, single-stem palm that looked like a ready-moulded spear. '*Ponee-a*', he called it. Had he sculpted this, it would have been a beautiful piece of craftsmanship. But the art was in the choosing of the wood, not the crafting of it. Pablito's skill showed, even in a piece of stick. There's so much to learn – it makes you want to pack up and go home. But I'm settling into the timeless way of things.

16 NOVEMBER

Again, I was off in the forest with the children this morning. I'm beginning to enjoy these nursery days, running off together out of sight, and then stopping while Lucy makes leaf bands and decorates Roberto and me, her playmates.

A monkey gave its early morning growl, and we all called its name together, '*achoo!*', and then ran off further through the trees. Even with all the noise we make, Roberto managed to surprise a junglefowl, a perdís, and zap it with one of his toy arrows. In the bird's insides was a bright turquoise egg.

Although I can't help wishing I were spending my time with Pablito, not Lucy, sometimes I see her little black eyes looking around at the forest, and I'm reminded that she's all I need in a tutor.

She stands gazing, lets her mind travel wherever the forest takes it. The Indian 'relaxes within his universe', Adrian Cowell wrote in *The Heart of the Forest*. 'He does not struggle through it like we do.' One might imagine the author had in mind someone of the stature of Pablito, but here's a child doing this magic thing he described, and she knows more than I can ever learn.

17 NOVEMBER

I've been fishing for piranhas all morning with Roberto. He wouldn't let Lucy join in. She accepted this, but went away rather sorrowfully. The piranhas here are dozy. Someone has been over-feeding them or something.

Now, back in the camp, Lucy is sitting playing with a cluster of palm spikes, about five of them. She's toying with the idea of tattooing her face. At present she is unmarked. Her mother is encouraging her, wiping her fingers over Lucy's clear cheeks, which seem as white as ivory in the dark of the forest.

Her mother is now patterning her with soot from the fire [the ingredient for tattoos], marking a delicate track across her small face.

Roberto is pretending not to be interested. He's perfecting his new, grown-up size (almost) bow – from 'nyi-ha', a palm with spines.

Lucy has lost her nerve. She went to see her face in the reflection of the water, and came back having washed the soot off. Roberto, who was climbing a nearby tree, teased her for not daring, chucking down twigs at her like a monkey.

Now their mother is swinging on a vine, sitting as gracefully as an Edwardian lady on a garden swing, though of course she's topless.

Pablito just a moment ago brought over a stem from a giant palm and fashioned from it a sharp, aseptic knife. From his wife's sign language I understand it is used to give women a Caesarean section. I'm impressed that these people have everything they need here, of course, and I'm having fun pottering with the children, but my old fears are coming back again. Time is ebbing away, and I'm learning little of immediate use. For example, how likely am I to need a Caesarean section?

[From now on, this was continuously on my mind. Learning these things was the work of an ethno-botanist while my job just now was to learn sufficient to get out of here. I was still thinking in terms of words like 'survival'.

There followed seven exasperating days, in which I seemed to spend my time learning about medicines for fungus infections, or of 'miskee-panga' leaves which released a sweet fragrance like perfume, or 'klabo-waska', a liana for arthritis and rheumatism.

However, I tried to put a brave face on it, and take things as they came.]

24 NOVEMBER

Today I went into the forest with Lucy and Roberto, as usual entering into the spirit of things by skipping along like them, and feeling like a little boy on an outing. After playing about for an hour, Lucy suddenly turned to me, and said, in a whisper, '*Perdido*. Lost.'

*Lost?* I couldn't believe my ears. I stared at her in disbelief, thinking, 'But you're an Indian, for heaven's sake! Indians don't get lost.' I looked about us at the black, faceless forest, beginning to feel panic rising up in me.

But Lucy wasn't panicking. She prodded Roberto and instructed him to call out in the direction of the camp. 'Woooooooah!' he shrieked. I tried as well, but there was no answer.

Roberto, being a male, had always led the hunting games, but now we were in a crisis: he immediately handed the problem to a girl to sort out. Lucy got down on the ground, and stared at it, so close she might have been an animal sniffing for tracks, not looking for them.

This little ten-year-old was now inspecting the ground with her fingers. Stalking forward, she spotted a leaf which had been turned over by one of our feet – its wet underside showed. 'Roberto,' she noted to herself.

Next, she noticed an impression in the leaves. 'Lucy,' she said. After a few yards more, a large footprint, where some clumsy oaf had slipped in the mud. 'Beneeee,' she commented. We made our way home like this, Roberto chipping in when he thought he remembered a tree, or saw a leaf that we had bruised. Once we stopped for a rest while Lucy ducked off the path to gather food for us. When she reappeared, she had a handful of edible plant shoots, mainly fern tips. She carefully divided them in two, giving us half

each and taking none for herself. On we went. After a while, Roberto
and I just let her get on with it – useless men. After another while,
Lucy stopped to whack open an edible palm, and divided the white
core in two for us to eat. The little girl led us home.

We were saved. But, I have to ask myself, will I ever be able to
do what Lucy did? Hope to God I'm never tested.

What can I do, actually? I know how to eat the core of the palm
wa-sai-ee, I know of flaky barked vines to drink water from, like
pao-wheel chakee; roots from which you can chew water. There is
tami-shee, a stringlike vine used in construction, and even wakra-
pona – you skin off the white fibrous tissue of its spoke-like roots,
and make it into a poultice for a snake bite.

It's not enough.

I went hunting by myself today. Even before I could set out,
Roberto had to fix my arrow flights, which were mangled from
yesterday. [The arrow flights, or feathers, consisted of three feather
halves stuck on to the arrow with resin and further secured with a
thin cotton strand. I'd carelessly left the arrows in direct sunlight
and the resin had melted.]

Today, I was determined to come back having caught something.
*Anything.* Eventually I chanced on a sloth. It was only a baby. I
ignored it at first but after an entire day in the forest without luck,
I came back to find it. I shot three arrows. Missed. Tried again. In
the end I found it easier to shake the sloth down. However, in the
process of falling from the tree, the sloth landed in a muddy puddle.
It now looked like a drowned rat, except with big, friendly black
eyes.* I carried the poor creature back to the camp. Surely it was

* This most harmless of mammals, top speed one mile an hour, is from the same
scientific order as the anteaters and armadillos. It sleeps, mates, eats and gives
birth while hanging upside down with hook claws. The coat, too, grows upside
down, so that the rain runs off, and on it flourishes an alga which gives the sloth
a slightly green camouflage – and also attracts a population of moths. On the
rare occasions a sloth travels along the forest floor it is awkward, crawling along
spreadeagled. Some individuals spend their whole lives inching around just one
tree. Mine was a three-toed species, which feeds mostly on the leaves of the *Cecropia*
tree; it comes down out of its tree once a week, digs a hole with its stumpy tail,
and drops its faeces into it. The two-toed variety defecates, as it does everything
else, while hanging upside down from its branch.

better than nothing. When I arrived, Lucy jumped up and down, wheezing with laughter. Roberto danced around singing, 'cling-cleng,' the sound my ridiculous camera makes.

Now Lucy has given me a nickname. It seems to mean 'the catcher of poor sloths'.

The worse thing is, they've all seen this particular sloth many times already. Roberto took the docile creature all the way back to its tree.

25 NOVEMBER, NOON

Pablito must think I've progressed in some way though, because today, at last, I've been honoured to go hunting with him, not dumped with the kids.

Leaves are splayed over us, the light in spindles from the canopy, and insects, true kings of the forest, jiggering about. I'm alone with Pablito and his wife, at last. We're following the new track of a tapir.

It's mid-afternoon and the forest is sizzling. We've stopped for lunch and rest. Pablito used tree resin to help the fire catch, while I made myself useful by cutting leaves for us to sit on. We have fish to cook. With no children here we are strongly aware of each other.

*Later*

Soon after, Pablito took some achiote pods and began painting his wife with red cheek bands; she then did the same to him.

Pablito spun palm leaf stems into the holes in his lips to make his whiskers and the woman placed long whisker strands into her nose, decorating them with red bands.

Afterwards, Pablito started decorating me. It was an intimate act that you might, in the west, do for your child. It was the first time he has done this himself, and it felt like an investiture. I watched his fingers as they worked. He is very loose-knuckled. His fingers bend, giving to the pressure of the surface of whatever he lays them on.

208

RIGHT: Pablito as a
'jaguar man'.

BELOW: Pablito during the
journey up the Galvez – his
'jaguar whiskers' visible as he
heads into the interior.

LEFT: Pablito's third wife breast-feeding the latest of his thirty-odd children.

BELOW: The author's forest tutor Lucy brandishing some of her healing herbs.

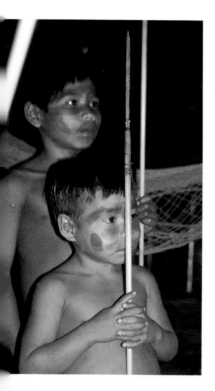

ABOVE: Pablito, with bow and arrow.

LEFT: Two of the author's fellow pupils of the forest – Roberto at the rear.

BELOW: 'Escapee' mission Indians, during a grooming session at Santa Rosa.

LEFT: An armed Helena, at Anushi.

BELOW LEFT: A young sloth, wet from a fall into the water after hot pursuit by the author.

BELOW RIGHT: Roberto and his brother, bathing at Anushi.

ABOVE: The girl of the Santa Rosa *maloca*.

BELOW: The author receiving the jaguar stripes from Pablito.

ABOVE: A Matsés hunting party on the upper Javari.

BELOW: A quiet moment with Pablito during a hunting expedition.

OPPOSITE:

ABOVE: Administering mind-clarifying snuff to Pablito.

BELOW: Matsés child with a play canoe on the River Javari.

ABOVE: The author emerging from the Amazon at the Mato Grosso – after seven months and 5800 kilometres.

RIGHT: A cattle rancher in the region of the Mato Grosso.

Maybe I *have* learnt something all this last week. I'm well aware that the paint is not just a badge to tell you you're a Matsés, it's seen as a protective layer against malicious spirits, a coating of invisibility. Outsiders aren't painted, because the spirits have no hold on them; now I am considered a little more visible to the spirits, and I need the protection. I feel something a bit like pride. Time stilled a little for me as he painted.

On the walk I was conscious of the guiding hand of this man Pablito. Always near, always with me. He really is fond of me, he really does care. Being led through forest brought me closer to him. We were united under the sensations it poured at us – the steady quavering of insects, the chirruping of frogs. The red paint makes me part of his family, and also part of the forest. However, as we walked on, our attention moved away from each other and to the forest, as we settled deeply into the arrangement.

I've taken encouragement from Pablito's inclusion of me.

My senses are certainly sharper. I can pinpoint sounds better. And I've just been watching a snake, the way it betrays its presence only by the slow thickening on a ridge of muscle as it moves.

This is what I've learnt – how movement is the great betrayer in the forest. If an animal does not move, it's fairly safe. Insects rely on their mating calls to locate each other. The movement of the larger animals, rodents and other mammals, is done at night.

The sloth doesn't move much at all.


26 NOVEMBER · *In camp*

Now I've learnt two traps. One is made of a log which drops on rodents when they remove the bait and trigger the mechanism. Effectively, it's a 50 kilo mousetrap.

The second trap is a springy pole tied at its upper end against a tree trunk. The lower, free end is spiked and sprung to slap against the tree by means of a trip wire. Could kill a jaguar, or – if I wander across it in my absent-minded way – me.

Something happened today which made me stop in my tracks. I was fishing with Roberto, trying to summon those piranhas by threshing the rod in the water, and Roberto caught a small fish. Before I knew it I had killed it. Not by thumping it on a root, because one wasn't available, but by raising it to my mouth and biting through its neck.

It's what a Matsés might have done.

All the forest's strangling plants, bitings, betrayals have been – *are* – changing me. I am becoming something more like the forest. Tenacious, a survivor. Have hardened myself to be able to kill, to be able to be part of the forest process. By copying these people who rip insects apart for fun I am being hardened into a forest creature. Scares me.

Just as well I'm harmless to most wildlife.

So what does the jaguar mean to these people? It doesn't seem to be a 'god' or 'spirit' to them, something they might want to pray to. It is simply an animal that happens to favour the wetter reaches of the forest as they do, and one they'd do well to copy. It suits them – stealthy, powerful, nomadic.

They imbibe the character of the jaguar in the same way that the Niowra [who I lived with in Papua New Guinea], seeking to survive in tough head-hunting country, have copied the top animal of their forest, the crocodile. The Niowra have formalized the arrangement, putting their young through a crocodile initiation ceremony. They take them to a ritual Crocodile Nest, and with beating sticks toughen their children into that voracious reptile.

27 NOVEMBER

[The next day we were suddenly on the move, the camp abandoned. I wrote the following while we came back down the Galvez in the canoe.]

Nomads will be nomads. Now we are off downstream without warning. We have only two paddles, and Pablito's wife is happy to steer in the stern, Pablito ahead. We children sit in the middle.

Seem to be going to 'Santa Rosa', a place I've never heard of. It's on the Choba [highish on the Javari] so I suspect he's hoping for help from Armando and my trusty motor.

210

A pleasant day, watching the turtles flip into the water from the riversides, the bats blow away silently from their log eves.

## 29 NOVEMBER

[We made very fast progress over two days, and just past Bien Peru we came to a track on the left bank. No sooner had we arrived, than the family unit went into action. Lucy and her mother automatically set about gathering wood for a fire and Roberto went to the river bank to catch some fish. Pablito, however, began preparing himself for the forest, painting broad red bands across his face. As I was trying to take a photo, he reached over and smeared paint on my cheeks. I guessed then that he had brought me here specially, to take me to see something.]

Pablito has just called Lucy to come and translate what he was trying to tell me earlier. She said, '*Serpiente graaaaande.*' Biiiiig snake. '*Casa de serpiente.*' She pointed with one finger into the forest. 'Snake's house.' Pablito looked around for a tree to indicate the snake's size. He was having difficulty – there wasn't a tree around here that was big enough.

As I understand it from Lucy, a giant snake lives in the lake, which is often poisoned with barbasco [and something called *wáká*, which has fruit like elderberries and grew in a garden plot around the home]. All in an attempt to kill the beast.

Also running through my head was a memory of something the crook Fidencio said: that the most prominent of all the spirits and bush demons in the Mayoruna forest is a monstrous water snake.

'So it's not safe enough for us,' I said, now hoping to cancel the visit.

Pablito, meanwhile, has now settled for a tree of about two feet or more in diameter. That's the size of the snake.

Oh gawd. Do we have to go and see this Thing?

Pablito led off down the track. The forest was dark and thick, the ground cover sparse and the floor wet, as if it had recently been flooded. I watched Pablito's eyes as they moved slowly about him – he was sensing more than watching.

Now, still within earshot of the camp, Pablito slowed. He was bent, slinking forward, holding his breath, his feet absolutely quiet as he placed them down on the leaves. Suddenly I had forgotten about the spines and hard roots that were hurting my feet, and was holding my breath too.

'If Pablito's afraid, I should be,' I thought.

Pablito moved slower and slower, so I knew we were coming to something. I looked up and around, trying to keep up with Pablito, as he watched, and smelt, and listened. Now I wasn't enjoying myself. This was my guide, and I could see he had brought me to a place he wasn't certain of. And to my amazement – not to say horror – I found I could no longer take comfort in my western· upbringing, the questioning, doubting world from which I had come. I'd left it all behind. I too could believe in this giant serpent.

'No buen,' Pablito said, suddenly, making me jump. It was so rare to hear his voice in the forest.

He spread his arm in front of me, a way of indicating the small lake that was shining with silver light beyond the black trunks. The light reflected on to his face, playing geometric patterns on the painted skin and shiny black eyes.

We stopped at the base of an extraordinary, rooted tree. The roots were giant snakes in themselves. It was unnerving just to look around. This monster was so vast we might not even be able to see we were standing somewhere in the middle of its coils.

I stood with Pablito, waiting as his instincts filtered the waste noises – the background wood-crickets, the frogs – and assembled a picture to do with the flux of the forest itself: the patterns of disturbance created by the merest breath of creatures, their consciousness resounding on other animals which lay in wait, or fear.

Infinitely slowly we tiptoed forward to the lake. It was calm. Not a ripple in all that silver water.

CRAAASH! There was a resounding smack of a giant animal's belly hitting the lake surface, then the whoosh of this animal surging through the water. Before I knew it, Pablito was off out of here. He sped past me, screaming 'Beneeeeeeeeeeeeeeee!' and bounded off back up the track.

I was already at his heels.

When we came tearing into the camp we found the rest of the

family already throwing themselves into the canoe for a quick getaway. It was an impressive team effort.

Whether it was 'just' a cayman that we heard, I don't know. But ironically enough, that creepy spot has helped me see how much more at ease I've become in other, normal forest. I feel this *could* be a home for me. I don't ever need to panic, when I'm up there in Brazil. Not unless I encounter a creature like that one . . .

*Later*

However, I do wish I could take Lucy on my journey. I'd gladly swap her for the mustard.

# XI

# It Looks Like Suicide

### BASED ON MY DIARY

30 NOVEMBER · *Anushi*

Armando was fetched from Angamos. He hadn't heard of 'Santa Rosa' either. However, it was clearly a community favoured by Pablito, so we agreed to go on an expedition up the Javari to visit the settlement, which was on the Choba, a Peruvian tributary.

Armando's very first words were not, 'Hello, how are you?' They were, 'Can you live off the forest yet?'

'Not exactly,' I said. 'But I feel better about it. The forest even feels a little homely.'

'Homely? How very nice for you,' he said, drily.

Two or three weeks more, I can allow myself. Such is my confidence in myself that I've now gone through my luggage [which Armando had brought up from Angamos], desperately trying to assemble a survival kit: heavy duty fishing line, packets of blades, fishing hooks. Gone are my dreams of taking it easy on my walk through Brazil's forest. It's now just going to be a question of getting by.

Still, Pablito hasn't given up on me.

*En route south up the Upper Javari, to the Choba tributary and 'Santa Rosa' with just Armando and Pablito*

On either side of me there's a pretty forest billowing high up on either bank. This is the jungle just as people back home like to

214

draw it – dangling fronds, vines, shrubby palm clumps, leaning palm trunks. The reality is generally far less gracious.

In places on the Brazilian side of the river logging teams have been at work, selectively felling, and hoiking out trees along occasional paths that are the width of main roads.* Otherwise, fairly 'virgin' forest – or rather *silent* forest, emptied of Indians.

On the right hand side, we have just passed Cashishbi, a Matsés settlement said to be dangerous.

The Cashishbis have many tin roofs, but are no calmer for that. Hearing our engine, they crowded down to the river and began waving their fists like the chorus of a bad drama company.

'No buen,' Pablito said sadly. 'Santa Rosa,' he said. 'Buen.'

Is Pablito *really* sure Santa Rosa is friendly? I now recall that Louis wrote HOSTILE INDIANS on the Choba, the tributary where we are going.

1 DECEMBER

We slept overnight at a remote hunting shack. Piums, the biting flies, were everywhere and merciless.

We've now turned off to the right (west) down the Choba.

Two felled trees have blocked our way so far. Armando hacked through them. He thinks they have been laid there on purpose, but Pablito seems undaunted. He is in the prow, so I expect he'll be the first to be shot.

A twiggy insect, like a mottled briar twig, is plodding about on the lip of the canoe. If it falls in, that means I won't succeed in my lone journey out of here . . .

The insect has speeded up – apparently feeling alarmed and out of place among the petrol cans. It has fallen in. Dramatically, the hapless invertebrate jumped overboard. It looked like suicide. The little incident seems all the more tragic because the insect was so much just a frail twig. Perhaps few other species recognize it as even

---

* So far, not much damage on the Javari – but in total 400,000 km² of the Amazon Basin has been deforested. See *Manchete* magazine.

belonging to the animal kingdom. The twiggy creature struggled half-heartedly as a fish came to the surface, and removed its legs, one by one.

We have slowed right down. There's a canoe moored against the bank. Two dead curassow are hidden under a wide paddle, and two magpie-like scrounging birds are hopping about, trying to get at them. Also here, a set of arrows made with – appropriately enough – arrowreed stems. Pablito is busy assessing what this all means. He is looking about at the forest, reading its leaves.

Is he *really* sure this place is friendly?

*Later*

Around the next river loop was a village, set on the right hand bank beyond a muddy lawn. There was one *maloca* and also a line of new rectangular houses. It all seemed horribly silent.

'Santa Rosa?' I asked, hoping it wasn't.

But it was. Adults were eyeing us from their houses. At the back of the buildings were a sprinkling of children tugging at each other in anguish. Clothes were hanging off them like tired Christmas decorations, or ripped flags.

While Pablito again assessed the situation, the tension was suddenly broken by the arrival behind us of the canoe we'd seen downriver. In it was a crotchety old man who wasn't going to have his day ruined by anybody. He paddled right on by. Behind him in the canoe was a lithe and yet extremely bosomy girl. Blue beads were strapped tightly across her bare chest and shoulders, bunching her puppy flesh.

Pablito signalled us to tie up. And then he saw a man, a teenager, emerge from the *maloca* and he let out a whoop of greeting. The young man whooped back and gave Pablito a shy smile.

We walked up the bank, tailing Pablito towards the *maloca*. We ducked and entered its gloom. Suddenly we were unbothered by the biting piums and we were embraced by coolness.

'Buen,' said Pablito, holding the teenager around the waist.

This turned out to be a son of his. We sat in hammocks around him, while one woman, the boy's first wife, ran outside to fill a pot of water to boil yucca, and a smaller, younger wife kicked logs into the fire to raise some flames.

One of the wives had been weaving a string hammock and it lay stretched, half-finished between two poles. Maize was stacked up on a shelf near the roof. There were no inner walls, but a few structural posts which gave the *maloca* two partitions and two fire-places.

We've been here all morning. Now the fire is hurling out an orange light. Pablito is talking to his teenage son, joking about how I hunt – my height, my heavy feet.

In a moment he'll tell the story of my sloth, and I'll be even more of a laughing stock.

*Later*

The young second wife spun a pot of boiled yucca on to the clay floor for us. Armando and I have eaten some of this and retired to our hammocks, feeling sleepy from the journey. We're listening to Pablito talking, and watching the wives run about. The older wife has a large ant hanging from her chin. It stays there, clamping its jaws on her, motionless. Armando says it's a treatment to get rid of a mole.

The younger wife keeps herself even busier. Pablito's son, who speaks some Spanish, says he's taken the woman into his house because both her parents have died. As far as we can see, she isn't really a 'woman' at all – she's a girl of perhaps twelve. She had a firm, rounded-out stomach and the way the navel rests high on it she might conceivably be pregnant.

She has a way of looking up through her fringe with an alarming coyness, wondering what we are saying about her.

2 DECEMBER

Last night we were woken in the dark by our host, Pablito's son, who said that a hunting party had arrived and was planning to steal our canoe and everything in it.

217

Apparently this Matsés village was founded by escapees from the Two Harriets' mission, which is not far from here. The thief is the latest escapee. 'Thou shalt not steal' doesn't seem to have sunk in.

We went out into the night, walking back and forward in the rain as we collected our stuff. On each trip we were attacked by waves of snapping dogs.

This morning I'm sitting writing outside – the strips of mist around me falling away like protective wadding from the trees. A dog is eating a fish head that's bigger than mine. A line of Indian women are picking lice from each other's hair.

Around the village, captured wildlife stalks. There's a curassow that has fallen in love with another curassow, which has fallen for a parakeet, which has fallen for a sun bittern [a relative of the heron]. And this has fallen in love with a chicken – any chicken it can jump on. The dogs, though a desperate mob, are pecked viciously if they don't get out of the way when the preening parade comes by.

Pablito is outside with me, squatting with another older man, who is smoothing the flights of the arrows. The companion is the man who wanted to rob us. He sits there, shifting his shifty eyes, but Pablito just takes him as he comes – as he does the world.

The little wife is coming up from the beach, carrying her pot of water on her head. She's the height of my solar plexus, and with raggedy-gypsy hair.

Pablito and the older Indian are fascinated by her. Now she's with a little boy, playing with a knife, hurling it into the sand. She has quiet but lit-up eyes. She moves like a model, angling her face at me, matching my glances. A girl's ungainly legs, her face well advanced, and her bosom in between.

Any minute, Armando is going to fall in love with her – I just get a feeling.

[Soon after, Pablito and I went off hunting with bows and arrows. I found another sloth. Although I didn't bring it to the village Pablito certainly ensured the story came back with us.]

I've come back to find Armando forlorn, listless. He's in love with the girl/woman. Trouble is, we all are. She walks about, well aware of the effect she has on us men. All we can do is stare. *'Champee!'* sighs Pablito.

I could hardly believe what I saw next. She stood outside in the sunshine, innocently playing with other children, while sucking on a condom.

Armando, when he had recovered from the sight, explained that these are just curiosities out here – in fact they are curiosities even in Angamos. They are easier to get than party balloons. It was the first the girl had seen of anything balloon-like and she was trying to learn to blow it up – the milky rubber expanding and deflating between her pink lips. It was too much for Armando. 'I'm going on a long walk,' he said, and left hurriedly.

A heavy rain came in the afternoon. She danced as the water tumbled down, skipping about, intoxicated by the effect she was having on everyone – Pablito, Armando, old man, and even me, who has other worries on my mind. TIME IS TICKING AWAY. Meanwhile, she is fascinated by this new power she has. Now she's watching me out there in the rain as I write under a palm shelter. Her hands are full of powdered milk that Armando brought with us, and are raised above her head catching rain drops off the *maloca* roof. While her eyes study me, she lowers her hands to her mouth and licks at the wetted milk powder.

*Later*

Armando has brought out some Christmas fireworks, sparklers that he's brought up from Angamos. When the first sparkler burst into life the girl let out a shriek and, just like her husband and Pablito, ran for cover. Armando handed her one, carefully taking the opportunity to hold her hand as comfort. She stamped on his foot, and he went away limping. Now her husband is painting the girl's face red. He seems to think the fireworks signify a festival.

Armando is watching a little boy coming and going. The child has access to this second wife and Armando does not. She calls out to the boy, roughly, and he comes. A shock: the 'little boy' is in fact about her age.

*That evening*

Pablito sits on the *maloca* floor, talking with his son and a couple of older men. A torch of resin is burning in a leaf, placed on a log on the damp clay. It smells of incense, a scent that seems to warm the *maloca* and the night. The men talked about the good old days – the fights, the raids on the Marúbos, the Remo-aucas, the *mestizos*.

The son translated for me, telling me how they learnt to grow manioc by capturing *mestizo* women and making them show them how. Pablito remembered Sophia, the woman who taught Harriet their language. He didn't capture her himself, but he remembers her kicking and screaming. She hardly taught them anything, but he'd heard she made a good wife. Then she ran off. Before they could snatch her back, she had built a raft and was away.

Pablito remembered his childhood as being one of movement. They were always abandoning camps, and moving on. In those days they had occasional small gardens of yucca, maize, peanuts, sweet potatoes and pumpkins, but these were kept only irregularly and they preferred the freedom of wandering between the palm stands, and climbing for the fruit of palms like assaí and chonta – the tree that also provided their bow wood. They also had wild cotton, and the women spun fibres for string bags and hammocks. As the Matsés adopted a more formal horticulture, with large slash-and-burn gardens of maize and manioc, the Marúbos were able, in turn, to learn from the Matsés – by the practised method of capturing their women.

The girl is watching me write, her head angled in curiosity. Just now, she brought out a bowl of yucca. It was for me, not Armando, and she barged him out of the way with her elbow.

Pablito is now telling his son how he ate his grandparents.

'All of them?' Armando asked. It did sound almost greedy. Apparently not, because in answer to this Pablito let out a throaty roar, imitating how he had been sick as a child, when handed a piece of grandfather.

'It's the best bit!' Pablito's aunt had said to him.

The little Pablito had looked at the flesh. 'But it's a penis!'

His aunt snatched it from the ungrateful boy and brought him another bit, slapping it crossly into his hand.

'But it's a vagina!'

The story-telling is still going on and all the time the wife/child is at the central fire, stoking it with her immaculate toe. Sometimes she looks up in this direction. Wish she wouldn't, because her husband laughs about this with his first wife. Their eyes move between the two of us, watching for developments.

## 3 DECEMBER

I've got up early. The clouds are towering. There'll be rain.

Something strange has happened. Pablito's son squatted himself down at the fire, dressed just in his shorts. He put a bit of cord in the fire, and then, drawing in a deep breath, took the burning end in his hand, and stubbed it into his upper arm. Seeing me gawp, he laughed. He showed me circular scars in rows on his arm. The same marks are on the breasts of his older wife, from rituals gone by.

The son has now applied a secretion they call *sapo* to the wound, a clear substance secreted by the skin of a toad or frog. The *sapo* cleared his head, he said, and allowed him to get 'nearer', *más cerca*, to the forest. These were his last words of explanation. As I write he is squatting by the doorway with a feverish look on his face. He can't talk. His mind has gone. Sweat is pouring off him. The dogs are edging away from him. And now . . . yes, he's retching all over my luggage.

## In the afternoon

Pablito has guided his son safely to the forest – he still looks a shivering wreck – and left him there. I hope he knows what he's doing.

## That night

The son returned to the village after dark through the yucca garden, and with no torch. He didn't succeed in hunting down anything in his purified state, but that he found himself home at all seems to me a miracle.

I indicated to Pablito that maybe I should resort to *sapo*. It might help me get 'nearer' to the forest. Pablito thinks it's a bad idea. Perhaps he thinks I couldn't handle it. Perhaps he's right. The son, though, is now full of energy, and can't stop talking. Clearly he's still under the influence.

While we talk, the girl-wife-child is spinning cotton. Armando's eyes are on her fingers as they work a puff of it into a thread, teasing a strand out to a spinning bobbin made from the top of an old tin can. She lifts the bobbin up and down, up and down in front of her chest, which also rises and falls, raising her year-old bosom. For a child, she's quite a woman.

'When do you want to leave Santa Rosa?' Armando said, watching her. 'I don't think I can stand it any longer.' He really is smitten.

I've been wondering why there appears to be a lack of any formal initiation ceremony, a time when children, in the timeless forest, are marked as adults. However, Pablito's son is telling us about a time when, as a boy, Pablito was invited for the first time to a feast held by the men, when all the forest spirits were 'invited' in out of the darkness. As the men chanted a song, calling on the harpy eagle, the jaguar, the cayman and other creatures of the forest to come and share the festival, the animals did indeed appear. Their different spirits entered the bodies of the men, who took on their physical characteristics, putting on decorated hoods made of bark skin and dancing in front of the assembled company.

There were no formal rituals of manhood, though the young were tested to see if they were ready to join the adult raids on other tribes – and on rubber tappers, for that matter. Pablito recalled the day two older brothers brought him an alligator, hoisting the giant beast in front of him. They asked the young Pablito if he was brave or a coward. Pablito knew he was about to be tested and said he was brave – he was too scared to admit he wasn't. The alligator's mouth was prised open by the two men and Pablito was invited to show his bravery by putting his hand down the alligator's throat. He was so scared, at first he couldn't do it with his eyes open – they had to steer his hand. Into the mouth it went, into the warmth and slime. Deeper and deeper, while the alligator kicked and thrashed, staring with its cold, furious eyes. Suddenly, when it

222

looked as though the alligator would break free, the men yanked Pablito away. He was man enough.*

The men will talk into the night as usual, and the girl will stay up for them, dark eyes soft in the firelight. She spreads light around the *maloca* – I mean that literally. Her job is to tap the resin lantern when it grows dim, and to jiggle it into life.

I remember very clearly making a rule that I wasn't going to get drawn into the Dusky Maiden Syndrome – that is, see innocent beauty in these Amazon females, fall victim like so many previous travellers to half a millennium of mythology.

But there again, Pablito is an Indian, not a white man – and he can't take his eyes off the girl. It just must be *her*.

4 DECEMBER · *In the forest, around midday*

Early this morning I went off into the forest with Pablito, his son and *her*. Armando stood on the bank like a sick puppy, watching us go. He had better pull himself together soon. She's a third his age, and younger than Lolita.

We drew the canoe up at the hunters' path not far away. By the river bank was a jaw of about the same size as mine, but this one belonging to a fish. It lay on a mossy trunk, picked clean by a forest cat or even otter.

Pablito sat me down and painted my face, while the others painted each other.

Afterwards, we paired off. I went with Pablito. The last I saw of the girl-wife she was burrowing into her cane daypack, unfurling a fish from a banana leaf, already treating herself to our lunch.

With Pablito this morning I learned how to stalk while clearing the path before me using a spear. [With this technique I could

---

* Among the wife-stealing Panoans women were always under threat of abduction, and perhaps because of this their puberty is considered of greater significance than the men's and is marked by ritual. Among other Panoans, girls were whipped or subjected to forms of circumcision. The Mayorunas, though, observed the first menstruation simply by secluding girls and feeding them a restricted diet. At the end of that time their bravery too was tested – for example, in the dark they were handed a parcel containing an electric eel, and invited to unwrap it.

advance my feet rapidly and silently through noisy and sharp sticks and leaves. Later, it was to prove a vital lesson.]

We have met up with them again just now, and are having lunch by the river. Pablito handed the girl a curassow which he had shot, an easy target while it was cold and damp from the mist. She began plucking it, then yanking its guts out. As she worked, jewels of sweat appeared on her nose. Now she's laid the bird in the fire, and has gone to wash her hands – she folds neatly in two as she bends to splash her arms.

Above us just now, there was a sudden crack – a branch had broken maybe a hundred feet up above us. As we ran for cover, the descending pieces struck lower branches and exploded overhead. The air began raining with chunks of tree, crooked javelins and massive clubs that shattered around us on the ground.

We're sitting about on palm leaves, waiting to eat. Pablito is trying to repair my arrow flights. Twice this morning he had to climb a tree (shinning up it) to get my arrows down. Now he's having to take over my work again, spinning the arrows in his fingers, warming the tar, re-sealing the flights. They are laid in a spiral, so the arrows spin as they fly. Not that it seems to help me.

I'm going to get an ulcer if I think about how long I've got left to learn in.

Giant bumble bees with foxy fur shoulders are examining the discarded bits of bird. If disturbed, these bees bully you, making a series of noisy passes.

Soon after I wrote the above, while we were all sitting about in the forest, Pablito produced a tube that he'd made by curling a palm leaf. With him he also had a dishevelled leaf wallet. 'Ner-nér,' he said, pointing at the green powder inside it. He pointed to his eyes, and told his son to explain. 'You eyes not so good.'

'There's something wrong with my eyes?'

He made me understand that there was something wrong with my eyes. Also my nose, my ears, my tongue – every part of my anatomy.

'You no good.'

I can't argue. Countless days I've spent hunting, and I've only caught a couple of sloths. Pathetic.

Pablito had, it now seemed, decided that I would never hunt

like a Matsés, a 'jaguar man'. Not, at least, without a little extra help.

'Now you try *ner-nér*.'

'What's *ner-nér*?' It was in fact a blend of coca, tobacco and *curupa* (leaves of the *Mimosa* genus), but by now I was ready to try rat poison if it would help me shoot straight.

Pablito gave his son some, so as to demonstrate. The two men squatted facing each other, and Pablito tilted his home-made tube to his son's right nostril. He placed a pinch of the green snuff into the other end of the tube, and – the son bracing himself – gave a short, sharp puff. Both men disappeared in a cloud of green smoke. It seemed to come out of the son's ears. The process was repeated for the other nostril and, before I could see through the green haze to tell if the son was crying, it was my turn.

I glanced at my audience. She was sitting with her legs out across the forest floor giving me a little peer through her thick fringe.

Pablito raised the tube and blew. The *ner-nér* seemed to hit the back of my skull, not the back of my nose. And when I had recovered from that blow, I found the rasping powder had left a dry track not just up my nose but also into my mouth, turning my tongue into a dry and leathery toadstool. I wiped my tongue on my wrist, and it left a jade green smear which irritated my bites.

Pablito wasn't finished. He blew again, this time into my left nostril. I kept my mouth shut, to stop the *ner-nér*'s passage. The powder chose a separate route, and went out of the other nostril, rasping as it went. I tried to get up – just to get away. But Pablito held me by the shoulder.

'*Más*,' his son said. More.

I was feeling drunk. There was green soot in my eye. 'I don't think –'

'*Más*,' said the son harshly. I suddenly wondered if I was being tortured for looking at his wife.

With the practised thumb of a pipe smoker, Pablito separated out yet another pinch and pitched the tube towards my nose.

I took two more doses, and stood up, bewildered, sniffing and spluttering in my green cloud. Seeing me stagger, the girl snorted, clapping her hand over her mouth to restrain her whinnying laughter, intertwining her toes as she tried to get a grip on herself.

Her husband was laughing even more uncontrollably. There was a look of profound satisfaction on his face.

Pablito also took *ner-nér*, and we all sat there a while, like country bumpkins at harvest time after too much scrumpy.

More than tipsy himself, Pablito began talking about Inti-shí, the moon. 'He look after time,' the son translated. 'He guide the good Matsés.'

The sun is of little importance to Pablito. God was the moon – '*Noheen papá*,' he said. 'Our father.' The forest, as perceived by Pablito's son, is not male or female, it is the forest. There's no mother earth, just the forces of the spirits around us, tugging, pushing, steering life along. Some are dangerous, devil-like and invisible, some simply the spirits of the dead that have lived on – we sometimes catch sight of them in the form of deer and other fleeting creatures. And some spirits we see as jaguars; this is the form taken by accursed people, who by day are men and by night transformed into stalking cats.

Pablito was now beginning a chant. It was a song to the heeke erapé, or harpy eagle, the regal bird that looked part owl, part eagle and was king of the air, as strong in its element as the jaguar, king of the land.

'Come, father harpy eagle . . .' This was the song from the feasts of the men, when the nature spirits were drawn out of the night into the *maloca* to be among them.

He sang away in happy drunkenness, and I looked about the humming forest around us and I felt sad. It was a happy scene, and I was going to break away from it in only a few days now and endanger myself; I was suddenly on the point of tears.

Our minds settled and it was time to go. Pablito pulled off his shorts and ripped off some soft tree bark for a belt with which to hang up his penis. We picked up the arrows and walked off together. I walked stiffly at first, trying to rope in my senses, kill this drunkenness.

Then I was aware of Pablito ahead of me, stalking an animal. My mind sharpened steadily as I watched. His head was down, and he was walking stealthily, hunched and taut. He was creeping forward, and then staying himself, stock still as he watched, poised, with his black eyes gleaming. I watched him go – stalking, checking himself, a prowling cat that was sliding out of sight through the greenery.

I was aware that my own mind was alert now. The forest was resonating just as before, but my senses did seem sharper, as if all the different intermixing sounds, all the strands of noise, had been unwoven for me. Just as I was adjusting myself to this new clarity, I found I had caught up with Pablito. He was bent over the leaf litter, examining some tracks of a paca, the nocturnal rodent that is like a tubby, well-meaning, almost tailless rat, with speckled white markings along its dark bronze sides.

The trail was lost but we returned to the riverbank and made a platform of sticks a short way up in the tree. We would wait for the paca here.

Now almost dusk. We will be out here in the dark without any light source. My mind beautifully clear. Movements seem magnified by the snuff, and I can pin-point the direction of sounds. So this is how a jaguar sees the world: a midge cloud moving like a fishing net, ants trickling like treacle down a tree, a cicada like a castanet on the bark above. Details are visible, yet there's only a grainy infusion of light now; a sprinkling of silver dust on every insect and leaf.

Girl, leaning her head on her arms, holding tight still in the last light. Those bright eyes large; face tilted to listen.

So young, so proficient. She is half sitting on the platform, her back to me, feet splayed against the treetrunk for support. When I concentrate I can hear her breath – as if we aren't in the midst of a croaking forest at all. Feel the warmth off her back, and a sort of hayloft comforting smell rising into my face from her.

Have to keep picturing myself in the school playground as a little boy in shorts playing conkers: that was what I was doing at this girl's age.

I could write and write, but it really is dark now.

*Later that night*

There was a huge splash. We jumped in the air with fright. My immediate thought was that Pablito's son had fallen into the water.

In fact it was a dolphin jumping – we all laughed, recovering from the shock.

In the dark too, an owl shriek that sent a chill through me. We waited, everyone silent.

The paca came without warning. I heard its rustle, but I only knew it was different from the other rustles because the girl touched my arm. It was time.

Suddenly, I heard the thwack of a loosed bowstring. There was a squawk. Pablito lit up a resin torch, and we found a paca pinned to the ground through its mouth. Pablito went to beat it with a stick, but too late: it had already died of fright.

Now we are back in the *maloca*, telling Armando about our adventure. We've already roasted the paca, which looks even more like an oversize rat than they usually do.

Armando, meanwhile, is more interested in watching *her* running about, as she looks after the *maloca* – one moment whacking the dogs to make them go outside, the next trimming the resin candle.

I said, 'I'm sure she's also a neat little sorter of firewood, and a busy little thing in the kitchen as well, but I don't think you ought to get involved.'

'You did, with *your* Mayorunita.'

'Didn't.'

'Did.' This childish bickering went on for some time.

Finally Armando sighed. 'Another night here and we'll all be killing each other over her.'

'Speak for yourself.'

Later, Armando became sombre. He said, 'Benedito, the water level is getting low here.'

It's his way of telling me that time is running out. It's time for me to face the horrors of Phase Three. I feel sick at the thought.


7 DECEMBER, DAWN

Pablito is down on the shoreline, scooping water from the canoe with his instep. We're off, just the two of us. Last minute coaching?

Correction. Not just the two of us. As I got into the canoe I was joined by the woman-girl-child-creature. She slotted in neatly

behind Pablito. I waited for her husband. But he wasn't coming –
I saw the girl's eyes flick to the mooring rope. She was wondering
why I was hesitating. I undid the rope and we cast off without
him. I wondered – briefly – if this was a good idea . . .

Now, mist is rising lazily off the water, the slate blue glassy
surface is looking about to burst into flames. Frogs are crackling
like electrical static. The leaf screens of forest on either side of us
are hardening in the sun. As we duck under outreaching boughs
the leaves flap over us like leather strops.

*Later*

Pablito walked off to the picnic spot [where last time we took
*ner-nér*]. When we had secured the canoe I followed him, and she
followed behind me. I was very conscious of the order in which
we were walking. With the Matsés you walked through the forest
playing follow my leader: I was the girl's leader.

Up until today I've been used to placing my big clumsy feet into
the short, wide footprints of Indians. But now Pablito was too far
ahead and I was having to feel my own way along. I couldn't hear
her movements, only my own, but I could imagine those cunning
little feet of hers parting the ground flora neatly behind me.

Already, by her quietness as we walked, I knew she was
responding to this world – I was still searching for it. I dreaded
the moment when she might hear a bird and signal me to zap it.
I tried to reassure myself: 'Think what you were like a few weeks
ago. Probably you're not too big a disgrace nowadays. You walk
quietly, you even move nimbly – for someone who's six foot four
and who can't even shoot straight.'

Pablito was at the picnic site. Oh dear: I noticed that he had
brought along a foot-length tube for blowing *ner-nér*. He squatted,
sorting through a leaf pouch like an old man thumbing through
tobacco.

I got down beside Pablito, and took my dose. Two blows up
each nostril. Pablito then gave me the tube to blow up his nose. I
put a large pinch of the stuff into the tube with my thumb, then
hesitated. How hard should I blow? But I hurried now, feeling my

own drunkenness coming on. A Dr Jekyll panic: my character was changing.

After giving Pablito his dose, I moved a little way off and squatted down. I felt a warm feeling all over. I was very woozy and happy and aware that I was laughing.

Suddenly, a little shriek from beside me – the girl. Hearing that noise of alarm, my mind sharpened. Pablito had yanked her to the ground beside him to receive a dose. She didn't squat, she sat down on the leaves, legs straight out, her short feet with their big white pads right under my nose.

Her brow wrinkled as she braced herself. Her eyes then fixed on Pablito's face as she held the tube to her nose, pleading with him to be gentle. She only took one blast. She coughed and spat, and walked in circles shaking her head. I think it must have been her first time.

After waiting a moment for our drunkenness to clear, we moved off. And before long, Pablito was off stalking again. He hunched down, slinking away out of sight, a big cat that hunts by itself.

As we walked on, alone, I now became aware of the girl. The effects of the snuff had been to give my senses a greater resolution and this should have given me confidence to hunt with her. But the *ner-nér* had made me aware of every feeling not just in the forest, but also between us.

In short, just when, at the end of my training programme, I felt empowered to hunt, I couldn't. I was far *too* conscious. For a while I tried, and I did enjoy the focused view of the forest, and – something unexpected this – a wonderful security. In this state I felt I could wander anywhere, and find myself home.

By chance white flowers began to percolate down from the tree tops overhead, falling on us and around us. As I stopped to look up, she began laughing and spun about, catching them. For perhaps half a minute we were showered by flowers. They had come from way up above us somewhere. We couldn't even see the higher branches from down here. Perhaps, outside the forest, there was wind, the sign of the onset of rain.

Then the flowers stopped coming, and the girl and I were facing each other. I went very hot, wondering what was going to happen next. She was watching me, hesitating, sorting through her feelings, a quick smile like a twitch, then frowning, and another sharp smile.

The rain came down then, slapping the leaves overhead, and spinning chains of water on to us.

Her hair was caught by the beating rain, but, as in a D. H. Lawrence novel, she let the elements do what they would with her. The rain teased out the strands, which played shapes around her eyes. She was still watching me. Then a smile broke into her eyes, and we were both laughing. We stood giggling in the rain together as it beat down on us. I was happy then; we both knew we would come away from this just friends.

We turned around and made our way back to the river through the rain. There was still that contented feeling, tucked away deep in my stomach. I'd had the privilege of a secret moment, access to a different world, and neither of us had destroyed it by seizing it.

She stopped once and bent to show me something. 'Mi-sha-maon'. It was a print from a tapir, now a muddied fist-mark, gathering cloudy water. Then she looked up into my eyes and gave another little chirrupy laugh.


9 DECEMBER

We are leaving this morning. The rains that came yesterday don't seem to have done anything for the water level of the Choba. We may get trapped here. Besides, I'm only delaying the inevitable. It's time to see what lies beyond the dreaded Batá . . .

The girl is sitting by the fire in the *maloca* refusing to look up. She's bent over and stabbing the uneven dirt with a knife. The little boy who normally pulls her away to come and play is standing back, giving her room. Who is she pining for? Armando? Me? Pablito? Or her husband? We are all leaving today and last night she was sharing her favours fairly evenly, even allowing Armando to draw his name on her with a biro.

Armando lit a sparkler to try to cheer her up. I left my hammock and lit another, forcing it into her little, unyielding hand. She couldn't help looking at the sparks, and she leapt up and danced about the cramped *maloca*, keeping the firework at arm's length.

'Buen *champee*,' Pablito said to me, seeing the girl dance and laugh. Good girl.

'Yes, good,' said the husband – although his eyes were on his inflammable *maloca*.

'*Too* good,' said Armando, packing our gear.

But the firework has done its magic. She is a child again.

[First Armando and I would conduct a short recce of the Batã, which was not much further up the Javari. Pablito and his son would come with us only some of the way, because of Pablito's fear of the rubber tappers. We would pick them up from somewhere on the Javari as we passed back down to Angamos. Then it would be time for my big launch.]

After we were out of sight of Santa Rosa, I said to Armando something to the effect of, 'Trouble with child brides is, I suppose, they are children. I mean, as in all arranged marriages, they never face the rough and tumble of competitive love, the trauma of love-pains, rejection, the loss of the ideal, the inevitable compromise, the coming to terms with life. That's the trouble with child brides.'

'Yes,' Armando said, disconsolately. 'I find that.'

He's still feeling rather sorry for himself, I'm afraid.

We've just passed a bird that looks like a heron; it has a pale blue beak, black cap on its head, a thin plume – I think white – foppishly hanging down its neck. It's a beautiful creature of its type, I'm sure, but unfortunately, because I don't recognize the species, it just reminds me how little of the forest I know. And the final countdown has begun.

I mustn't think like that. I've felt at home here with the Matsés, and I can do so again. However, the truth is, I have more than just the forest to worry about. I can make the quick dash that I've been preparing for. But I've got murderers/robbers and other miscellaneous villains ahead and I need their help with the tricky rubber tappers' paths.

As the river twists, the sun is moving around us. Sitting in the open canoe, it's like being cooked on a spit.

Pablito says Armando and I mustn't travel upriver at night. He says a 'black boa' will attack us. Only a month ago a huge snake climbed into a Cashishbi canoe and overturned it, he says. The black boas will 'eat our heads'.

The black boas are perhaps a myth – for the Indian, as well as white man, the forest creates symbols that represent our very real fears. Less mythical, however, is the light aircraft that has just flown low overhead. It's heading upriver. It's landing at an abandoned airstrip [built by oil prospectors] towards the head of the river. Drug traffickers – and we know all about them, don't we . . .

Armando thinks we'll be perfectly safe, as long as we don't see the traffickers at close quarters. They are certain to have gone by the time we pass there, *he says*.

*Camping on the river bank, that evening*

Pablito is padding around us in the forest, vacuuming up the edible things. What'll it be like without him?

We have the shotgun, which Armando keeps by him – a touch over the top, but it makes Pablito happier. I wish he would relax. Seeing him worried about the black boas and the rubber tappers doesn't do much for my confidence at this time.

Two million species of living things out here in the Amazon, less than a third of them classified. What am I doing, entering into the thick of them?

10 DECEMBER

We have just passed Trinta e um, the large Brazilian Matsés settlement that expelled the boat-load of evangelists and raided the Harriets' mission for wives.

The settlement doesn't live up to the stories – from the river you can even see some tin roofs – but we didn't linger to find out. The women were flapping skirts, waving us away.

The river is narrow now, the forests stacked above us. It's like being in a corridor.

An hour or so later we saw two Indian children, a girl and boy, on the Peruvian bank. They both wore skirts made of cotton left-overs, and were gaping at us from the trees. As we came nearer, they started screaming. We watched as they ran chaotically along the bank, and then we spotted a *maloca*, a dark brown hump in a small clearing. In clear view was a naked man and also a woman wearing a skirt that looked like an old tea towel. They were retreating sideways, watching us stiffly over their shoulders and apparently not wanting to offer their backs to us. Then they saw Pablito. They didn't know him, but they came forward. It was white people they were scared of.

The woman ducked through the one open entrance, at the south end, which has a thatched lean-to on it. She came out and waved meat at us. She wanted to trade.

Pablito looked at Armando, wondering if we were going ashore. All of us were in two minds about it. 'Good people?' I asked. '*Bírambu?*'

Pablito pouted, unsure.

Armando said we might as well risk going ashore: he thinks I might need them as friends, if things go wrong with the Brazilians on the Batã. Pablito went first, not saying any greetings, but murmuring a few words to the man. Armando passed forward some salt, and Pablito gave it to him. The Matsés handed over a rather ancient, smoked howler monkey.

Pablito and his son have decided to stay here to await our return from the recce. Before my departure with Armando, I went off to the forest gardens to gather yucca for our trip. I found myself guided through the forest by the wife, who had friendly, round eyes, a mask of red paint across her face and leopard spots over her chest. She sat down patiently and preened my arrows whenever I paused to take a little look around the forest.

REMEMBER: no matter how the journey goes, this tricky bit of forest is still a home for people. Can be a home for me.

[Now we were to continue with our recce into the rubber tappers' country. We left Pablito with his son to await our return, and after a few hours' travel stopped for the night at the 'abandoned' landing strip.]

Dusk now, and we're at the airstrip, a giant concrete slab beside the river and tucked into the forest. Weeds are battling through it, but it looks flat and alien here among the tangled vegetation. Like a dead river. It's too late in the day for planes to come (Armando claims), and no one has been here since yesterday. A cigarette packet has been dropped, and there's disturbed grass by the river bank, but otherwise no sign. Seems a silly risk for us to stay here – why don't we just camp in the forest with the black boas?

'People only come here before four PM,' Armando told me, still scratching about for signs of the drug people.

'Only before four PM,' he says – as if this continent is known for accurate time-keeping.

11 DECEMBER · *En route to the Batã tributary*

Return of Fidencio's Revenge. My normally cast-iron stomach is now in its fourth week of protest. It doesn't feel like mine any more, just a donor's organ that my body is now rejecting.

Further south (ahead) there was a storm last night – electrical mayhem in the sky. Now the river is swollen; it's rising and buckling – no longer moving on a level plane, but swinging around the corners, a viscous mass, dragging against the forest. Whirlpools and sudden gushes, waves pounding as if on a beach.

*River-bank camp, Javari*

Have stopped early – danger of capsize. A papaya sunset and mist in the dusk. Here we are on an outer bank in an abandoned hunter's shack, the river below us flexing up and down, largely silent, a slippery bulk of something solid and unstoppable.

12 DECEMBER

The aftermath of the storm: a huge beetle is marooned on a stick in mid-river, clinging to the forest wreckage. A homeless-looking capybara* swam by desperately, even with its partly webbed feet.

* At over a metre long, the world's largest rodent, a semi-aquatic animal which was the Amazon's ecological answer to the West African pigmy hippo.

Only its blunt nose and eyes were visible. Logs sweep on by.

We are at the mouth of the Batã, once the scene of an Indian attack.* Now there is no sign. The forested bank is just one more stretch of remote, ceaseless vegetation that I must learn to call my home.

And, finally, up the Batã and into Brazil.

[We came at last to two solitary, slipshod houses, up on a high left bank. This was the start of the path through the forest.]

The family here are what the Brazilians might call *caboclos* [much the equivalent of Peruvian *mestizos*, peasants of mixed stock]. They look harmless enough, but, because of ferocious insects called piums, they are clothed as if in high fever, all swathed in jump suits, shirts and socks. The only person who isn't dressed up actually does have a fever.

There are two families, mostly babies and old, but also a girl of about fourteen who put on lipstick when she saw us. They are quiet, skulking people, but this might be the fault of the piums. They look tired, weary from a long battle; the girl alone shows life, largely because of seeing Armando – it's like a desperate last bid to get out of here.

This is the spot where Armando is meant to be leaving me in a few days' time.

We've given them some meat. Even though it's only a bit of old howler monkey, they seem grateful. The older man said, in Portuguese of course, he's been in this dump around fifteen years. I'm the first *gringo* that he's seen here in that time. He says that

---

* Hemming tells how, in 1866, the first expedition to demarcate the Peru–Brazil boundary set off up the Javari in dread. Finally, at the mouth of the Batã tributary, Indians, perhaps of the Panoan tribe called Capanawa, fired off their arrows. The party retreated, with the death of one Brazilian. Another expedition tried again, eight years later. Having harassed the surveyors all the way upriver, sometimes crashing trees into the water, the Mayorunas finally surrounded the expedition, dispatching arrows and shouting defiance while the intruders were hauling their boat against the current. Captain von Hoonholdtz ordered his men to open fire. The Mayorunas, exposed on a beach, were easy targets and many were killed before they could scatter. 'We asserted through today's victory our supremacy in this region of indomitable natives,' said the Captain, and took the chief's headdress home as a souvenir.

Cruzeiro do Sul is two weeks' walk away. If I can find my way up the track, the loggers might help. Or they might not. I will need them – it isn't the distance, it's the maze of old rubber tappers' paths.

Armando asked, 'What about the robberies?'

'Just stories.'

But then, he would say that, wouldn't he?

I tried to coax these people to help guide me. Then Armando tried. It's no good. We can't offer too much money, because I'll be an even more obvious target for robbery then. I'll just have to do the best I can alone.

I've gone to bed early, watching the flies trying to bite me through the mosquito netting, and watching Armando [still eating supper] chewing the massive voice-box of the male howler monkey. Wondering what I'm going to do without him, his craftsman-like ways – craftsman-like except when he fell apart over the Matsés girl, that infant.

I think that this push, when it comes, is going to be just too much for me. Should I stop now, go back home? What would Jita say? And mum. And how much forest *after* Cruzeiro do Sul and the Juruá to face? Mustn't think about it.

16 DECEMBER

[Having proceeded back down the Javari, picking up Pablito and his son, we arrived at Anushi.]

I've been greeted by a series of nicknames.

'The man who has no fear,' giggled the third wife.

'The hunter of sloths,' Lucy said.

'Cling, cleng!' called Roberto.

With time running out fast, I got down to a week of vigorous training in the forest with Pablito's family.

I took *ner-nér* and it worked its magic, guiding me out and guiding me back, and flexing my six foot four frame into some semblance of grace. But the children always laughed when I came home. 'Cling-cleng!' Roberto imitated my stiff gait as one might tease an old man, and every time I came indoors Lucy asked how many sloths I'd caught today.

Pace, pace. Speed and alertness: this is what will get me out of here. I'm sure I'm right in thinking this. I mustn't waste time hunting for creatures that will already have heard me coming.

There was one thing I wanted to know, before leaving Pablito for my journey: his name. I don't mean 'Pablito', the name which he gives us.

He's told me it is Shává, brave one, valiant man.

## 22 DECEMBER

There were no goodbyes, just Armando coming at dawn, and taking me away from Pablito to Angamos, to inform the governor that I was leaving for Brazil.

I grasped Pablito by the shoulder, and he grasped me by mine. Then I turned and left . . .

But he then jumped into my canoe, piling in half his women as well. It is, after all, a free ride to Angamos.

We've just passed Paowheel, the village where Helena is ensconced with her husband. On the roof of one hut, Helena's only known article of clothing, a bluish home-made skirt, hanging there like a little farewell wave. Armando insisted on blowing it a kiss on my behalf.

### Angamos

Pablito is still wearing his red paint and whiskers – and the soldiers at the checkpoint are new conscripts. The corporal, instead of challenging us, went green. Then there was the sound of rifle butts slipping to the ground. Other soldiers, washing their fatigues in the river, froze, like rodents spotted by a predator.

'Pass,' one soldier at the back said, faintly.

Pablito sat back, a satisfied smile on his face.

Angamos came into view. The plaza was there as usual – red cement benches, little yellow shrubs in lines, Amazon mud filling them. As usual, there was no flag up; it was like a deserted ship in a sea of silt. The governor stood in the middle like a doomed captain.

I went to see him straight away. Spotting me coming, he looked cautious. Last time, I had produced Fidencio.

He told me about a party planned for Christmas Eve. Everyone will be playing bingo he said, proudly – then he saw Pablito walking across the plaza, and lost his thread.

Pablito was soon causing a commotion over at Angel's store. He was in the centre of a circle of men, holding someone's banknote between his fingers and studying it. Angel was calming everyone down, saying Pablito meant no harm, he just didn't understand what money was.

I'm spending the rest of the day indoors with Armando, discussing the logistics of getting out of here. I don't even have enough cash to get me to the Batá and pay Armando.

Outside on the waterfront Pablito has got my camera and is taking photos of all the young schoolgirls. '*Champee!* Girls!' he keeps sighing.

They love him, and pose in the rain, their shirts stuck to their chests, and he has now begun wolf-whistling, copying the *mestizos* who've started to gather for the spectacle. [Later, when I developed the photographs, I found they were shot on a slant, just as if he was aiming arrows. The targets were the girls in their drenched shirts, doing cartwheels and backflips for him.]

All those times I've had with Pablito in the forest, but I'll remember him here in Angamos with his red jaguar paint on. He's master of this world that should be so alien to him. I'm reminded of something said by Joseph Campbell [the American authority on mythology]. 'The way to become human is to learn to recognize the lineament of God in all of the wonderful modulations of the face of man.'

I'm not here long enough to understand what Pablito's god is, but here is a man whom the average person at home would have called primitive – a Jaguar Man, with tattoos and whiskers. Yet he's as civil as anyone I've ever met. He's a specialist in an animal's environment, and what's more has the confidence to cope with the west as well. An extraordinary person yes, but more important, a *person* – one of us.

23 DECEMBER

Angel, the store owner, has agreed to help. He has very quick, sparkling eyes, but Armando says I can trust him. Angel says in exchange for the outboard motor, the canoe and the shotgun, he'll get me as far as the Batã.

24 DECEMBER

Last night I went to a party in a palm shack. Everyone drunk, and Rosa, the sophisticated girl from Iquitos, was fighting, lashing out with her mighty fists. The hut almost collapsed under the strain, and a teacher, while teaching me to salsa, tried to pull down my flies.

I came back to the house and described the scene to Armando, detailing vomitings, punchings. Pablito suddenly appeared, jumping up from out of my hammock. He said, excitedly, 'Champee? Girls?'

It seemed to be his idea of heaven.

# XII

# Leaving for Oblivion

## BASED ON MY DIARY

24 DECEMBER · *Angamos*

The luggage I must take is far too heavy, thanks to the video, that *máquina horrible*. Having sorted through all the stores [that I'd left down here in Angamos], I have selected: a spare machete, two pairs of long trousers and two shirts, my little towel, my sleeping bag 'inner', hammock, water bottle, mosquito net, survival kit, notebooks/pens, toothbrush/paste, one plate, one spoon, my hat, and the much coveted Kitchen Devil. There's also my boots, socks and the shorts, which I'm wearing.

Oh yes, and the mustard.

Also, a 'starter pack' of food – sugar, *farinha*. Enough energy there for only seven days, and it's a 'fourteen-day' walk. I'm planning to trot – in fact, I'm counting on it. Seven days . . .

I've made an additional rucksack out of two spliced palm leaves: in it, additional sugar, *farinha* for two guides (fifteen man days).

If I get to Cruzeiro do Sul, then I can think about the next stage across the Amazon. And the next . . . I do so need a holiday.

Can't face leaving for oblivion today, and besides I've been invited to the most prestigious event of the year, *el comandante*'s Christmas party.

[The arrangement was that two of Angel's workers would accompany Armando and me up the river to the Batã, and that we'd use Angel's big boat and *peque-peque*, the standard engine of the

Amazon which used less fuel and which had a characteristic thumping sound.]

The character of Angel's two men is a source of worry, but there's no choice. Antonio has pale skin and glassy eyes. He has been kindly to me so far, but I think he's a potential villain who, for the moment, is just kept honest by the bonds of his peasant state. Lucio looks more reliable, but is totally lacking in energy. If the canoe capsizes, I'm probably going to drown trying to rescue him.

Preparations for *el comandante*'s party: Armando has been down by the river, helping me wash my shirt around the armpits, and dunk my boots to wipe off the worst of the forest mud.

He says I'm to ask after the health of the mayor's daughter; apparently she's exquisite. 'Absolutely everyone is after her,' he said.

'You mean *you* are,' I said.

### 25 DECEMBER

I marched over the rickety bridge to the army camp and was stopped by the sentry. He smiled, maliciously. 'You're a friend of the criminal, Fidencio?'

The smile dropped from his face when he learnt I was a VIP for the day. He looked very miserable having to salute me. I think I've ruined his Christmas.

At the officers' mess, a lieutenant handed me a beaker of pineapple juice, and I was ushered in front of *el comandante* himself. He was in fatigues and had his big black revolver attached to his side. Attached to his other side was his wife, no less frightening.

The mess was like a children's classroom, with paper Christmas trees on the walls but with the little desks removed. A crib occupied a corner of the room, a sad little farmhouse scene with home-made houses of paper. Polystyrene packing material represented snow. It was a story from the Middle East, enacted here in the heart of the Amazon with European snow.

Everyone was still arriving, the cream of Angamos society – which meant the governor, the mayor and his wife, Angel from the store, and four 'representative' village families, the same ones every year. They had been squeezed into their best clothes. Ties had been found, cuffs stitched. They nervously deposited their children at the trestle table outside, on which was heaped cake and cocoa, and came indoors, looking around warily to avoid their first social gaffe. They were as nervous as the Indians walking across the plaza and couldn't stop their hands shaking.

I had wet soapy patches around my armpits, and felt no more at ease. *El comandante*'s party was not meant for fun, I now realized, it was an ordeal; we were just trying to make the best of it. There were heavy silences, in which we swigged our pineapple juice from our plastic beakers, wishing we were drunk. We looked about for things to say. To help fill the next silence, the mayor drank our health. We soon discovered that this was a way of filling silences, and copied the formula. '*Salud!*'

The pineapple juice that we were gulping down was now found to be alcoholic. As the drink took its evil hold, *el comandante*'s wife became steadily more flamboyant. She also developed ugly, clumsy features; raven hair, large, aggressive nose. *El comandante* hugged her passionately as they led off the dancing.

The conversation became strained again, and again the mayor drank everyone's health. And again. He kept on doing it – a nervous habit. '*Salud!*'

*El comandante* was now also the worse for wear, his heavy black army boots clonking on the floor as he danced, his wife helping swing him around. He still had his pistol at his hip. I thought, 'Shouldn't someone disarm him?' But it was his wife who lost her grip in the end, shoving him into the crib.

It was time to wind things up. The mayor gave a speech, proudly flashing his good teeth from his short but wide mouth. He was accompanied by excruciating feedback on an entirely unnecessary microphone. The speech was thorough in the extreme. I should think there was hardly a dog in Angamos that didn't get a mention.

*El comandante* was manoeuvred to a table stacked with presents of beautifully wrapped panettone and a liquid that claimed to be champagne. One by one, the honoured guests were called forward by microphone and handed the hampers. After each received their present, they were applauded by the other guests. Everyone in the room went home with a present except me. I left feeling miserable, like a forgotten spoilt child.

I helped get the governor home across the rickety wooden bridge. 'I am the Number One person in Angamos,' he kept saying. 'Number Two is *el comandante*. I am the Number One.'

'Yes, yes, of course you are . . .' We were proceeding slowly. The mayor was trying to overtake us, and I remembered that Armando had told me to ask after his beautiful daughter. 'Do please send my best wishes to your good family – and of course the *señorita*,' I quipped.

My season's greetings had an extraordinary effect on the mayor. 'I've heard about you and your Indian girls. My daughter is thirteen years old and I'll thank you to remember that.'

I made a mental note to strangle Armando.

[That night there was electricity in Angamos, and free drink and a dance. At midnight, the mayor took the microphone and made another long speech to wish everyone peace and happiness. As if this was a signal, rival clans of Matsés started a pitched battle across the plaza.]

No arrows available thankfully. The Cashishbis versus the rest. Couldn't help but be fascinated by the cohesion of the Matsés forces, young men flying in to help brothers, taking running dives into the thick of the ruck. Then combat by fist and foot.

The Angamos ladies began screaming, reining in their husbands. Girls ran around collecting bottles and other potential weapons. It was as if this was well practised. Armando appeared, looking for me. He was paralytically drunk, but had still come to make sure I was safe.

Later I told Armando I was going to sleep, because we wanted a dawn start. He danced on, hugging a soldier, saying into his ear, 'Benedito, I won't fail you!'

That was last night. Now we are heading up the Javari and Armando has a terrible hangover, along with Antonio and Lucio. I'm still getting dark glances from everyone for pulling them away from their hammocks so early.

[My exit to Brazil was not a triumphant one, with the excitement usually engendered by explorers on their departure for the interior, it was made in glum silence. While the crew members were sick overboard, or merely clutched their heads wishing they were dead, the sound of the *peque-peque* engine thumped across the glassy river, the water brightly reflected the low morning light – and all the while in the plaza, the governor shaking his head sadly, watching us go. Soon he would walk back to his empty office, and look again at his empty IN tray. And, like everyone else, he would be waiting for the next plane, and the medical officer would come round and issue his sick-note.]

At last, after two months, I'm on the move again – never mind that I'm heading towards disaster. My ribs, at least, are now in good condition. They feel about the only bit of my anatomy that is.

Suddenly feel gloomy. My strategy is simply to make a run for it. If I do the walk quick enough, the theory seems to go, then the forest and its lurking occupants won't have time to notice me.

I've had to take an aspirin, the first medicine in all my journey. Hope it's a hangover, but it's more like a dizzy fever. Wonder if I can keep going even to the Batã. And then my Fidencio's Revenge – is it five weeks now? Mustn't think of it.

It's too pathetic for words. Armando has begun nursing me with sugar and salt solution and dry *farinha*. This isn't going to give me the energy to walk, or run. Postpone journey? Maybe it's just my nerves.

[We travelled day and night, the river narrowing, the forest pressing in on us. On beyond the Choba tributary with its girl/woman, and on past the Matsés *maloca*, which was empty. On beyond the abandoned airstrip, and finally, at midday on 27 December, we came to the little house on the Batã.]

Biting flies are as bad as ever, but that's the least of my problems. I have Fidencio's Revenge, and the residents are unwilling to conduct me to the loggers, even for substantial cash.

'And people say the *English* are unfriendly,' I said to Armando. We stood together in silence, looking at the bleak settlement and the path leading away vaguely into the dark forest.

Armando said, 'Well, I can't leave you *here*.'

We're to give it a go: we're going to leave with Lucio, just to the logger's camp. Antonio will guard the canoe and motor here. Leaving right now – late midday. Must keep the pace up.

*Later*

Lucio was very slow, and I felt that if I didn't run I was going to collapse. I kept clipping his boots from behind, harrying him like a sheep dog. We stopped for him to rest, and I examined my bows and arrows, knowing already they were a hindrance. Better to concentrate on edible plants. At least plants don't move. This is the logger's camp: a riverside shack beside the Hospital tributary of the Batã. The 'loggers' are three ragged scouts who are working under Victor Braga. Also here, a young *caboclo* [peasant] family composed of mean, grumpy characters.

When we turned up these people were smouldering and snarling like a pack of feuding dogs. Even our unexpected arrival out of nowhere couldn't disguise that they'd just had a really bad argument – the sort you can't afford to have if you're living together in an alien environment. From this desperate lot I'm going to have to find a guide.

The youth in charge I would perhaps trust, but not the other two loggers. One called Jaime is skulking about. He's Peruvian but I can't understand his accent. He has only a few teeth – they are remainders, bits and pieces which fit into gaps in his gums. The other logger, a loud youth called Pasarin, also speaks Spanish. He has challenged Armando to arm wrestling, just as he challenges everyone. I have refused. I'm feeling vulnerable enough without showing myself up as a wimp.

The head of the *caboclo* family is the only other option as a guide. He's a grisly man who says he won't come except for a lot of money because, so he claims, the forest is full of anacondas, caymans, and other carnivorous creatures. It's true that it does look as if he's been bitten by something, some sort of bloodsucking fish. It's a large round scar on his calf, like a hateful love bite.

I'm passing myself off as a scientist working for Victor Braga. So far we are believed, because they know Armando once worked for Braga, and we keep hinting that word will get back to him if something untoward happens to me. I even photographed the loggers, and loudly asked Armando to forward it to Braga.

All this effort, but I really do feel scared. Armando does as well: he wants me to return with him.

These people are poor people, *mestizos* from the town: like every-one – the missionaries, the tourists, the gold miners, the travel writers – they look to the Amazon as a place to fulfil their dreams: and the poor man's dream is to make money. They are opportunists. And I am an opportunity.

[The father seemed the best of the bad lot, and negotiations as to how much he should be paid continued into the dark. Between bouts, I kept up my diary.]

Possible guide has a growling voice, black stubble beard and a lanky, plain wife whom I feel sorry for. He looks just like a murderer should, and admires my machete too much. He has a sorry collection of children. The bald face of one of them is blotched with a birthmark, another is as skinny as a refugee. The third kicks him around, his hair amateurishly cropped to start treatment of a scalp infection.

It seems the wife has given up motherhood and she lavishes her affection instead on a baby capuchin monkey that she's hung up in its own miniature hammock, swinging it to sleep. I'm sure the love won't last. While Armando talks to the 'Murderer', I watch the monkey peeping out from under its own blanket. In delivering the creature to these people, fate has dealt it a cruel blow. I know the feeling.

Late at night now, and the Murderer has decided not to take me – even for the equivalent of $20 a day, which is more money than I have anyway. He's swallowed the story of Victor Braga, and is scared. Get the feeling I've had a narrow escape.

The two loggers have agreed to take me. In addition to receiving valuable extras, such as machetes, and continuing to receive their normal wage as loggers, I'll pay Crs 200,000 a day [$20] – this cash alone many times the national 'minimum wage' (Crs 40,000 a month, or a pound a day) that they'd hope to get from a *patrón* – here in Brazil called a *patrão*. The boss says they are not to be paid more, and he insists on looking after their money – i.e. he doesn't trust them.


28 DECEMBER · *En route to Cruzeiro do Sul*

This morning I said goodbye to Armando. I went off with him behind the bushes so that I could extract my money from where it's hidden in my boots, my trousers, my waistbelt, my pack. I gave him his wages plus all I think I can risk parting with. Also my water bottle, my hammock and my spare long trousers.

'You'll need them,' Armando said.

But the guides are refusing to carry anything more than their food.

Finally, I gave the Kitchen Devil to Armando and he promised to hand it to Helena. 'One last chance to kill her husband,' Armando said, trying to cheer us both up.

Departure time, and now Pasarin, the louder of the two horrible guides, was crooning over a fancy watch that Armando had been given by one of his Angamos girls. Armando handed it over, and Pasarin shook Armando's hand and hugged him. Armando wasn't impressed. 'Just take good care of el Benedito.'

I didn't know what to say to Armando – just goodbye? Like me, he seemed to be putting it off. We stood facing each other, and he reached out as if to shake hands. But instead he touched my bow and arrows. 'Hang on to them,' he said.

On impulse, I said, 'Here, take them. Keep them for me. I'll try and pick them up one day.'

'But, all Pablito's lessons . . .'

I confessed how badly I had always done on my hunting trips. 'See that big tree over there?'

'The huge one? What about it?'

'I'd miss it.'

Armando was shocked. 'What were you doing all that time then?'

I told him that I'd learnt plants to eat and all sorts of fascinating things, but I supposed what Pablito really taught me was confidence to move around the forest.

Armando looked at the tree again – the one I couldn't hit if I tried. And then he looked at the guides sitting together, watching us. It looked like they were already plotting.

Pasarin got to his feet and shook Armando's hand again. (Large brutish hands, he has, and a very slow turn of thought.) We had to wait a good few seconds while his brain prepared him for speaking.

'Don Benedito is safe with me.'

Armando took me out of earshot. 'He's not a fool,' he said.

'Good,' I said.

'I mean, watch out.'

With these words still in my ear, I walked away into the forest.

Pasarin took the lead, playing the chimes of the irritating watch. He has a short gait, and walks with his stomach out, shuffling, his insteps outward. A fag in his hand. He has pale skin that will burn easily in the sun – if we ever reach daylight . . .

Now we've stopped, and are resting – though I'm the only one who's carrying much. '*Escucha!*' Pasarin said. 'Listen!'

I waited while he got his brain into gear.

'Don Benedito,' he said. 'In the night, I saw one of the *Peruanos* opening your bags. Is any of your money missing?'

Last night I was awake with my worries and also Fidencio's Revenge, so I know that he's lying: no one touched my bags. Pasarin just wants me to check my money so that he can see it. So now I know for certain: he's after my cash.

As we walk, I keep looking at the forest, feeling like a child at a swimming pool, standing on the top diving board. I'm going to have to take the plunge, I know I am.

### *Early evening*

We are now camping in a little shack used by loggers. It's right on the edge of a swollen stream. Sweat bees, a reek of bad meat, and a bedraggled and starving dog which couldn't care less about life any more.

On arrival, the two men immediately began looking for a supply of meat hidden by that man I nicknamed 'The Murderer'. First they looked to see if he had hung it from a vine. Eventually they found it salted and stashed in a camouflaged clay pit. These people don't even play fair with each other, God knows what they will do with me.

A sliver of new moon, rising, so if I do have trouble with these two, there's very little moonlight in which to escape with my belongings. Pablito and Lucy and Roberto are only a few days away through the forest, living happily in it. Must keep remembering that. I must remember the forest is a friend and these two loggers, and any *seringueiros* I meet out here, are from the outside world and are probably its enemies. The forest and I are on the same side, sort of thing.

[In the night I thought a lot about the loggers and the rubber tappers. Could I totally blame them for whatever they were planning to do to me? With the Brazilian inflation rate of 1 per cent a day the cash part of their wages would lose about half its value by the time they'd returned to the camp. It would be almost worthless before it was ever spent.

They occupied this Indian land, but their lives were not those of conquerors. Rubber tappers, like the loggers Pasarin and Jaime, and like the gold prospectors all around the Amazon Basin, were only the hopeful poor. Often they were slaves to a *patrão*, or more specifically the *aviador*, the men's immediate boss who kindly advanced them food for their lonely months ahead in the forest – and thereafter kept them in debt, tied to his service. The *seringueiros* weren't much better off than the Indians who had been made slaves in their own forests. Each day, the *seringueiro* had to rise in the dark and milk his allotted wild trees in the first hours of the day, before the heat thickened the sap and sealed off the cut. Trudging back to his hut with the latex he had accumulated – about five kilos for an average allocation of a hundred trees – he could begin curing the day's yield. The latex was solidified over a fire of palm nuts, the liquid poured steadily on to a rod as it was turned in the acidic smoke. Once done, it was time to go out to find more fuel for tomorrow's fire. In the rainy season, when it was too wet to work, the *seringueiro* left his shack and floated his 40–50-kilo rubber bales downriver to his *aviador* boss. Replenishing his clothes in the *aviador*'s trade stores, seizing the simple pleasures for which he had been craving during months of solitude, he got himself in greater debt and tighter bondage before setting off alone into the forest again.]

29 DECEMBER

Woke in the very early morning to hear the others putting their boots on. They'd teased my pack away from my mosquito net. Five minutes more, and they would have been out of here.

When I got up and snatched my bag back, they laughed off the incident. I went back to my mosquito net, put the damp, muddy bag in the net with me, and curled around it as if to go back to sleep. They could walk out if they wished: I was daring them.

'You really work for Victor Braga?' Pasarin asked, still standing there. He had his machete in his hand.

I insisted that I did.

'If you did not, then we would just leave you here.'

I gave a hearty laugh. 'But we are friends! I'm sure you wouldn't do that to a friend.' This sounded very weak.

Pasarin said, yes, we are friends. 'Shake hands?' We shook hands through the mosquito netting. Now, dawn, they've taken my spare machete. They've hidden it somewhere. Have one machete left, and my survival kit and my pack.

We're just about to start our walk. From now on I must sleep in my boots and clothes, my pack under my head and with a string from it looped around my wrist.

I'm right where he wants me, in his fat hands.

MUST believe that the forest is his enemy; it's my friend. I'm noting details now – the tread of their boots, the style in which they cut saplings, clearing a trail. It's all in case I have to follow them. I must be ready.

Resting by a river now. All morning, the loggers ran ahead of me – they have no hindrance of a pack. I had to run behind, jumping streams, crashing through bushes to keep up.

Pasarin isn't trying to lose me – that would mean losing the money as well. No, they're testing me. Pasarin wants to know how far he can push me. He's also weakening me.

So tired. Not really from walking, I just want to sleep. Feel I'm being baited and taunted.

I've seen giant dog footprints here. The tracks are old, but someone else has been out here a matter of weeks ago – a comforting thought, though he may of course be of the criminal fraternity as well.

Pasarin is sitting right by me, being charming. (By the way, I

251

see he's got a scar through his left eyebrow, as if from a knife wound.) He's telling the story of a giant black cat that he believes lives in this forest. It calls out a 'wooo' sound in the night, and this sends the rubber tappers to sleep as they sit over a fire in their shacks, curing the latex into a bale. The *seringueiros'* necks can be seized easily that way. Pasarin is trying to scare me, I suppose, but he's only succeeded in scaring himself. More worrying to me is the story-teller: Pasarin finished his tale with a little silence, and then a tale of how life is hard for him, and then a straightforward demand for $200. He says he'll let me think about it.

Evening, and we've made a shelter from palm leaves. Pasarin was visibly shocked when he saw me select and cut the palms. 'Lived with the Indians,' I said casually.

He repeated this information to Jaime. Wish I'd brought the bow and arrow – give them something to think about. I showed them my New Guinea tribal initiation marks instead. This shameful display has at least bought me time.

Now realize that Pasarin has been feeding me misinformation. He's been confusing me with names of smallholders and distances ahead of us. It's not incompetence – I don't believe that any more. I'm mentally preparing myself to make a run for it. But where to? I have no compass to help with directions, nor any map.

I keep reassuring myself that I'll be all right. That I don't need these things now. I find myself testing my skills – for example when I saw some dark shapes moving on the ground far ahead, I knew they were birds – because the shapes were, in side view, triangular: head, tail, and legs form the corners.

30 DECEMBER · *At a rest point on the trail*

I'm being stripped down – feel so weary. My survival kit has gone. They take things in the day, and hide them in the forest. I can't guard my things every minute. When I was washing they took my survival kit [attached to my belt] from my clothes pile.

Already I'm like an SAS soldier on active service: I'm wearing my boots day and night now – my feet rotting away inside them – and I sleep on my machete.

Will I be able to look after myself when the moment comes? Saw a peach-palm along the trail today, just coming into fruit. Can they be eaten raw? Running for your life is not the time to find out.

I try to get back at the loggers with little punishments. Last night I mixed heaps of mustard into their food, ruining their meat. So it does have its uses. Also, at each opportunity I try to destroy that watch. I told Pasarin it was waterproof, hoping he would cross a river and it would be 'drowned' by his own hands. I told him to dry it out by the camp fire, hoping its plastic works would bubble. I want that watch to stop its bleeping for ever, and in some violent manner.

All the time now, a physical confrontation is on the cards. Both have machetes for the trail, and I have to keep mine at hand. I don't know how I'd ever whack anyone with it. If I can just keep moving this fast, I won't have to. Very soon, surely, we'll reach the *caboclo* settlement they call Julião – witnesses.

'They've made their move,' I wrote simply for my next diary entry. I'd taken off my pack as we felled a tree to make a bridge. Because the bridge was wobbly I had to trust them to carry the pack over to the other side. Then a perfect opportunity arose – the tree collapsed into the river, separating me from them. The bridge was gone. And very soon, so were Pasarin and Jaime. It made it all too easy for them. After a few moments' thought about my predicament, I recorded:

> Now I'm alone out here, my blood is racing around and I'm trying to calm myself by writing my thoughts down. I should be prepared for this, but I'm still in shock. Can't take in that this situation is real. That I'm up against it.
>
> Six or seven hours of daylight left. But I'm going to make myself take this slowly. One slip, one wrong trail, and I'll end up like Fawcett. Disappeared.
>
> I'm slowed by not having boots – they were in the pack, temporarily. I don't want to think about what else I don't have.

Specifically, I had a machete for building a shelter, but no medicine, no sleeping gear, no footwear, nothing to light a fire with. I was standing in the forest just in my shorts. But I did have a daypack with my long trousers, and also miscellaneous items of no survival use such as my notebook.

'This is your home,' I remember saying again and again, as I paced around, unable to calm down enough to think, and all the time aware of time running out. Soon there'd be the usual mid-afternoon rain, and the tracks would be rubbed away.

'This is your home. Your home.' It became like a chant as I did start to get a grip of myself. Where would the tracks of Pasarin and Jaime lead me? If they were going to 'Julião', then that made Julião suspect as well.

Again I sat down to write, hoping it would clear my thoughts.

I'm sitting in my shorts, trying to conjure up Roberto and Lucy – that day when we got lost together. She calmly took charge, and leaned forward to the ground, and began to sort the problem out. She looked for leaves that'd been flicked over, depressions in the thin leaf litter. She could tell even where her own little, light feet had trodden. You would have thought I could manage following the clumsy boots of loggers . . . Give it a go?

Must make a decision: it's time I was gone.

I'll do my best to track the loggers to Julião, where they must be heading. Then – if I get that far – I'll skirt the settlement and keep going.

Where are you Pablito, now I need you? But I knew I'd have to face this situation one day.

Crossing the river proved surprisingly easy without the hindrance of a backpack. Only after I had edged along the submerged log bridge to the far side did my problems start. Where to now? I cut a spear as Pablito would have done, and began using it to point out the tracks to myself. I talked my way through my actions, as Lucy used to. 'That's Pasarin's boot. And there again. And now the heel of Jaime's boot – narrower, and with fancy crenellations. And the flat tread of Pasarin's fat boot again. Well, "Beneeee", you're not doing too badly so far . . .'

After some hours, my back aching from being bent double over the mud, I saw some ferns and gathered some shoots to eat, copying Lucy's example as any baby brother might.

'*Bírambu*. Good,' I said aloud, standing there alone in the forest. It was a silly fantasy to believe she was with me, but it was keeping me alive.

However, I began to encounter wide old paths used by the *seringueiros*, and also the occasional, huge, long-forgotten rubber tree, still with old criss-cross scars where the sap had been milked. Sometimes, by the foot of a tree, lay the rusty remains of a metal collecting cup, once fixed to the fresh wounds on the tree-trunks. Far from being reassuring, these ancient human signs gave a ghostly quality to the forest. All the other outsiders except me had gone home, leaving behind just their scratched rubber trees and empty paths. The scratches looked like the desperate markings a prisoner leaves behind him in his cell.

The further I went, the deeper I entered into the maze of paths. This was a forest full of the ghosts of outsiders, rather than ghosts of Indians, and now I was fighting hard to keep that vision of the Matsés in my mind. 'You're with them now,' I told myself. 'Lucy is inspecting this sapling, noticing the crease on one of the leaves. Roberto is shrieking that he's found a boot mark. '*Mirambó!* Show me,' I said. And in my mind they did.

I progressed like this, trying to be like them, a lost Indian child in the forest, but before long the *seringueiro* paths almost defeated me. I hated these towering rubber trees with scars made by people like Pasarin and Jaime, men who were dominated and scared by the forest. I was surrounded by ghosts of other outsiders who had failed – even that huge oil company airstrip had been abandoned – and couldn't believe the forest was a home for anyone any more.

'Thus, an aged tree falls and moulders into dust,' the Victorian naturalist Charles Waterton wrote, 'and you cannot tell what was its appearance, its beauties, or its diseases amongst the neighbouring trees; another has shot up in its place, and after nature has had her course, it will make way for a successor in its turn.'

I'll moulder into dust as well, I thought, sitting there surrounded by the abandoned things of outsiders. I'll disappear just as Colonel Fawcett did.

And Fawcett had two companions!

After some considerable time, I picked my way through the worst of the old gardens, and slowly, keeping my nose to the ground, I was in less disturbed forest and could again pretend to myself that I was in the company of Roberto and Lucy.

'*Mirambó!* Teach me.' I began to speed faster, finding a rhythm at last. I heard the grunt of a pig, a stray peccary, and this too lent me encouragement: it helped convince me that this was a place to live in. I recognized things around and about me – a butterfly with wings like golden stained glass; in a clearing a mealy parrot, its greenish yellow body dusted with a powder; a small, stout bird with a gaudy yellow breast and black cap and wings – I think, a golden-collared manakin. With my newfound confidence, I earned the luxury of being able to stand up straight and look for edible plants. As my confidence grew I was able to veer off the track to gather up tree fruit thrown down by monkeys.

*That night*

Have found my rucksack. Just off the track, camouflaged with leaves – not very well camouflaged, either. Clearly they didn't think I'd track them this far. Feel indomitable. If Pasarin comes back now, I can simply run off into the trees. Now he, not the forest, is my threat.

I've sorted through my pack. All the food gone. Also the stash of money. Have my machete now, and boots, and mosquito net and sleeping bag. Also malaria tablets. But no survival kit. They've left my ordinary camera here and – typically – the indestructible video camera (with no battery power).

Important thought: they must be expecting to come back shortly, before rain ruins the cameras.

Another point: they've only found a bit of money. They may come looking for me.

Too dark to get to Julião, and too dangerous? Risk it, before I lose the tracks?

[The decision was made for me by the sudden onslaught of rain which, within seconds, washed over the paths. I decided to move off the track a short way and make a camp. Nowadays, shelter construction was second nature to me. The palms were located, and assembled like a shield over an area cleared for bedding.]

I'm in my mosquito net, dry and secure for the moment. But from now on, hardly any tracks: one mistake tomorrow and I'll go wandering off and that'll be the end of me.

'Come on, *mirambó*, show me.' It sounds like a prayer. I think it is. '*Mirambó*.'

<br>

31 DECEMBER, FIRST LIGHT

And a Happy New Year's Eve to you, too.

I must take courage in my hands, and try to track them – with no tracks. Very, *very* slowly now. I don't even know the Matsés for 'good luck'. '*Mirambó*' will do . . .

I've had a breakfast of palm stem. Sad, eating alone in this predicament, but I'm far from beaten. Lucy and Roberto are going to show me a way out, aren't they?

Tree smells are in tight clouds at dawn. Many are sweet – sometimes damp-seeming, sometimes dry. Roar of monkeys signalling oncoming rain. Keep the pace up. I am an outsider. Time will run out for me, as it did for all the rubber tappers.

Pace, pace. Keep moving. Come on, Beneee.

[I headed off along a track that seemed to run approximately south-east, the direction of Julião, I thought. After some hours, occasionally encouraged along by the sign of some blurred tracks.]

With my spear, I've brought down a nest which had five or six sparrow-sized eggs. Two broke, but I swallowed it all down raw. It's not really what you would call dining out. I should have married Lucy and put her in my backpack.

I've stopped in a clearing made by ants. An area of about ten paces square has been stripped of leaves. All that remains, apart from the stark trees, is a clay mound, their home. They make a bivvy camp, just as I do, and move on.

Be like those ants. Be like a jaguar. Keep moving.

*Mid-afternoon*

As I was walking, heard a knocking sound, someone ahead of me in the forest. My heart thumped – PASARIN!!

But no one was ahead of me in the forest. I held my breath, and looked around once more. Then the sound again. And I looked down and saw a tortoise at my feet. It was nudging against a root, its shell making the clonking noise. All by itself, it looked lonely. Like me, I suppose, clumping along.

No means to light a fire to eat the tortoise. Not desperate enough to eat it raw – yet. It bangs against my head in my rucksack, which I'm carrying the Indian way, weight taken by my head.

[As the afternoon wore on, I moved faster and faster. I now knew from their prints how the men walked: Pasarin went straight through puddles, his feet splayed out. Jaime was more cautious, and edged around the muddy areas, his softer footprints lost in the leaf litter.

I walked faster and faster. Then I stopped. I could distinctly hear the sound of children. I had reached a settlement, probably 'Julião'. I ducked around the gardens, moving very slowly so the dogs wouldn't hear me. I saw just one house, and one family. I stood watching through the sugar cane, wanting so much to be able to go to them.]

Writing quickly now: update only.

From what I see it's just a simple *caboclo* home; they have two *peles* [rubber bales] in their veranda. Pasarin and Jaime not here, I think. They have two or three young children, but there are also three youths – sons, perhaps.

Hearing the happy children shrieking makes me want to cry. I'm so lonely out here, just in their garden, looking on like an escaped convict.

Must be strong, not make my presence known. It's the youths that worry me. Pasarin will have covered himself by saying that I've done some crime.

The homesteader's wife is large, and with a delightful laugh which comes in two modes – a normal chuckle, and a higher geared shriek of exaltation. Has big biceps, and probably hair on her chest. I bet Pasarin didn't challenge *her* to arm wrestling.

\*      \*      \*

I set up a little camp, and crept into it, feeling miserable. I departed before daylight the next morning, 1 January, finding Pasarin's trail continued on the far side of the settlement. I kept moving, able to trot now.

Spotting a newish side-path I turned off, and suddenly this track was opening into a garden. The maize here was newly planted.

I hid my pack, and proceeded forward carefully. It was a single *caboclo* house, again, this one situated on a small river. The piums bit me, and the sunlight began to burn, but I stayed watching to see how many people were here. In the house there was one woman, a little girl and boy and perhaps another child. I waited for some time, listening to the girl singing to herself as she swung in her hammock, her gentle tune making me feel homesick. As I listened, it became more important than anything in the world to be with the family, sitting around a supper table with them. I couldn't stand this loneliness any longer.

I would risk it, I decided.

I walked straight towards the camp, calling, 'Hola!' I didn't want to appear like someone running away.

The woman came out. She was wary, but she beckoned me forward into the shade. Things would be fine here, I decided.

Later I wrote:

From the woman's face, I must look like a foreign lunatic. I feel like one – like a veteran of the SAS, a soldier just emerged after years lost in the jungle.

When I produced the tortoise, she did cook it up for me, but she looked me over, silently. The children regard me in dumb hostility. This place – just one house – is called San Miguel, she says. She keeps saying her husband is coming – I'm sure he isn't. She's scared. I look a mess. More to the point, she's seen the way I keep looking over my shoulder. I keep expecting Pasarin to emerge with his machete.

I tried to stop myself tapping my fingers as the tortoise cooked. Sitting at the table I wrote, 'The woman is no fool. There's something odd about a lone person walking through this forest. Especially a foreigner. And I'm all too obviously nervous. I shouldn't have risked stopping here. She keeps asking questions: "How did this happen? You've no friend to travel with?" She has warm, loamy brown eyes but a way of seizing my arm to emphasize her words. I think she's just protecting herself and her brood. In normal circumstances, she'd be a pleasant person.

She's trying to tell if I'm the victim or the cause of a disaster. For now, she's presuming the worst. I've decided to tell her everything – her husband better not be involved with the loggers.

When I did tell her, she said, 'You are in trouble if they find you.'

I said I knew I was.

'The police have never been out here. No one from the government has. They are too scared.'

I thought to myself: They're right to be.

Then she told me everything: Pasarin and Jaime were here last night. They said they were working for a foreigner. Pasarin had said I was a liar and a cheat, and she wasn't to believe anything I said. 'So when I saw you,' the woman said, 'I thought, "Oh, here he is. Here's the American –"'

'– Briton –'

'"He's the one who's made slaves of two poor people." But now I can see I got it wrong. It's you who's a slave.'

'How can I get out of here?'

'Stay. You've got to rest – you should see a mirror.'

I should see a doctor, I thought. I told her that I'd be all right.

'They might kill you,' she said.

This seems to me to be an argument for getting out of here, not staying. She thinks Pasarin has gone back to Julião to look for me. We've crossed on the trail somehow.

'Stay. It's safer than walking in this forest. How far away did this happen?'

She was expecting me to say just an hour or so away. When I said I'd found my way along two days' worth of trails, she said, '*Dios!*' Or a Portuguese word to that effect.

She said I must not push my luck further. 'My husband will be back here in a week or so.'

'In a week or two I'll be dead and buried,' I said.

260

*Later*

DECISION: I will leave. The nearer I get to Cruzeiro do Sul, the more witnesses there will be to any violence. An americano out here is news.

Haven't left yet. Calculating they couldn't get back here from Julião for another hour at least, I've just had a wash in the river. She set her ten-year-old son to wait on the path to shout if Pasarin came. The boy loves the excitement, thinks it's just hide and seek.

I'm leaving now. The woman has given me hard-boiled eggs for the journey. One day I'd like to meet her, and thank her properly. *Pace, pace,* Beneeee.

[Soon I was in the old routine again, making my way along the paths, now tracking the boot prints of the woman's husband. I was moving faster than ever, spurred on by the knowledge that the outside world was in this direction, and that I was doing all right, supported by my bank of Indian memories. After a few hours, I came to another settlement.]

Another woman scared out of her wits at seeing me. She wouldn't talk. She just wanted me away from her.

The speed I've been going, there's no danger Pasarin will catch me. As I travel, the paths are getting fresher. These signs are like whispers of the outside world, louder and louder, urging me on, out of here.

*At dusk*

Now it's twilight and I should be making a camp for the night but something has happened. I've come to a really decent sized river, and am in direct sunlight. And another thing, the forest is different here. At my feet are pretty flowers, much like lilies of the valley. Behind me is a tree like a cherry. It really is most peculiar; this is an old European garden, yet I'm in the Amazon forest.

I've just walked on a bit and have found, cramped by encroaching trees, an abandoned house which once had tiles on. In front of it,

261

two graves. Both the same age, and marked in the same way with a primitive cross. These two people died together.

No one has a grave on their front lawn. These were the occupants of the house and both met a sudden (violent?) death.

As for me, this place means life! I've made it to the outside world. Must have. The tiles and sawn planks have come from the outside. This is the frontier.

Suddenly, after the forest dark, all this daylight. The sun is on me – the outside world is on me. A rising feeling, a feeling that I've got away with it.

## XIII

# The Day of the Jaguar

I CUT A SAPLING to help me bridge a stream, and within minutes, sooner than I'd dared hope, was at a homestead.

'Are you a . . . a *gringo*?' were the first words of the man who came out to meet me. He looked me up and down, and was relieved to see that I was.

He told me I had reached Augora. I was on the Ipixuna, a tributary of the Juruá, the river on which stood Cruzeiro do Sul.

His family fed me and gave me a place to lie down, but they were unhappy with me here. 'We can't have doings with strangers,' the man said, putting me in a canoe for downriver the next morning. 'We have our families to think about,' his wife chipped in. 'You understand?"

With neighbours like theirs, I could quite understand.

Their canoe took me away downriver before the sun had even burned off the mist. I sat among a cargo of tortoises, and after two hours of being butted and scratched by them we drew up at a clearing, and the rough road to Cruzeiro do Sul. The crush of the insect noise was gone. There were no bird twitterings. The forest was behind me.

As I walked off alone up the road, a wide mud track with the sun and the outside world pouring in on me, I kept on telling myself that I was free. But it was like the freedom felt by an escaped prisoner. I seemed to have cheated the system. I expected to be hauled back. Think of Fawcett, I thought. Perhaps he thought he'd made it out of the forest too.

I kept walking quickly, as fast as ever. Never mind the glare of the sun after all the dark of the forest, never mind that the skin of my hands was blistering. As the air began to throb with heat, I came through rolling hills of destroyed forest, the cattle lands of Acre. With no trees any more, there was so much room in which to see.

And yet there was nothing much here. A reed bent and swung, telling me that a grasshopper was landing on it, perhaps to avoid a squad of predatory ants. That's all. Otherwise it was stiff grass, solitary palms and blackened tree remains, like the weathered masts of shipwrecks.

Dusk came, and still no one had dragged me back into the forest. But I didn't yet dare to think forward. I had not completed Phase Two, not until I was safe in the town. Then I could award myself a shower, I thought. I could buy shampoo, perhaps. But I mustn't think of these things yet.

Now there were cattle out there, and sometimes cowboys galloping around them. As the dusk came on the sky became yellow and puce, colours which I had not seen in such large spreads for months. That night I was sheltered by a farm worker, who killed a chicken in exchange for my last cruzeiros. I walked on again under the moonlight, before the heat would begin to bake me again.

As the first light came, I discovered that I was walking by a big *fazenda*, a large ranch. The land looked the same as everywhere else here – dead – but there were also businesslike black and white fence posts. I stopped, staring at them. They stretched ahead along the road to the horizon, lines of regulated wood, disciplined forest. Then I heard a vehicle engine. It was coming in this direction, across the *fazenda*, meandering towards the gate that I had just passed. It came into sight, a white pick-up truck. The driver slowed as he came alongside. 'Hop aboard.' He was looking straight ahead up the road. 'I'll take you back.'

Back? He thought I'd come from the town. No one came from the forest.

I climbed into the rear of the pick-up and we lurched off. As I bounced along, watching the frontier open up, I thought, 'Perhaps I've made it now. Perhaps it's safe enough to say that.' And I began to hold out hopes for the future. 'Soon I'll be in bed,' I thought. 'I'll get medicine for Fidencio's Revenge. I'll have a shower.'

But the rancher stopped after some miles, and got out of the vehicle. He was a short man, with a white cowboy hat.

'I'm lucky you were passing,' I said. 'It's not a busy road exactly, is it?'

He cut through the chatter. 'Lucky? The fact is, you're a journalist who's come out here to snoop, and I don't want you around. I'm taking you off my land.'

I sat there, slightly in shock. I'd thought of this man as my salvation, my help from the outside world; he was telling me I was his enemy. Limply, I told him that I wasn't a journalist.

All he said was, 'I don't want any trouble.' He took a swig of water from a container which had been sitting bouncing with me in the back. 'If you want trouble, I'll take you right the way back to Cruzeiro do Sul.'

'But that's where I want to go!'

He stopped swigging water and gave me a bit of a snarl. 'Are you trying to make fun of me?'

We drove off again, and stopped at a second *fazenda*, swinging in through huge gates. He sat me down under the shade of a lime tree. He said he wanted to tell me about the 'real' Francisco Alves Mendes.

I knew who he meant well enough. Chico Mendes had founded the Brazilian Rubber Tappers' Union and had campaigned for all those dependent on the rain forests. Soon he had consolidated the rubber tappers and little men into a force substantial enough to stand up against the power of the ranchers and owners of *intifundios*, large land holdings, people very much like my host. On 22 December 1988, just as his crusade had caught the imagination of environmentalists all around the world, the landowners lost patience and had Chico Mendes killed.*

My host said, 'He was a crook, a trouble-stirrer, corrupt.' These were only some of the Portuguese words I could understand. 'And don't pretend you don't speak fluent Portuguese. How did you get here from Cruzeiro do Sul, if you don't speak Portuguese?'

---

* 'They would have to kill us to destroy our movement and they can't. I don't get that cold feeling any more. I am no longer afraid of dying.' From the book of Mendes' thoughts, published seven months after his murder.

'But I haven't got to Cruzeiro do Sul yet.'

He thought I was mocking him again.

I had been trotting for a week through the forest and was too tired to argue. I sat in the shade, while sweat steamed off the rancher. 'You make me sick, American. You're not even trying to listen.' From time to time I tried telling him I'd come from the Javari but he wouldn't listen. He walked up and down, making himself hoarse, trying to get through to me.

'Only too obviously, you came up here from Rio. The Earth Summit. You are snooping around, causing mischief. Just say it. I'm not asking more. SAY IT!'

Finally, we were leaving for Cruzeiro do Sul – or so I thought. Beyond more acres of cows and scrubbed-out forest, we pulled up at the isolated house of one of his farm hands. 'This killed Chico Mendes,' he said, patting a rusty barrel of the farmworker's decrepit shotgun. It looked as if it would be more of a danger to anyone pulling the trigger, and anyway Chico Mendes was killed with a rifle – the fifth such union leader in Brazil that year. 'Are you getting the message, now?' the rancher said, rearranging his point for the umpteenth time. 'You, Mr Journalist, are not wanted here.'

'But I don't want to be here either,' I said.

The rancher couldn't stand it any more. He yanked open the door, ordered the workhand into the driving seat and told him to drive me to Cruzeiro do Sul. 'I've had enough of this!'

'At last,' I thought.

I was on my way now, surely. That shower. 'Thanks for the lift, anyway,' I said, cheerily. 'And by the way –'

'Think about it,' he said.

I was only going to tell him a wheel nut was coming undone.

I worried about the nut all the way, but the driver was a huge man who smelt of violence and I just sat there looking at the oncoming world instead. Small cattle herds blocked the road and men on horseback cracked whips over them. And then we were entering the main town itself. Even here cattle clattered along the roads, but there were also boys playing with kites. Two nuns stopped their car in the road to have a think, and stalled as they jerked forward again.

Town life, I thought. Man-made security for a while. That shower, and then sleep.

The pick-up stopped. I got out. 'By the way –' but the vehicle was moving off, tail gate flapping. 'One of your wheel nuts is loose,' I said, my voice trailing away.

I looked around. The central thoroughfare, layered with frontier sand, was marked out as a sports track. A boy wandered about with a white paint can, touching up the town tree-trunks. I saw a clock for the first time in almost three months. To my surprise it was still only mid-morning.

I walked to the nearest hotel, excitement welling inside me. My shower was minutes away. A quick glance in the hall mirror explained why the ranch owner, at least, thought I was after trouble. I had a desperate look in my eye – ten days of yearning for the safety of the outside world.

Just as I was about to go to enjoy my shower, I saw a map on the wall. It showed I was on the Juruá river, as planned, but I couldn't help but notice that the final phase of this journey kicked off with a good thousand kilometres of forest – not a road in sight. Indeed, there wasn't even a year-round road from here to the provincial capital, Rio Branco.

I wanted to cry.

Better not to think about Phase Three just now, perhaps. Now was holiday time.

But I couldn't resist a closer peep. The Juruá was a substantial river and would have lots of traffic. So far so good. I would take a boat south, downriver to the settlement of Eirunepé, and there ask around for help getting east through 300 kilometres of forest to the next river along, the Purus. Having survived this I could think about getting through 200 kilometres of forest to Pôrto Velho, on the Madeira river. It didn't bear thinking about, and I decided not to.

The good news was that after that I'd be able to zig-zag along dirt roads across the Mato Grosso to the Xingu tributary called 7 de Setembro, the source of which marked the furthest reach of the Basin and the end of my journey – but it was already too late. I'd heard too much about what was ahead of me: my shower was ruined.

I had a quick splash in the washbasin and, knowing I wasn't going to have the energy once I had collapsed on a bed, I staggered off to have my passport stamped, to change my money, and phone Jita: no reply. At the riverside I glimpsed a leaky little *colectivo* passenger boat set to cast off its moorings. It claimed to be going down the Juruá, past Eirunepé, just my destination.

'Coming aboard or not?' asked the captain. The boat was seething with passengers, and looked part wood tug, part open boat – the sort you'd catch if you don't mind risking a short river crossing. In my state, I wouldn't have minded risking it across the Atlantic.

But not today. Apart from needing to buy equipment – forget the shampoo – I needed a nice long rest. I probably needed a nice long look over by a doctor as well. I said, 'Sorry, no time to get my supplies.'

I expected the captain to say, 'Bad luck then, *gringo*. We're off.' He said, 'We'll wait.'

'Food,' I said. 'I'll need food for the voyage.'

'You'll be served three meals a day. All included.'

'No, really. Better I wait for the next chance. Tired.'

'Next boat's due in a month.'

Wearily, I gathered my things from the hotel. Perhaps the tide is now running my way, I thought. Perhaps that's what it is.

After more disastrous black market dollar dealings, I walked down to the waterside, with three quickly purchased machetes. I'd just have to buy more equipment downriver, I thought, as I threw myself aboard.

As the deckhand cast off, I remembered I hadn't bought antibiotics for my Fidencio's Revenge. As the boat swung into the midriver my bowels made a portentous burbling noise.


It had been my agreement with myself that I'd have a rest after the forest. I had been trotting ten hours a day, sometimes alone, and always silent, and now I was trapped on a boat with dysentery – I think after more than six weeks we can reasonably call Fidencio's Revenge dysentery – and losing my seat to the throng every time I went to queue at the loo.

Opposite me was a grandmother, her daughter, and her

daughter's daughter, each with the same long bleached hair on their arms, and each with large African buttocks – each female a tribute to the way the Portuguese colonialists had intermarried with the Indians and plantation slave descendants. They wore the tight half-length blouses currently in fashion, and together paraded the skinny, russet navels of three generations.

Had I been thinking of sleeping, that was not an option either. I was English, and that made me a curiosity. England was America, and America was what Brazil wanted to be – America was where dollars came from. Here in Brazil, inflation being what it was, the descendants of the country's great pioneers refused to allow their faces on the banknotes. 'Let our corrupt politicians be put on them instead.' So the Brazilians dreamed of America; the school uniform was blue jeans.

My neighbour, who had a very sharp elbow, said, 'English? I can speak that.' He taught his friends a proverb. 'You can't get help for love or honey.'

'Money,' I corrected him. But it was no use. He wanted to be seen to be understood by an American.

'See! He understands.'

He had Hitler's greasy hair and parting. As the days passed I grew to know him – the horribleness in the way he handled his cigarette. His lips puckered as he took a drag, as if they found the proximity of his skinny fingers distasteful. Worst of all were his eyes, which played around the young women on board, feeding on the way they moved – the granddaughter, stroking her hair, assembling her long locks on her shoulder like a pet; a girl on her boyfriend's knee, blowing her bubble gum, a pink that matched her lipstick.

I hung on, gritting my teeth. I saw the forest go by, and wanted to be back walking through it again.

I wasn't the only one. We were carrying too much animal life as well as too many passengers, and most seemed to be trying to escape. There was the goat on the roof, the chickens in baskets, parrots in cages under a cotton wrap. Sometimes the goat let out a mad cry of despair, and this was faithfully imitated by the parrot: 'baaaa!' Dogs were also here in force: dogs that sat on my feet, dogs that looked abandoned, dogs that looked rabid, dogs that looked dead. The one sitting on my foot was a diseased mutt of doubtful parentage whose lower lip had once been removed by a pig. Consequently saliva dripped out of its mouth and down our legs.

'Doggy?' asked a child who was wanting to learn English.

'Doggy,' I confirmed, sadly, and the mutt licked my foot gratefully.

The night came on, and under cover of darkness, we each tried our best to shift the dog away from our spot. The dog spent its time swaying sleepily on its feet, moved to and fro by our wet toes.

On the three-day voyage to Eirunepé the only friend I made was the cook, Mirlena. It was Mirlena who rustled up a set of nondescript antibiotics and put an end to Fidencio's Revenge. And eventually, still sitting in my one shirt, with sweat in it from days running through the forest and red dust in it from the road – just when I was beginning to want to chuck the dogs, and myself, overboard in despair – it was Mirlena who secured me a way through the forests to the next river along, the Purus.

Her job was to serve us meals cooked in the muddy water. She earned much less than the minimum wage, about enough every week to pay for the hotel bed I'd promised myself – and not got. By the time she reached the boat's destination, Manaus, it wouldn't be worth even half a night's stay. I'd moaned to her how much I'd felt like a prisoner here in the little boat but now I felt ashamed, for Mirlena the cook really was a prisoner.

She was a stout girl with an unfocused look to one eye, but the captain was after her and some of the passengers as well. She came over to sit beside me just to get away from them. Together we looked out from our prison hulk, extracting what entertainment we could from the passing world. We watched the bats, how their wings caught the sunset light as they swung through the air.

The second evening we stopped at the little town of Ipixuna for a few hours, and I walked ashore towards the sound of a party. Now I can have a decent wash, I thought. And scrub my clothes. Now I can have my shower, even.

I ran towards the lights and music. Ribbons had been strung on power lines over a dirt dance floor, men leant against the tin walls with bottles in their hands. Or they yanked girls to their feet and danced a primitive salsa with stiff movements, like the backwards-forwards duel of two insects. Not a word was said between partners as they parted at the end of a dance; the men just reached for their drink.

I tried to ask a serving girl where I might wash my clothes and have a shower. But the serving girl appeared to come with the service, and disappeared down a dark passage with a customer. Most of the men were very drunk. A mad boy opened up the contents of his shorts for everyone to see, and the men just saluted his health. No one shouldered him away. This *was* away. There was nowhere else to go.

Just as I found someone coherent enough to ask where I might wash, the captain emerged – he was the man who had been down the dark passage with the serving girl. He said to me, *'Oba!* Wow!' and plodded back down the river bank, taking me with him. We were off again.

Presumably as the result of some of these parties, three of the eight unmarried girls on the boat had babies. Mirlena told me that hers was being looked after by her mother in a settlement she called Envira, on the Envira tributary, near Eirunepé. She already knew that I was heading in that direction, east, and she said I might do well to head up there. A week ago a party of hunters had come all the way from the Purus, where I was heading, and down the Envira. They were resupplying their expedition at Eirunepé and would be going back in a few days. If Mirlena was right, then I might do this leg through the forest to the Purus in a matter of weeks, rather than months. Sitting here on my prison barge, it was an exciting prospect indeed.

Mirlena said she'd show me on my map.

'Don't carry one,' I said. 'I want the local view.' But for the first time in six months I really regretted it.

She drew a sketch in my notebook.

However much I wanted to put my feet up for a few days, we agreed that I just couldn't let this opportunity go by. And there'd surely be time to have a shower in Eirunepé. 'Just as long as I get that.'

I had great hopes of Eirunepé. It was a regional headquarters of the New Tribes Mission, American missionaries of a Protestant, clean-cut persuasion – they were bound to have a shower there.

Just when Eirunepé was at last in sight and it was time to gather up my few soiled belongings, Mirlena spotted a childhood friend of hers travelling along the shore in a canoe with a *peque-peque*. He would know if the hunters were still resupplying their expedition in the town. She told the captain to slow our boat, letting the canoe come alongside. Close up, Mirlena's friend looked mean, even cruel. It took time before he had any kind of smile for her. He said the hunters had already left the settlement, and were probably at their shack on the Envira, about to head back to the Purus by way of the Pauini tributary.

The name Pauini meant only one thing to me: it was one of the areas of conflict between rubber tappers and the Indians. I remembered reading in *Amazon Frontier* of how the Indian populations of the headwaters of the Purus and Juruá had been systematically wiped out as men penetrated the forests in search of wild rubber or Indian women. Alfredo Lustosa Cabral witnessed a reprisal raid on the Katukina of the upper Juruá. They were shot in turn as they came out of their hut. Fifteen children were captured and on the return journey home, when they cried too much, abandoned in the forest. They were still tied up. Some men fired off their Winchesters, 'taking off the tops of the children's heads with bullets'.

On the Pauini too, the Indians were being forced to retreat further into the headwaters. 'The owners of the seringals [the rubber stands] exact a heavy penalty for massacres, and the reports of killing are becoming less and less frequent,' noted Henry Pearson, editor of *The Indian Rubber World* around the turn of the century. 'The remaining wild tribes, as a rule, live back in the forests above the limits of navigation.'

Which was where I'd be heading to from this side. But I suspected that, as usual, if there was any hazard it was not going to be from the Indians.

It sounded as if it was too late to catch the hunters. 'Never mind,' I said to Mirlena, 'I'm exhausted anyway. Better I call in at the town, plan this properly. Buy some food.' And the shower, I thought. Maybe the American missionaries had a tiled bathroom. I savoured this pleasant prospect for a second.

'My friend here is a kind man, he'll help you catch up,' Mirlena said. 'You're both strong. You could run, catch them on the trail.'

'No, really,' I said. I'd introduced myself to her as an explorer. I couldn't tell her that all I wanted was my shower.

Mirlena was suddenly cross. 'You are prepared to kill yourself trying to get through the forest without a compass – and alone – when you could be taken through the forest in days?'

For a shower, I thought, yes. But I couldn't say so and I was soon aboard the canoe and turning off up the Envira, leaving Mirlena behind, waving back from her prison.

By dusk, we had arrived at the hunters' shack on the Envira. Or rather, I had arrived there. I stood alone on the river bank, dumped without assistance. The hunters had left by foot for the Pauini, and there was no knowing how far they had gone. 'But you can't leave me here,' I said, as the glum boatman chucked me a small basket of *farinha* and some sugar, and took one of my machetes in exchange.

'The three hunters must be just up the trail,' he said, pulling away. 'Their boss is a good man. He's waiting for them at the Pauini before leaving in their canoe.'

'Supposing the three men have got there already? That would mean there's no one out here in all this forest.'

'Not my problem,' he said. His voice was beginning to fade. Straining, I could just make out his final words. 'You asked to be taken here, and that's what I'm doing.'

I looked about me. A string of butterflies with zebra-striped, oval wings descended to the ground attracted to the salts left where the hunters had urinated. Other butterflies came as I watched, some with the colours of a miniature peacock, though with not so much to display about. A sparrow-sized bird, a tanager, spun by, the last light of day warm on its mossy head, its cream breast.

Things would work out, I told myself, as I lay in my mosquito net listening to the whistle hoot of the owls, the swooping tones of the nightjars. After all, they always had. The broken ribs, the cocaine dealers – the list went on and on. Yes, things would work out. Being abandoned was par for the course, nowadays.

\*       \*       \*

I got up early, and felt less sure of things. The hunters had left yesterday at the latest, and that was a long time ago in a place where rain showers came every day and wiped the ground clean.

Slowly, I began investigating the forest for new trails – bruised saplings, snapped leaves. At last I tilted my pack on to my back, took a deep breath and, with only enough food for two days, struck out, walking quickly up the new trail cut by the hunters, wondering if there was anyone at the end of it. In a couple of days they'd already be descending the Purus, a hundred or more kilometres away. If I didn't catch up with them today or tomorrow, then I might never find a way out of here. I charged on, head to the ground, once again trying to be as good as Roberto and Lucy, with their toy arrows and quick senses.

A trumpeter bird scuttled away on its skinny black chicken legs. A tree that I brushed gave out a fleshy tang, the strong pungent smell of meat. These things were important to me, as I trotted along. They were things I knew about, familiar pieces of furniture belonging to a place I had to believe I could live in. Somewhere ahead of me now were a group of white-lipped peccaries. They left a wide track through the forest, and later I found a muddy pool where they had wallowed. Then I heard them – a piglet squealing, and the huge teeth munching through the forest.

I stopped only once, to eat sugar and *farinha*. On a tree beside me was a dense cluster of caterpillars. They bore silvery hairs on their black and white backs and together their colony formed a mat. When I tapped the mat with a stick, the caterpillars squirmed. The weaker ones fell to the ground, easy prey for birds, wasps and all the other hunters.

Perhaps I was being really stupid. Perhaps I should go back and wait for any passing river traffic. Think of Colonel Fawcett. 'The forest,' wrote his son, 'in allowing him a peep at its soul, claimed his life in payment.'

But I found myself on the move again. Faster, faster. I kept walking through the still hours of midday, and now sometimes saw a boot print filled with clouded water. I wasn't far behind. Probably I would catch them in time. Probably.

Finally, I stopped. I must now have covered two days' walk. It was dusk and still there was no one. I was in the middle of nowhere, alone, and I felt I was about to burst into tears. Slowly, trying to be strong, I went about making a little camp, tiling my shelter with leaves from a wild banana. Soon after I heard a knocking – regular, persistent, unmistakably a human sound. I ran to investigate and soon I saw a tall man inspecting a tree, looking up a giant buttress. I called out, and got a return call from him, and also from another man further away. I'd found the hunters.

They had a camp only a few hundred paces from mine, in which was a third member of their party who was flat on his back with a fever. Most of their equipment was with their boss, but they had a shotgun and box upon box of cartridges. They sat me down to eat their pork with them, and I found a malaria pill to give the sick man.

However, soon I was wishing I hadn't found the hunters at all. One of them was short and lean and the other tall and lean, but both kept talking about how poor they were and how I was a rich American and could help them out. They kept asking where I was camped, and was I really alone. Did I have any cartridges? I suspected they wanted to know if I was armed.

'I'm in trouble again,' I thought.

It was getting dark. They told me to bring my equipment over. They'd look after me, take me along to the Pauini, the Purus tributary two days' walk from here, where the boss and one other man were waiting with a canoe and motor. 'One hundred dollars,' they said.

'Here we go again,' I said to myself as I walked away, wearily taking a direction to my camp that would mislead them. It was just like old times. Through the night I thought about it. Really I had no option but to go with these people, but the situation didn't look good. I lay awake, listening out for them. All was silence, except for the scratching of a tree-rat above me, and the hiss and tinkle of a gathering wind and a million hoppers and scratchers. Before daybreak, I got up and went for a little walk. I still needed to think.

Half an hour later, when I came back to my camp, I found nothing. They had taken the whole lot. All I had now was the pair of shorts that I was wearing.

I shook my head in disbelief. 'As I was saying,' I said aloud, 'just like old times.' It was impossible to take this expedition seriously any more. I mean, Fate, what the hell did it think it was playing at? Once again, I was going to be following thieves, looking for the trademarks of big boots. Once again, I was up against it.

But there was a difference between this occasion and the last. This time I wasn't feeling afraid. Perhaps I'd just had too little sleep for too long, but I felt in control. This time I was hunting people down, not escaping. This time, they were the ones running away, not me.

I saw that they had taken a route that ran along parallel to the Pauini path. They were hoping to lose me.

Well, they wouldn't succeed – not unless they sharpened up their performance. I settled down to the old routine, craning forward and walking. The forest, so big and relentless, was on my side. I really believed that; maybe as a Jaguar Person I was a non-starter, but I belonged here a good deal more than these hunters knew. And although when it began to rain I did slip about in my bare feet, and when there were palm thorns across the path I did walk more like a skinny-legged heron than a big cat, I was good enough. I was even rather enjoying myself.

Within the hour, I had them in my sight. I watched their progress. They were trying to hurry, but they seemed slow, heavy-footed – even allowing for their sick man. They were meant to be hunters, but they looked like easy prey.

Creeping behind them, following at leisure, I bided my time. Then the third man must have become much weaker because they had to stop to make a camp. Suddenly I realized I didn't know what I was going to do next. I stood there watching, crouched, being bitten by mosquitoes. The sick man moaned a bit, and they fetched water for him. This told me there was a stream on the other side. I went for a drink there myself – still with this new feeling that, dealing with these outsiders, these hunters, I had all the time in the world. Up in a tree, a Spix's guan, from the same family as the curassow. And I stayed to watch a kingfisher; coming away from a dive it gave a shake of its wet head.

I returned to sit behind a tree. A konga ant marched by, an inch long and shiny black. Its sting could inflict pain for several hours, enough to cause me serious problems. It was a sobering reminder as I sat just in my shorts. I was far from safe, as yet.

A short distance from the camp I wrenched open a palm to eat and found a fruit like a peachy mango. Now the light was beginning to fail and I began to feel nervous about what I was about to do. I remembered how Helena, Roberto and Lucy had played jaguars, stalking me from behind, and measuring themselves off against my back. Well, now it was my chance.

First I worked out a route in. I'd use that trick Pablito had taught me, using a spear to clear sticks that might crack underfoot. As important as my route into the camp were routes away, and I now worked on these. I made two piles of leaf bedding, alternative places to which I might flee.

As the light dimmed, they lit their little paraffin lamp. I checked: there was my rucksack, lying half opened; and there was my machete, stabbed into the ground by the camp fire. The orange flame of the lamp spread a bowl of light that even reached me out here. I would wait until they blew it out. That would be my time.

They had finished their supper and fireflies were shimmering through the darkness. Now the time was getting near, and I was feeling sick in my stomach. The light was suddenly out. Time to go. I crept closer, unable to see twigs ahead, but feeling my way with the stick, using it instead of jaguar whiskers. I darted in. One quick swoop, and I had my rucksack and was bounding away.

I waited for the cries of shock, the men to scramble to load their shotgun and blast blindly into the night. But there was no sound at all. They hadn't even noticed me. So I pounced in a second time and swiped away the machete. I was away again, and again I had not been noticed.

Suddenly it was all over. Out of reach, I fingered through the rucksack, feeling my boots, and the rest of my kit, including mosquito net, diaries, film and camera and documents, and half of the *farinha*. It was too dark to erect my mosquito net properly and in the night I was bitten by ants and mosquitoes; damp, spidery things ran over me in the dark. It didn't matter: I was on my way out of here. I had actually pulled off something that Pablito would have been proud of.

The next morning, I sped along the track towards the Pauini, and the 'good man' who was the boss of their party. After an hour, though, I started to reflect. I wrote in my diary: 'I'm far from out of danger myself, but I'm starting to worry about that sick hunter. There's someone dying out here in the forest and it might have been me. I let him die? Law of the Jungle? I could have left him some of my malaria tablets . . .'

I walked further, scared by the change in pitch of the cicadas. It was already the thick of midday. I stopped again.

'I've been thinking about that sick logger,' I wrote. 'Is he dead by now? It's not reasonable to expect me to go back, is it? Back into danger.'

Soon I was on my way again, but not for long. I sat by a stream, thinking about the man. I watched a wounded cockroach rise heavily into the air and then drop into the water. A surge, and it was eaten. 'So much life is used up in keeping the forest going,' I wrote. 'And the hunter's too?'

Typical. Just when I was on my way out of here, just when I was triumphing against the odds, and actually had something to celebrate, it had all been ruined.

I couldn't go on. The sick man would have to be rescued.

Hardly able to believe I was doing this, I hid my pack and turned round again. 'Just typical,' I said again, and plodded back down the track. Why was I risking doing this? I asked myself. I didn't even know. Perhaps it was because of that day with Roberto when I'd shocked myself with my behaviour, killing a fish with my teeth. Perhaps my worry was that I had been toughened into a hard forest creature – like Lucy, able to tear up an insect as if it was waste paper.

Then, before I knew it, the three hunters were standing there in front of me: we were staring at each other on the track. But how things had changed. They were pale, covered in mud from a day's struggle with the sick man. He hung limp, suspended between the other two. The tall man gave a wince of recognition, but they were all so tired, they hardly cared what happened next.

I got out the malaria pills and barged the men aside as a doctor might, trying to get through a crowd to a car crash victim. No words were exchanged. Soon I had handed over the pills and we were hobbling along the path, taking it in turns to support the sick man. Slowly, I got to know him, this person I had risked going back for, this man whose skinny arm was clutched around my throat, partially choking me.

He said nothing, unless it was to give me an order, '*Inglês*, water!'

His left forefinger was cut off a little at the end, making the fingernail stumpy. His face was tight-skinned, a little grim, and he had only a thin patch of hair growing on his head.

'*Inglês*, cigarette!' He seemed excessively self-centred, even for someone who had recently been dying.

'*Inglês*, water!!' As he gave his orders, his stubbly chin moved, flicking the home-made cigarette that one of the other hunters had put in his mouth. They had probably shoved it there to shut him up.

This man demanded we stopped to give him a rest, though the dark was coming on. 'You want to know something?' He began a long, rambling story, a long tale about how, walking in the forest, he'd seen a skull of a giant man. He'd hit it with a machete – it cracked and a giant egg yolk came out. 'I thought you were meant to be ill,' the lean man said afterwards, voicing my thoughts exactly.

We started walking again.

'I saw an animal graveyard once,' the short man said, his head protruding from the sick man's armpit. 'Some bones were more than a metre long.'

'Don't you start,' the other man said.

An hour beyond the place where I'd hidden my backpack was the camp. The whole gang of us left together the next morning and the day after reached the Pauini and their motor and dugout. We left straight away for downriver.

It really did look as if I would come out of this unscathed. We made our way, day and night towards the settlement of Labrea, occasionally popping malaria pills into the mouth of the sick man. After Labrea would be more forest, a battle to get to the Madeira river and Pôrto Velho, start of the notorious Madeira–Mamoré railway.*

* Promised by the Brazilians in exchange for Bolivia giving up the rubber-rich territory of Acre – including the forest I'd tramped through from the Javari – the railway, which cut through remote, disease-ridden forest, was never fully completed. What there was of it came too late to help the country exploit the rubber boom. From 1912, the market began to collapse – rubber seedlings smuggled out of the Amazon thirty years earlier had grown into the huge plantations of Malaya. Bolivia was left with a useless railway that had cost 6,200 lives, one for each hundred sleepers. They had died for nothing.

But after two days the sick hunter had recovered sufficiently to talk full-time. '*Inglês*, got a girlfriend? I have. Told her she wasn't coming out here for a year. Want to establish myself first, so the other men can't get her.'

He described how his previous girlfriends had been 'got' by other hunters. 'Lost a great many friends that way.'

There was no end to this man's stories and soon I was beginning to wish I hadn't gone back for him. My machete had already disappeared and now I found my only spare shirt was gone. Where were they hiding these things? I never worked it out. A fish jumped into the canoe and before I could kill it the creature left an unwashable smear on my one remaining shirt. That day the hunters also took my fishing tackle and I caught the sick man rummaging in my backpack.

At last, one night, Labrea appeared in the darkness. We drew alongside the river bank, I stepped ashore and said goodbye, and as they disappeared into the shadows I found they had stolen my last cash.

All was quiet, and very dark.

A man was sitting by the water. He had lifted his shirt to his shoulder to scratch his stomach.

A big black bug blundered against the man's paraffin lamp – 'whack!' – and slid down, in insect unconsciousness.

'From where?' the man asked. As usual, it took some explaining. 'God, you're lucky!'

'Lucky?' I didn't feel lucky. Exhausted, robbed, yes. Lucky, no.

'You've got here from Cruzeiro do Sul in two weeks!' he said. 'Without those hunters, it could have taken you the rest of your life.'

'Without the hunters I'd still have money, and a way out of here.'

However, one had to count one's blessings. I did, after all, have my backpack. I opened it up, gratefully – and found that the man whose life I had saved had pinched my camera.

A solitary giant toad was messing about under the man's lamp. Its eyebrows were thick leathery shelves. In this darkness, a mad Indian boy was trying to construct a huge cross on the riverbank, tying poles with bark string. At least I presumed he was mad.

'Where are you going now?'

I told the man I was going in the direction of Pôrto Velho, the city on the Madeira river, but I was in dire straits. It was 150 kilometres east through the forest to the main highway leading there.

'God, you're lucky.'

'I wish you wouldn't keep saying that.'

'I mean, they've now built a road from here, all the way through the forest to the Pan-American Highway. My lorry is leaving when the daylight comes.'

That wasn't the end of the Amazon, and that wasn't the end of the struggle to get across it.

But I had been through so much; the momentum I had gathered was enough to enable me to surmount obstacles that normally would have reduced me to a sobbing heap. Now, the journey carried me along with its own force.

There was Pôrto Velho, where I had been intending to have that shower and get some money but which I accidentally passed through in the truck at night; next, the more modest town of Vilhena, where I climbed off the truck, brushed myself down, and uncovered a forgotten stash of money in my trousers. Tacking south-east towards the Mato Grosso, I cadged a lift on the back of a cattle wagon.

Sleep would solve a lot, I decided, as I bounced through the road dust and the goldmining country of the upper Juruena. My eyes, which I could feel with my hands were sunk back into their sockets, would soon resurface. Just as soon as I had a good long rest. Yet rest was one thing I couldn't allow myself. Luck had carried me through too many disasters. Whenever there was an opportunity to keep going, a truck ride, a lift on the back of a jeep, I felt I couldn't afford to ignore it. I must hurry on out of the Amazon while it was still giving me the chance.

I kept my nose out of the window, watching the forest for its surprises. However, this was forest dissected by white men and it frequently looked a bit second-hand, misused by careless owners. Often it was low, dented, scrubby, and sometimes, where the forest had been ripped open completely, the land had disappeared along

with it. There were banks of pure clay on the roadside and sometimes what separated these banks from others was not trees, but
gullies, gaps where the rain had carried away the landscape as well.

Between lifts on the backs of lorries, there were waits on the
edge of frontier towns, sitting in dry ditches by the now barren
pastures, with the ants and coarse grass.

On I went. I took a lift, was dumped in the middle of nowhere,
picked up again. On past *fazendas* with signs bearing the German
names of their owners and telling strangers that they were pro-
hibited. Boys with waste-paper kites. Girls in their school jeans –
one girl with a top button undone for her pregnancy. A policeman
slept, and a passing child put a plastic beaker on his head. And
couples in tin-roofed villages without a plaza did their best at seren-
ading, getting a year or two in before marriage. Madmen whom
the dogs loved to pursue, hoteliers left standing in the doorway
while I moved onward, not daring even to stop to have that shower.
I hung on, hoping against hope that luck would hold long enough
for me to survive whatever other bizarre instalments were to feature
on this expedition – I knew I was due for another one soon.

It came as I neared Novo Horizonte and my lorry driver
demanded cash and then dropped me on a marshy side-road. There
didn't seem to have been another vehicle here for years. Beside me
in the ditch, a dead dragonfly was suspended in a cobweb, swinging
stiffly, like a mobile. Further along, small alligators were sunbathing
in the road. As I walked to whatever might be the nearest house,
the alligators picked themselves up, and with a tick-tock, clockwork
motion moved over into the ditch. With the light fading I began
to wonder if their bigger brothers would tick-tock back on to the
road again.

A Toyota approached at last and came to a halt. The driver
cautiously wound down a window to examine me. He was a government official working in conjunction with IBAMA, he said, the
'Brazilian Institute of the Environment and Natural Renewable
Resources' which sought to establish and maintain forest reserves.
He'd gladly put me up for the night. He promised to tell me more
about his laudable work, but when we arrived at his quarters, a
prefabricated hut off the side of the road, he instead showed me a
photo of a girl from Glasgow. 'I miss her,' he said.

Soon, even before I had managed to have that shower, I found out how much he missed her. He dropped his supper into my lap and insisted on wiping up the mess with a damp cloth. After a few wipes he came to the area of my crotch. Suddenly the deprived man could control himself no longer. He was on me, his hands wrestling with my flies.

It was not his lucky day. I hadn't come across the Amazon Basin – chased, shanghaied, robbed, pillaged – just to be molested by a sex-starved civil servant. But as I threw him off, I was alarmed to see he had already got his trousers down.

Now he was back on top of me, using his weight. His fingers were very strong and I couldn't peel them away. He began shouting. 'Shit you, shit you!'

After peeling off his fingers one by one, I seized his hands, and heaved him away. He didn't give up. Effectively, his trousers had hobbled him around his ankles, and he now propelled himself on top of me like a skydiver. 'Don't be afraid. Nothing's going to happen. I just want to touch you. Nothing's going to happen.' He was absolutely right it wasn't. After another scuffle, quite violent now, I rolled him off me. He collapsed on the floor in a sorrowful pile.

Time to leave. Outside, it was very dark. It must have been my imagination but I thought I could hear alligators snapping their jaws.

The nearest habitation was a good deal nearer than it might have been and a man with a hairy mole on his nose beckoned me in for the night. His wife, speechless with delight at having a guest, sent a child to clean a glass and pour their prize bottle of warm Coca-Cola. Her hair was in a plastic bag, being bleached blond, but she cut short the operation to cook some meat. It had the fishy taste of the alligator meat walking about outside.

Quite unable now to imagine what would befall me next, I caught another lift in a lorry, meeting the huge road that was slicing south to Cuiabá and at Sinop carrying on east into forest again – the Mato Grosso. I took a breath. This was Fawcett country. He had launched his last expedition from Cuiabá, coming north through the forest, in this direction.

The road was shrouded by trees once more, as I bounced in the cab of an empty timber truck. We surged through the mud, the engine roaring, as if hungry to devour more forest. Ahead now would be the Xingu river, and somewhere in this forest 'Dead Horse Camp' – the site at which Fawcett dismissed his porters and walked on alone with Jack and Raleigh Rimell, expecting, he had said vaguely, to reach Indians and a great waterfall in ten days. It was difficult to know when exactly my timber lorry would be nearest to Dead Horse Camp, or indeed if we were churning right over it. Fawcett had marked it as 11° 43' South, 54° 35' West – but this was one of the secretive man's attempts to disguise his trail. The last authenticated sighting had been at Bakairi Post (around 14° 10' South, 54° 15' West) on 20 May; although he was last seen heading this direction, north into the Mato Grosso, it was too far to have come in nine days. My road turned south, then east, then south again, taking me towards Bakairi, back along Fawcett's alleged route. Somewhere here were the last remains of Fawcett and his companions, somewhere, in my estimation, not far from his departure point, Bakairi and the Xingu tributary called the Culuene. As I thumped along the forest road, I thought of Fawcett's last letter – 'you need have no fear of any failure' – but even in this final message he had been complaining of the trail's discomforts, the insects they were enduring; he expressed concern over Rimell's foot, already badly swollen. The lorry pounded on, so easily carrying me out of the forest that claimed Fawcett's life in payment for a peep at its soul.

From Paranatinga, a town near Bakairi, now an Indigenous Reserve, I found a better road north-east across the Culuene river. And here it seemed that the Mato Grosso, the 'thick forest', was largely ranches with the sporadic forest often reduced to copses. So much forest had been peeled away – and still not a hint of Fawcett's Golden City. But after all, wasn't his legacy in what he dreamed of finding, rather than in what he found? In mirroring the quest of El Dorado of 300 years before, he had become an enduring symbol of the Amazon's hold over our imaginations, a sobering reminder of the way we have all, as outsiders, projected on to those forests whatever we desired – a lost city of gold, a Green Hell or an Eden.

\*     \*     \*

Towards the end of that same cattle-ranch road, we crossed the River 7 de Setembro, whose source marked the far end of the Amazon Basin. One day, into February and a little over seven months since I began, it was all over. I stepped out of a cattle truck, and was in the new frontier town of Agua Boa. Here, and only here, I could reach for the second of the two local maps I had brought with me all the way from England. The first had shown the start of my journey, the bleak countryside around Cotopaxi, and this map showed the other end of the basin, the source of the river called 7 de Setembro. I had all but finished my journey.

I heaved my backpack to a bar, and sat down, utterly dazed. All the energies that I had nurtured so carefully over seven months were suddenly gone. I had a drink of water, and asked for a basic meal – 'anything' – and collapsed beside a cowboy who was spooning beans into his mouth. I sat there in a stupor, smelling like a cow, unable to absorb what it meant to have got here, a stone's throw from the other end of the Amazon, a little brook in cattle land that was so far – it would prove to have been 5,800 kilometres by my route – from that little brook in the windswept Andes.

It wasn't a poignant moment, going out alone into one of the wired-in fields, and satisfying myself I had found the trickle of water at the end of my journey. I knew the Amazon enough to know it wasn't behind me. The Amazon was too big. I've said it before – its influence spreads further than just its physical boundaries.


I climbed aboard a flight to Rio and, before even having that shower and making myself presentable for Jita's arrival the next day, I took a walk down the Avenida Rio Branco wanting to feel the security of a city, a man-made place. No more rapacious wildlife – no ants scrambling over me, no more fungi establishing colonies on my skin. I'd been living on my nerves for weeks, terrified that the Amazon would digest me. And here in Rio, just when the Amazon had kindly spat me out and I was ready to welcome the outside world again, I was jumped on by two youths with knives.

Like the desperate civil servant, the robbers were out of luck. Coming at the end of this particular journey, two youths with knives presented no very great problem. I bashed them away with my bag, using the weight of the video recorder. A police car, seeing the scuffle, swung around in the street. An officer jumped out with his gun and seized one boy. The other robber slipped away. Then I saw that the policeman was drunk. I tried to slip away too.

Too late. The policeman waved me into the back of his car. I sat beside the boy who had, moments ago, attacked me. The policeman jammed the knife to the boy's throat to get him to tell him where he lived; afterwards, he tried his gun. It was no good at all asking a homeless boy where he lived, even at gunpoint, and after a while the policeman turned his attentions to me and – just as the robber had, moments ago – asked for my wallet.

I sat beside my robber in the police car, pretending not to understand Portuguese and wondering why, attacked by armed robbers, I had felt virtually no surge of adrenalin. Could it be that the jungle had finally made me an efficient fighting machine? Could it be that, after all the forest had thrown at me, I have graduated into a sort of lesser jaguar? I toyed with the unlikely possibility while the policeman tried his best to menace me. It should have felt very strange to be threatened by a policeman while sitting next to a boy who had tried to knife me, but on this journey it was absolutely to be expected. On this journey, only the Amazon itself, that great misunderstood mass of trees, had proved reliable.

The policeman noticed my arm was bleeding. Time was running out – he needed a translator. He turned on the siren, and cut through the traffic to the nearest hotel. While the boy made his escape into the street, I was marched to the foyer. The hotel manager took one look at the policeman's bloodshot eyes and understood the situation, immediately trying to fob him off with a false name and passport number. 'This is to be the conclusion of the great journey, the first crossing of the Amazon Basin, is it?' I thought as the restaurant waiter hid me in the loo.

I was surprised I hadn't expected this: I had been looking forward to hot and cold water for seven months, and now I had all the water I wanted. I was trapped with it, hiding from a policeman in a washroom of the Hotel Aeroporto, wishing I was back in the forest where I was safe. Sometimes, I ducked outside to see if the coast was clear. The restaurant diners waved me back in again. The waiter now had instructions to move me to the Ladies, 'for safety', and a whole new range of farcical possibilities opened up. I leaned against the tiled wall, holding my loo-paper bandage. Now I was graced with the company of an American tourist, who'd come to assist me.

I could see that Sally-Anne didn't believe much in make-up; she had a large chunk of crystal hanging on a chain from her neck and she clicked as she walked – the sound of vitamin pills in her pocket. While we waited for the all-clear, Sally-Anne told me she was a Libra and that she had seen twenty-six countries around the world, and had recently returned from the Amazon. That was why she was here in the loo with me, she said. 'Because the Amazon has strengthened me. It's almost as if the forest has given me some of Mother Earth's life force – and now I feel able to help you in your crisis, Benedict.'

'This isn't a crisis,' I thought. Being hunted by cocaine dealers, that was a crisis.

She had just been to Lake Titicaca, up in the Peruvian Andes. The water-level was abnormally low. She feared it was symptomatic of the whole world. Mother Earth was suffering. 'It looks like She can't take much more of the treatment we hand out,' Sally-Anne said. 'She's about to shed Her human load.'

While we were waiting for the policeman to be arrested, Sally-Anne told me about the Amazon, how the basin was the most vital organ of the Earth. 'Her lungs,' breathed Sally-Anne, reverently.

Actually the Amazon isn't the lungs of the world – that's another myth. The forest does not produce a net amount of carbon dioxide, or of oxygen. In the day it absorbs the former, releases the latter, and it reverses this at night, like all green things. She must have learnt about it in her school biology classes.

After a great deal more of Sally-Anne's thoughts on Mother Earth, she peeked out of the door. 'I'll fetch some food for you. Something wholesome.' She came back soon after with a plate of sandwiches laid on a bed of lettuce. It seemed that I could come out of the loo now. It was all clear.

In the street there were three cars with flashing lights. A senior officer was shuffling away the drunk policeman. Now we could sit down and eat the sandwiches; at last things would begin to settle back to something like normality, I hoped. I was safely back where I belonged, the western world.

'Don't touch it!' Sally-Anne said, seizing a lettuce leaf from my plate.

I said, 'I'm sure it's been washed.'

But it was the chemical content. 'It's poisonous,' she said, tossing it back on to the tray. 'It'll make you mad.'

'*Lettuce?*' I looked at the limp leaf as it flapped harmlessly under the overhead fan.

'Quite mad,' she repeated. She'd read it in her magazine.

All those countries, all those places Sally-Anne had explored, and she was prepared to believe a lettuce leaf would kill her. As if any more proof were needed, I thought, that travel does not broaden the mind.

It hadn't broadened the mind of Sally-Anne and it hadn't broadened the minds of the *seringueiros*, the *conquistadores*, the missionaries, the European explorers who had seen, in the Amazon, female warriors, child-like savages, dangerous piranhas, golden cities, nature-loving natives. Perhaps some travellers did glimpse the place as it really was; but I doubted it. 'The mind is its own place,' said Milton, 'and in itself can make a heaven of hell, a hell of heaven.' The wonder of it was that the Amazon was mighty enough to encompass our dreams. It gave us all we asked of it: that was its power, the magic it had over every single one of us.

And sitting there in Rio, still holding my loo-roll bandage, I had reason to be grateful to the forest for bearing with my dreams, letting me travel as a lesser jaguar, a little like a creature that belonged there. Like Fawcett, I could believe that the Amazon had allowed me a peep at its soul – but my life had not been claimed in payment.

# SELECT BIBLIOGRAPHY

Allen, Benedict, *Mad White Giant: a journey to the heart of the Amazon jungle*, Flamingo, London, 1992.

Anon, 'Rio 92: Environment and Development', *Manchete* Special Issue, Rio de Janeiro, May 1992. A wide-ranging survey of all the environmental problems facing Brazil – and the Amazon in particular. Printed to coincide with the Earth Summit, which, if nothing else, brought world attention to all the issues thus far ignored by statesmen.

Bates, Henry Walter, *The Naturalist on the River Amazons*, John Murray, London, 1891. Bates places the Mayoruna territory as a several hundred mile stretch of the western (Peruvian) bank of the Javari.

Bayard, Andrea, *Brazilian Eden*, Travel Book Club, London, 1961. Straightforward account by an amateur explorer, one of the many who have attempted to solve the riddle of Colonel Fawcett's disappearance in the Mato Grosso.

Beckett, John B., *Savage Interlude*, Hale, London, 1968. Unvarnished, simple text, about an expedition just off the Amazon's northern watershed, in Guyana.

Boom, Brian M., 'Ethnobotany of the Chácobo Indians, Beni, Bolivia', *Advances in Economic Botany*, 4, New York Botanical Gardens, New York, 1987. Anthropologist Jonathan Benthall mentions this project and discusses the potential value of indigenous knowledge – and the ethical issues arising from extracting it – in *Anthropology Today*, Vol.9, No.3, June 1993, 1–2.

Carmichael, Elizabeth, Hugh-Jones, Stephen, Moser, Brian, and Taylor, Donald, *Hidden Peoples of the Amazon*, British Museum Publications, London, 1985. Recounts cocaine culture of the Tukano, and includes an 1817–20 portrait said to be of a Mayoruna.

Chagnon, Napoleon A., *Yanomamö: the Fierce People*, Holt, Rinehart & Winston, New York, 1977. Perhaps the best-selling anthropological account of all time. See Knox-Shaw, below.

Clark, Leonard, *The Rivers Ran East*, Funk & Wagnalls, New York, 1953. The American traveller died while exploring the Amazon in 1957.

Cloudsley, Tim, *Shell's Search for Oil and its Effects on Natives in the Lower Urubamba Region of the Peruvian Jungle*, Research Report for Survival International, Glasgow College of Technology, February 1987. An insight into the impact of a development project on the life of tribes, in this case the remote Nahua and Machiguenga. For more detail on oil company projects in the Oriente, see Survival International's Urgent Action Bulletin, July 1992 and others.

Cowell, Adrian, *The Heart of the Forest*, Travel Book Club, London 1960.

Drown, Frank and Marie, *Mission to the Head-hunters*, Hodder & Stoughton, London, 1962. Concerning the Jivaro, who are a Montana Forest tribe, like the Panoans.

Duguid, Julian, *Green Hell: a chronicle of travel in the forests of Eastern Bolivia*, Jonathan Cape, London, 1931. A romping narrative, 'a record of a little band of men who went adventuring'.

Eichhorn, Franz, *The Lost World of the Amazon*, Souvenir Press, London, 1955. Spirited film-maker encounters the 'River of a Thousand Crocodiles', the 'notorious cannibal' fish (the piranha), a 'life-or-death' tussle with an anaconda, and much else besides.

Elliot, Elizabeth, *Through Gates of Splendour*, Hodder & Stoughton, London, 1957. Tells the story of 'the martyrdom of Five Ecuadorean Missionaries in the Ecuadorean Jungle'.

Erikson, Philippe, 'Ritual dos Matís', *Horizonte Geografico*, 16, June 1991, 12–24. A graphic, illustrated account – one of the first, and one of the last – of Matís life, as found by an anthropologist on the River Ituí.

Fawcett, P. H., *Exploration Fawcett*, Hutchinson, London, 1953. The posthumous account edited by his son Brian. Other sources include: Kevin Healey, 'The Road Less Travelled', *The South American Explorer*, 24, January 1990, 4–11; Paul Donovan Kigar, 'The Phantom Trail of Colonel Fawcett,' *Américas*, Vol.27, No.4, April 1975. Also, splendidly fantastic, by the grandson of Fawcett's wife Nina, Timothy Paterson, 'Percy Harrison Fawcett: a Forerunner', *The Beacon*, September–October 1980, November–December 1980.

Flornoy, Bertrand, *Jivaro: among the headshrinkers of the Amazon*, Travel Book Club, London, 1953. 'The first false image that must be destroyed is that of the feathered cannibal shooting arrows at the brave traveller armed with butterfly net . . . The first duty of those interested in the fate of the Indian should be, it seems to me, to restore him to his dignity.'

Frank, Erwin H., '. . . *Y se lo comen'. Kritische Studie der Schriftquellen zum Kannabalismus der panosprachigen Indianer Ost-Perus und Brasiliens*, Hollos, Bonn, 1987. Catalogues (in German) what Evans-Pritchard called our 'morbid interest in cannibalism' as seen among the Panoan tribes.

Gheerbrant, Alain, *Impossible Adventure: Journey to the Far Amazon*, Gollancz, London, 1953. Account of an arduous expedition, sympathetic to Indians, whom they find wondrous – 'barbarian Adam and Eve' and all.

Grubb, K. G., *Amazon and Andes*, Methuen, London, 1930.

Hanbury-Tenison, Robin, *et al.*, *Aborigines of the Amazon Rain Forest: The Yanomami*, Time-Life Books, Amsterdam, 1982. See Knox-Shaw, below.

Hatt, John, *The Tropical Traveller*, Pan Books, London, 1982.

Hemming, John, *Amazon Frontier: the Defeat of the Brazilian Indians*, Macmillan, London, 1987. The authoritative history of the Amazon frontier, with many accounts of skirmishes and massacres of indigenous groups, and a major source for this book.

—— *Conquest of the Incas*, Macmillan, London, 1970. Now considered a classic.

—— *Red Gold: the Conquest of the Brazilian Indians*, Macmillan, London, 1978. A much acclaimed study of remarkable scope – 'likely to stand alone for some time to come'.

—— *The Search for El Dorado*, Michael Joseph, London, 1978.

Hvalkof, Søren, and Aaby, Peter, *Is God an American: an anthropological perspective on the missionary work of the Summer Institute of Linguistics (SIL)*, Survival International, London, 1981.

Jane, Cecil, *Selected Documents Illustrating the Four Voyages of Columbus*, II, London, 1933. Quoted in Knox-Shaw, below.

Knox-Shaw, Peter, *The Explorer, and Views of Creation*, English Studies in Africa, 27, 1–26, Witwatersrand University Press, Johannesburg, 1984. A discussion of the whole subject of explorers' preconceptions on encountering 'Nature'. To illustrate this with my own examples: are the Yanomami the 'Fierce People' whom the anthropologist Napoleon Chagnon described? 'A high capacity for rage, a quick flash point, and a willingness to use violence to obtain one's ends are all considered desirable traits,' reads the introduction to his celebrated book. Or was the 'peace of the *yano* [communal dwellings]', encountered by tribal rights campaigner Robin Hanbury-Tenison closer to the mark?

Kuklick, Henrika, *The Savage Within: The Social History of British Anthropology, 1885–1945*, Cambridge University Press, Cambridge, 1992. Demonstrates how anthropologists' accounts about exotic cultures can be translated into commentaries on their own societies.

Lewis, Norman, *The Missionaries: God Against the Indians*, Arrow Books, London, 1989. Atrocities alleged by distinguished author who believes that 'in another thirty years no trace of aboriginal life anywhere will have survived', depicting the Indians as helpless against the Summer Institute of Linguistics and New Tribes Mission.

Macmillan, Gordon, 'Counting the cost of mercury gold mining', *Geographical Magazine*, Vol.LXV, No.11, November 1993. No-nonsense commentary on most recent research.

Marcoy, Paul, *Travels in South America from the Pacific Ocean to the Atlantic Ocean*, 2 vols, London, 1875. Quoted from Frank, . . . *Y se lo comen*. 'Paul Marcoy' was a pseudonym of Laurent de Saint-Cricq.

Mendes, Chico, *Fight for the Forest*, Latin American Bureau, London, 1989. Mendes' life and work in his own words.

Monbiot, George, *Amazon Watershed: the new environmental investigation*, Michael Joseph, London, 1991. A deep probe into the environmental catastrophe facing the Amazon by a writer dedicated to cutting through received opinion and information. Regarding the Yanomami/gold-miner conflicts, see also Survival International Urgent Action Bulletin, September 1993 and others.

Monge, Antonio Muñoz, 'Las Huaringas', *Somos*, 287, 6 June 1992, Lima. An article on the shamanic healers of Huancabamba, featuring none other than *el maestro*.

Park, Chris C., *Tropical Rain Forests*, Routledge, London, 1992. Provides up-to-date figures and a wide-ranging review of the environmental debate on rain forest around the world.

Popescu, Petru, *Amazon Beaming*, Macdonald, London, 1991. Concerning American photographer Loren McIntyre's Amazon travels, particularly his early contact with the Mayorunas and his intriguing relationship with a Mayoruna shaman. He mentions the Two Harriets and other local personalities.

Ribeiro, Darcy, and Wise, Mary Ruth, *Comunidades y Culturas Peruanas*. No. 13, 'Los Grupos Etnicos de la Amazonia Peruana', Instituto Linguistico de Verano, Lima, 1978. Summary by the Summer Institute of Linguistics mission of all the Peruvian tribes and our knowledge about them.

Ricardo, Carlos, *Povos Indígenas no Brasil*, Vol. 5, *Javari*, CEDI, São Paulo, 1981. Valuable description of the Mayorunas, Marúbos and other Panoans of the Javari region, with overview of their present and past lives.

Ricciardi, Mirella, *Vanishing Amazon*, Weidenfeld, London, 1991. Includes photographs of the Marúbos.

Rich, Paul, 'Mayoruna – Another Unreached Tribe', *Brown Gold*, New Tribes Mission, January 1981. One of the rare contemporary articles on the Mayorunas, this one by Protestant fundamentalists in search of their 'Brown Gold'.

Romanoff, Steven, 'Informe sobre el uso de la tierra por los Matsés en la selva baja peruana'. *Centro Amazonico de Antropologia y Aplicación Practica*, Vol.1, No.1, 1976, 97–130. A piece on land use, by one of the few anthropologists to have studied the Matsés.

Salazar, Fred A., with Herschlag, Jack, *The Innocent Assassins: primitives of the Amazon jungle*, Hale, London, 1967. Three Americans went in search of 'uncontacted', 'hostile' Waica Indians.

Seitz, Georg, *People of the Rain-Forests*, Heinemann, London, 1963.

Serrill, Michael S., 'Sendero's Turn to Lose', *TIME International*, September 1992. 'What the arrest of the century means to Peru and the Shining Path.'

Smyth, William, and Lowe, F., *Narrative of a Journey from Lima to Pará*, London, 1836. Quoted from Frank, . . . *Y se lo comen*.

Steward, Julian H., *Handbook of South American Indians*, Smithsonian Institution, Washington, 1948. Bible of anthropologists, a summary of all known about the tribes at that time.

Stoll, David, 'Qué hacer con el ILV?', *Amazonia Indigena*, 11, February 1986, 3–6, COPAL, Lima. An airing of the debate about the value/harm of the Summer Institute of Linguistics by the Peru-based indigenous rights group COPAL – 'solidaridad con Los Grupos Nativos'.

Strong, Simon, *The Shining Path: the world's most dangerous revolutionaries*, HarperCollins, London, 1992. A thorough study by one of the longest-serving English journalists in Peru.

Survival International, *Indians of the Americas; invaded but not conquered*, London, 1992. Includes the Putumayo massacre story and examples of other decimations.

Villarejo, Avencio, *Asi es la Selva*, CETA, Iquitos, 1988. Gives a brief run-down on the contemporary state of tribes, and rumours of 'Remos', 'Grillos', 'Capishtos' and 'Pisahuas'.

Waterton, Charles, *Wanderings in South America, the north-west of the United States, and the Antilles, in the years 1812, 1816, 1820, & 1824*, Macmillan, London, 1879.

# INDEX